THE PARENT EFFECT

HOW PARENTING STYLE AFFECTS ADOLESCENT BEHAVIOR AND PERSONALITY DEVELOPMENT

JOANNE E. CARLSON

WITHDRAWN

NASW PRESS

National Association of Social Workers
Washington, DC

Jeane W. Anastas, PhD, LMSW, President

Elizabeth J. Clark, PhD, ACSW, MPH, Executive Director

Cheryl Y. Bradley, Publisher
Lisa M. O'Hearn, Managing Editor
John Cassels, Project Manager and Staff Editor
Amanda Morgan, Copyeditor
Susanna J. Harris, Proofreader
Lori J. Holtzinger, Indexer

Cover by Eye to Eye Design
Interior design by Electronic Quill
Printed and bound by Hamilton Printing Company

First impression: July 2011

Library of Congress Cataloging-in-Publication Data

Carlson, Joanne E.
 The parent effect: how parenting style affects adolescent behavior and personality development / by Joanne E. Carlson.
  p. cm.
 Includes bibliographical references and index.
 ISBN 978-0-87101-417-7
 1. Parent and teenager. 2. Adolescent psychology. 3. Personality in adolescence.
4. Teenagers—Family relationships. I. Title.
 HQ799.15.C3735 2011
 649'.125—dc22

                                                      2010044557

In loving memory of my mother,
Loretta A. Carlson
(1926–2003)
I miss you

Contents

About the Author

Joanne E. Carlson, ACSW, LCSW, is a psychotherapist in Houston, Texas, who has specialized in treating adolescents and their families in a variety of settings for over 32 years. She graduated magna cum laude from the University of Texas at Austin with a BA in psychology in 1976 and received her MSW from the University of Houston in 1980.

Prior to starting her own practice in 1986, Carlson was program director at an inpatient adolescent psychiatric hospital from 1980 to 1986. She was on the board of directors of the Houston Advocates for Mental Health in Children from 1995 to 2000 and served as a consultant to the Special Education Department of the Fort Bend Independent School District for their emotionally handicapped student programs from 1991 through 1993. She also works closely with several family law attorneys, providing consultation and court-ordered family therapy for families dealing with difficult divorces. She is active in developing and presenting community education seminars.

Carlson has been married for 27 years and has two children—Michael, age 24, and a special needs daughter, Kelli, age 22—and three dogs. She lives with her family in Sugar Land, Texas.

Acknowledgments

Creating a book is a complex process. It starts with a dream, and the dream becomes an idea; the idea then becomes a reality with a lot of time, research, energy, and patience to turn that idea into a reality. This reality came about with the help and support of family, friends, and colleagues. Therefore, let me take just a few moments (and the last words I'll write for this book!) to extend my gratitude to everyone who gave their time and ideas to make this all possible.

To Pat, my loving husband of 27 years, who read every word (sometimes three or four times), corrected typos, reworked poorly worded sentences, and offered suggestions from a layman's standpoint: Thank you for all your support and encouragement—and for taking over many household responsibilities so I could spend my free time writing. There are soul mates in this world, and you are mine.

To my friends and colleagues, who offered ideas, encouragement, and editorial assistance—Lynne Watkins, MSW; Annette McMurrey, MA; Scottie Holton, MEd; Bill Wardell, PhD; and Charles Cox, PhD. A special thanks to Richard Newman, MEd, who coauthored the parent questionnaire and offered editorial assistance throughout this process: You are all wonderful friends and talented therapists.

To Rachael Hyde, my son's girlfriend, who painstakingly created my reference list and offered technical and editorial assistance: Thank you. We are so lucky to have you in our lives.

To my children, Michael and Kelli: I learned so much about parenting from both of you. Kelli, my beautiful special needs daughter, you taught me to see life from a simpler standpoint and showed me that the emotional changes of adolescence occur regardless of one's cognitive abilities. Michael, my bright, talented, and incredibly independent son, your adolescent years were fun, thought provoking, and occasionally challenging.

To my parents, Bill and Loretta Carlson, the original Easygoing parents: You encouraged me to follow my goals and have always been my biggest supporters. Thank you.

I must also extend my appreciation to the many adolescents and families that I have had the privilege of working with over all these years. Many of your stories (with details changed to protect privacy) are reflected in the pages of this book. Thank you for briefly sharing your lives with me. My gratitude goes out to my editor at NASW Press, John Cassels, for his patience and kindness to this first-time author—he was always there to provide information and support when I needed it. Thanks also to NASW Press for taking a chance on me and helping me turn my idea into a book. A special note of appreciation to Amanda Morgan—your careful editing made me all the better a writer.

PART ONE

ADOLESCENCE

Introduction

Adolescence is the most difficult developmental period for parents and teenagers alike. It is that period in childrearing that sends many parents searching for information or psychological help. This period can be an extremely difficult time or simply one that requires more patience, creativity, humor, and affection on the part of the parent and the teenager. Success at this stage also requires clear and compelling information that allows parents to be aware of the important role they play in the development of their teen's personality.

All parents have their own unique styles of dealing with their children. These styles are usually a combination of three forces: the parents' own upbringing, their personal needs and characteristics, and what they have learned from outside sources. The majority of parents will respond to their children in a fashion similar to their own (family-of-origin) parents' style. Some parents, unhappy with their own childhoods, may consciously parent in a manner that is distinctly different from that of their own upbringing. Another contributing factor is the parents' own particular personality characteristics, motivations, issues, and needs. These particular aspects are affected by a number of life events, including divorce, medical illness, psychiatric disorders, and substance abuse. Outside sources of information about parenting include books, magazine articles, TV shows, newspaper reports, parenting classes, and advice from friends and family.

All three of these factors help define an individual's parenting style. But the most powerful of the three is the parent's own issues, needs, and personality characteristics. This book does not intend in any way to blame parents for family difficulties, but it is designed to allow parents to see the association between their parenting style and their adolescent's behaviors.

Most books on adolescents address the issues that arise during this developmental stage from the standpoint of normal or problematic adolescent behavior and offer suggestions to help parents deal with their teens. Books on adolescents often discuss parenting style, but usually only briefly. This book aims to fill that gap by focusing specifically on parenting style and its impact. Hopefully, this will help parents to support their teens' growth and enjoy a warmer and closer relationship with them—as well as helping therapists and other professionals who work with adolescents to become more aware of the important role that parents play in their lives.

When an adolescent is brought in for psychotherapy, an assessment is usually made, identifying his or her psychological or behavioral issues. In many cases, a review of the teen's history and an exploration of the current family system are part of this assessment. However, far too often the focus remains on treating the adolescent as the primary patient and minimizing the role that other family members may play. Some insurance companies require at least one session with the family, whereas others decline to pay for any family sessions whatsoever.

The following is an example of two ways of assessing the same adolescent during the initial intake and highlights the differences between focusing on the teenager and focusing on the family as a whole.

An adolescent-focused assessment might look like this:

Rebecca is a 15-year-old who lives with her parents and two younger brothers. The precipitating event for seeking therapy was a highly emotional argument with her mother, during which Rebecca said that she wanted to talk to someone. Mom accompanied Rebecca to the initial session and reported that Rebecca has been increasingly irritable and disrespectful at home, that her grades have been dropping, and that she has been isolating herself increasingly from the family in the last few weeks. Mom also shared that efforts to apply consequences for Rebecca's behavior and poor grades have been ineffective.

As mom was talking, Rebecca appeared increasingly frustrated and finally blurted out that she has been sad and anxious for several months, not weeks, but no one had noticed until recently. During an individual session, Rebecca shared that she was sad and feeling lost. A review of her history revealed that Rebecca had been active in competitive cheerleading since age 4 but had recently quit. She was not interested in any extracurricular activities and was starting to hang around with teens who were involved in partying. Mom was seeking help in improving Rebecca's attitudes and grades.

An assessment that paid more attention to parenting factors might look like this:

Rebecca is a 15-year-old who lives with her parents and two younger brothers. The precipitating event for seeking therapy was a highly emotional argument with her mother, during which Rebecca told her mom that she wanted to talk to someone. Mom reported that she was seeking help for Rebecca because of her irritability at home, poor grades, and isolation from the family. According to mom, the changes had occurred during the last few weeks.

During the conversation with her mother, Rebecca appeared increasingly frustrated and finally informed mom that she had been feeling anxious and lonely for a number of months, but that the family had failed to notice until she started becoming more disrespectful and argumentative. A review of the history revealed that Rebecca had recently refused to continue competitive cheerleading, an activity she had been involved with since age 4. Rebecca reported that she stopped cheerleading because she was tired of the hectic schedule and the pressure from her mom. According to Rebecca, "My mom's whole life has been cheerleading, that's all she ever cared about," and she added that after she quit cheerleading, her mother had very little interest in or time for her.

Since quitting cheerleading, Rebecca has had difficulty finding a new interest or activity with which to align herself. She is no longer considered part of the cheerleading group and has found herself drifting toward the kids at school who are involved in partying. Rebecca's anger at her mom was evident in the conflict between them and appeared to be an attempt by Rebecca to get mom to pay more attention and acknowledge her. It is also likely that mom's anger reflected her resentment about Rebecca's leaving cheerleading, which was a significant part of mom's life.

This book is divided into four sections. The first reviews the basic characteristics and challenges of adolescence. The second identifies five parenting styles: My House, My Rules; Your Life Is My Life; Cool; Not Now, I'm Busy; and Easygoing. Parenting styles are identified, with the characteristics of each style provided. Possible etiologies of each of the five styles are provided. Each chapter then delves into the various adolescent reactions (both positive and negative) and discusses possible effects on teens' personalities and resultant adult characteristics.

The third section of *The Parent Effect* addresses some of the life situations that can affect parents' functioning and, through them, their adolescents. Divorce and remarriage, especially during a child's adolescent years, can result in significant changes in the teenager's world. Physical illness, psychiatric disorders, and substance abuse also create stressful home environments. The final section of the book provides suggestions and exercises to help readers become more balanced parents and improve parent–teen relationships by addressing the life issues that have affected the way they interact with their teenagers. Most adults can benefit from the insights derived from these exercises, becoming more aware and thoughtful and parenting with specific goals in mind.

Examples are provided throughout to illustrate the information presented. Although these examples are based on real clients' experiences, all identifying information has been changed to ensure client confidentiality. Some examples are composites of several situations.

Parenting style is not a new concept. Baumrind's 1971 identification of three primary parenting styles—authoritarian, authoritative, and permissive—has been the cornerstone for social research on parenting. In 1983, Maccoby and Martin further divided the permissive category into two subcategories: indulgent and neglectful. The resulting four categories are based on high and low levels of two elements, *responsiveness* and *demandingness*. Responsiveness is associated with warmth, involvement, and nurturing. Demandingness is associated with supervision, monitoring, expectations, and strictness. *Authoritarian* parents stress obedience and tend to be less responsive and more demanding. *Authoritative* parents are high in both responsiveness and demandingness, providing structure in an environment of openness and warmth. *Indulgent-permissive* parents make few demands and are highly responsive to their teens' requests and needs. *Neglectful-permissive* parents provide neither structure nor responsiveness. This book builds on insights from these categorization schemes but is organized around five parenting styles that reflect the various parent–teen interactions I have observed over the years in my work with families. The My House, My Rules parenting style is similar to the authoritarian style; Cool parents are permissive and neglectful; Not Now, I'm Busy parents are low in responsiveness; Your Life is My Life parents are high in responsiveness and expectations; and Easygoing parents are similar to those in Baumrind's authoritative category. Additional characteristics of each style are addressed in detail in the various chapters.

Even though *The Parent Effect* focuses on how parents influence their children's development, teenagers themselves play a pivotal role in parenting behaviors. Further, it is possible (if not highly probable) that teens will behave in inappropriate and even dangerous ways despite the best parenting efforts. Nonetheless, the fact remains that the most significant influence on teens' behavior and personality development is their relationship with their parents.

As I was writing this book, colleagues raised the question of whether I was going to write about abusive parenting. Parents who are abusive, openly hostile, or blatantly damaging to their adolescents' emotional well-being are not exhibiting parental behavior but are self-centered and often psychologically disturbed. Thus, I did not consider abusive parenting as a category of parenting style and did not include it in this work. This does not preclude certain abusive behaviors from being exhibited in the context of some parenting reactions. Often, one sees what I call "screamers"—parents who respond to their teenagers with yelling rather than calm discussion. Most parents are capable of yelling at their adolescent at one time or another, but when this becomes their primary form of communication, it is problematic and detrimental.

Thirty-five years ago, with a bachelor's degree in psychology, I began working with adolescents at a psychiatric hospital, and my passion for working with adolescents and their families was ignited. I earned a master's degree in 1980, and since then I have provided psychotherapy to adolescents and their families in a variety of settings. Although many therapists hesitate to work with teenagers, as they can be difficult, obstinate, dismissive, and even combative, I have found teens to be endearing, creative, funny, and genuine. Many have shared their pain with me, their struggle to understand their intense emotions, and their unique outlook on the world. I have worked with teens trapped in dysfunctional families, waiting to be old enough to move out and assume their own care; teens who struggled to meet unrealistic expectations; and teens who were dealing with the heartbreak of failed relationships. Most adolescents come into therapy reluctantly, denying any problems, but the overwhelming majority of them quickly open up and work hard to help themselves. Adults, on the other hand, often enter therapy identifying their emotional pain but are slower to make changes.

I have been privileged to work with many parents who have been open to making changes in themselves for the well-being of their children. I have also worked with parents who were unwilling or unable to address their parenting practices, and I could only hope to make some small inroad into their family struggles. Some were too afraid to face their own issues and insecurities but sought help for their teens. Others simply wanted their teens' problems "fixed," without much expenditure of effort on their part. However, the majority of these parents have been loving and concerned, dealing with their own flaws borne out of their own life struggles. Few have been completely disconnected or abusive. To all these families, I express my gratitude for sharing their most private lives with me.

This book has offered me an opportunity to provide parents and other professionals with valuable information on how parents and their teens interact. It is based on an extensive review of relevant literature, consultations with colleagues, and over 33 years of experience in treating adolescents and their families as well as the personal experience of raising two teenagers. It is my hope that *The Parent Effect* will be of value to parents, psychotherapists, teachers, and clergy, all of whom deal not only with teenagers but also with their parents.

CHAPTER ONE

Adolescence

I feel that adolescence has served its purpose when a person arrives at adulthood with a strong sense of self-esteem, the ability to relate intimately, to communicate congruently, to take responsibility, and to take risks. The end of adolescence is the beginning of adulthood. What hasn't been finished then will have to be finished later.

—Virginia Satir,
The New Peoplemaking

Adolescents, teenagers, tweens—these very words create stress in most adults. The primary message that adolescents wish to send to adults is this: "I'm not a child anymore!" The developmental period of adolescence is one of the most difficult life stages, for parents and teens alike. It is a slow, complicated, often stressful transition from child to adult, occurring between the ages of 11 and 21. Some children begin puberty as young as 11, and many adolescents continue to change and grow through their early 20s. The transitions that occur within the individual and in the family are fundamental and monumental. Adolescence has been written about extensively; however, this chapter endeavors to give only a brief and basic overview of the important changes and developmental tasks that occur during this time.

Changes

Biological, physical, emotional, cognitive, legal, social, interpersonal, and cultural changes occur during adolescence. Although there are significant differences in the way that different societies and cultures handle this transitional period, the basic individual changes that occur are universal.

Physical and Biological Changes

During adolescence, there is a significant growth spurt during which height, weight, and even organ structure change significantly. The most well-known and obvious change is the development of secondary sex characteristics. For girls, this includes the development of breasts, the addition of pubic and underarm hair, the onset of menstruation, and changes in body shape. For boys, it includes development of the sexual organs, growth of facial and body hair, and changes in the vocal cords that result in a deepening of the voice, a transition that can result briefly in uncomfortable voice intonation patterns.

Adolescence is also marked by a rapid gain in height, weight, body fat, and muscle mass. Changes in the respiratory system result in increased strength and stamina. These changes usually result in increased appetite, increased need for sleep, physical awkwardness, and increased physical endurance. When my son was in middle school, his friends would come over and head upstairs to play video games, leaving their shoes at the bottom of the stairs. I remember watching the shoe sizes grow dramatically within a very short time. During adolescence, such changes occur erratically and vary significantly from person to person, which can be a source of great concern and discomfort for teenagers. Girls also tend to mature earlier than boys, and in middle school many girls tend to develop in height before boys do, making both boys and girls self-conscious. During this time, teenage girls may become overly sensitive about their weight and body shape, whereas boys may become self-conscious about their physical size and facial hair.

Cognitive Changes

For years it was believed that changes between childhood and adolescence were primarily due to hormonal changes, but we now know that the cognitive changes that take place during this time are even more significant. Recent research has shown that there is continued brain development during the adolescent years. There is also a monumental shift in thinking abilities and patterns. The most significant recent scientific discovery is that the prefrontal cortex continues changing into the mid-20s. This area of the brain is responsible for impulse control, planning, problem solving, and making complex judgments. Research indicates that adolescents use their brains differently than adults do and that this results in more instinctive and impulsive thinking and reactions. Teenagers often misunderstand social cues and overreact to stressful or uncertain situations. They are more impulsive and less likely to think twice, change their minds, or stop and consider the consequences of their actions (Juskalian, 2010; Kever, 2006; Strauch, 2003).

During adolescence, there is a shift from concrete to abstract thinking. Jean Piaget's theory of cognitive development postulated that there are specific and sequential changes in thinking patterns over the course of a lifetime (Inhelder & Piaget, 1958). Piaget referred to the adolescent stage as the period of formal operations—the development of abstract and hypothetical thought and the ability to reason through situations in a more complex manner. What this means is that sometime during adolescence, the teenager becomes more able to think about things and concepts that cannot be seen or felt. During this time, teens develop more advanced reasoning skills; they become able to consider situations in hypothetical or imaginary terms and to consider multiple options and possibilities. They also become more thoughtful overall.

This growth in mental abilities, often referred to as *meta-cognition*, is what allows individuals to consider what they're thinking, how they feel about those thoughts, and how they are perceived by others. Simply put, adolescents began to think more about themselves and how they view the world around them, often becoming somewhat awed by their own ability to develop opinions and views independently of the adults in their lives.

This combination of changes often leads an adolescent to feel that he or she is the only person who has ever experienced certain thoughts and feelings. This also accounts for the intensity of emotion seen during this time. Teens have become able to react emotionally, acknowledge their feelings, and ascribe significance to them. This self-awareness and intensity often look to others like self-absorption.

Social Changes

The most obvious social change during adolescence is the shift from a focus on the family to identification with peer groups. Identifying with peers is extremely important during this time, in that it helps teens to separate their identity from that of their parents. Social changes are important in the development of identity, independence, moral beliefs, healthy interpersonal relationships, and confidence in one's self. This social transition is often filled with emotional struggles for teens and their families.

Families continue to play an important role during this time. As a matter of fact, some of the necessary social changes are also occurring within the family system. During this time, teens become more independent, more responsible, more opinionated, and more secretive as they strive to establish their own identity. Social interactions within the family, and parental reactions to teen changes, are of primary importance to an adolescent's success in moving through this time period.

The other social change that takes place during this time is the development of close friendships and eventually intimate partnerships. Often called "puppy love," the relationships developed during this time set the stage for the development of healthy relationships later in life. The development of romantic and sexual interests is an unstoppable phenomenon. Many adults have found it difficult or impossible to keep adolescents apart when they are emotionally drawn to each other. This force is the reason Shakespeare's *Romeo and Juliet* continues to be one of the most beloved stories ever written and one whose theme has been reworked in numerous formats.

Developmental Tasks of Adolescence

Several developmental tasks need to take place during adolescence in order for a teenager to become a healthy and responsible adult. Parenting style affects how a child carries out these tasks.

Individuation

In 1950, Erik Erikson (1950/1993) formulated his theory of the eight stages of development, beginning in infancy and continuing through adult maturity. These stages have long been accepted as essential to understanding the important changes that occur throughout one's life, allowing for the development of one's full potential. Erikson designated two stages of concern to individuals between the ages of 12 and 21. The adolescent stage is concerned with "identity versus identity diffusion," whereas the young adult stage is concerned with "intimacy versus isolation." In essence, the goal is for the teen to develop a stable sense of self, whereas the goal of intimacy is to have the ability to connect with peers or a life partner. Discussing Erikson's developmental stage of identity versus identity diffusion, L. Steinberg (2002) stated that

> the maturational and social forces that converge at adolescence force young people to reflect on their place in society, on the ways that others view them, and on their options for the future. Achieving a balanced and coherent sense of identity is an intellectually and emotionally taxing process. According to Erikson, it is not until adolescence that one even has the mental or psychological capacity to tackle this task. (p. 272)

This time is one of self-discovery, with the goal being a clear and stable picture of oneself. The process is anything but easy and takes several years, with many false starts and stops. This is why so many adolescents try different clothing styles, haircuts, music genres, and friendships. They may try on several identities, associate with different groups, and support different causes, trying to find those that feel most comfortable.

Teenagers are not predisposed to simply take on a role or identity established for them by someone else; they often actively resist the expectations of their parents and other adults. Identity is something you must establish for yourself; it cannot be handed to you or forced on you by another person. This does not mean that teenagers will not incorporate the opinions, likes, dislikes, and values of others, including parents, into their own identity, but they need to feel that they are making such decisions themselves. The process of individuation involves healthy separation from parents and development of a clear sense of self.

Achieving Autonomy

A related task facing the adolescent is to achieve autonomy, which involves becoming emotionally, cognitively, and socially independent. The terms "individuation" and "autonomy" are often used interchangeably but actually refer to separate, albeit interconnected, aspects of the transition from child to adult. During this time, teenagers spend more time alone, sequestered in their room, on the Internet, or out with friends. The need for autonomy results in teens wanting to make their own decisions about a variety of issues, including clothing, music, movies, friendships, and activities. In addition, autonomy involves being able to make reasonable choices and decisions for oneself, to plan and to follow through on plans, and to develop a strong sense of right and wrong. Teens need to accomplish these tasks in order become independent, self-sufficient, emotionally healthy adults.

Defining Social and Gender Roles

Whereas Erikson's "identity versus identity diffusion" is the most well-known developmental task facing adolescents, there are other important tasks adolescents need to accomplish. One, mentioned earlier, is to be accepted and validated by one's peer group. Connecting to a peer group includes developing and clarifying one's masculine or feminine social role. A few hours at the mall on a Saturday will illustrate this. From almost any food court, one can observe groups of teenage boys joking and swaggering and groups of teenage girls chatting, giggling, and observing their male counterparts.

Clothing and hairstyles, although personalized to some extent, also convey a sense of similarity that defines teens as a part of a particular social clique. Years ago, while I was working with adolescents in a psychiatric hospital, my small group decided to try an experiment. The teenagers took bandanas and tied them casually around their thighs on the outside of their jeans. Within one week, most adolescents on the unit were copying the style.

Social connection also involves the ability to socialize with and enjoy the company of others. This occurs in a variety of contexts: between classes, during lunch, at the mall, in neighborhood parks, at friends' houses, and in movie theaters. The modes of interaction have changed significantly over the years, with cell phones, texting, and the Internet now the primary methods of interaction. Texting during class has taken the place of passing notes. Facebook, MySpace, and YouTube are other primary sources of socialization. However, there is also still a need for face-to-face socialization practice.

During this period, social skills are practiced, conflict styles are tested, and social confidence is developed. Interactions with peers prepare adolescents for adult social interactions and obligations.

Becoming comfortable with one's sexuality and being able to develop and maintain interpersonal relationships are two of the important tasks of adolescence. This corresponds to Erikson's "intimacy versus isolation" developmental stage, which he considered a task of young adulthood. However, the practice relationships that develop the ability to successfully engage in intimate and romantic relationships take place during the adolescent years. During this period romantic interests are established, social skills are developed and practiced, conflict styles are developed, and sexual confidence is established. Same-sex friendships usually predate intimate love relationships and, eventually, committed sexual relationships.

Although young teens (ages 11 to 14) do develop close connections to peers, it is in later adolescence that the more intense and serious romantic relationships and friendships develop. During this transition, teens move from group activities to more individual encounters. As with other aspects of these developmental stages, the development of close interpersonal relationships is a process, with the earlier stages being somewhat immature and short-lived. Older adolescents often have developed the capacity to maintain complex, committed relationships. However, a tremendous amount of personality change continues to occur during the young adult years.

Productivity and Achievement

During the adolescent years, many teens are drawn to certain activities and interests, which may eventually develop into career interests. Discovering areas of interest requires a considerable amount of experimentation. Most teens gravitate toward certain activities and then align their identity and social relationships with these activities. Examples of these role identities are high school band members, athletes, drama students, and school nerds.

Although adolescent activities are not necessarily a precursor to adult career choices, there are often aspects of these activities that merge into later career interests. Band members may go on to major in music, drama students may become actors, and football players may become Monday morning quarterbacks. These activities, as well as schoolwork, provide adolescents with a sense of accomplishment and achievement. Ownership of one's grades, activities, and accomplishments is extremely important during this time. Although it is not unusual in many societies, or even in families, for career choices to be established for the teenager, the task of developing a sense of achievement is important to becoming self-sufficient.

Many adolescents take part-time jobs, which provide not only spending money but also a sense of independence and accomplishment. Part-time jobs and extracurricular activities help many teenagers learn organization, negotiation, and money management. Some teenagers find themselves juggling school, work, and activities, and caution should be exercised so that they do not become overscheduled and exhausted.

Acquiring Values

Another key developmental task is the acquisition of values, ethics, and a sense of social responsibility. This task actually occurs in tandem with the other tasks outlined previously. During this time, many teenagers develop a heightened sense of social consciousness and can be quite rigid in their beliefs. These beliefs may be religious, political, environmental, and personal, such as vegetarianism. When adolescents have an opportunity to explore a variety of values and beliefs, they will eventually be able to accept or reject them and incorporate these choices into their sense of self.

Normal Adolescent Behavior

Social scientists typically divide adolescence into three periods: early adolescence (ages 11 to 13), middle adolescence (ages 14 to 17), and late adolescence (ages 18 to 21).

Another way to conceptualize these age groups is to consider them in terms of school grade levels. Typically, the earliest adolescents, ages 11 and 12, are in fifth and sixth grade. Many consider them preadolescents, and there is often a concern about protecting them from the influence of older peers. Seventh and eighth graders typically range from 12 to 14 years of age. Ninth graders, typically 14 or 15, are a somewhat distinct category. Teens ages 16 to 18 are typically in 10th through 12th grade.

Many school districts have now recognized the need to separate teenagers into comfortable peer groups to allow for optimal educational and social development. Recently, school districts have started to separate sixth-graders into their own schools or areas within schools, and ninth-graders are also increasingly being segregated into ninth-grade centers within high school campuses. The concerns of the various age groups are different, and the need to protect younger students from the stress and peer pressure of older students is increasingly recognized, most likely on the basis of an awareness of the different developmental changes and stages that occur during the teenage years. Parents, teachers, coaches, the legal system, and the media should be aware of the wide variety of abilities that exist throughout the different stages of adolescence.

The following lists give a general overview of the behaviors, feelings, and conditions considered normal for early adolescence, middle adolescence, late adolescence, and young adulthood.

Early Adolescence (11 to 13):

- Onset of physical and sexual changes
- Thinking primarily in concrete terms
- Increased self-consciousness
- Beginning experimentation with style
- Increased interest in peer friendships
- Less tolerance of parents
- Beginning to develop "attitude" and challenge parental authority
- Boys become more obnoxious; girls become more melodramatic
- Increased intensity of emotions
- Feeling of being unique and misunderstood
- More time spent alone in room
- More complaints of boredom
- Continued dependence on family for social activities

Middle Adolescence (14 to 16):

- Continued but slower physical changes
- Increasing comfort with one's sexuality
- Increasing cognitive abilities, including the ability to think abstractly
- Reversion to more concrete and primitive thinking when stressed
- Increasing importance of social group
- Beginnings of interest in opposite-sex relationships
- Boys: amusement with sexual innuendos and insider jokes with other boys
- Girls: strong cliques and interpersonal drama
- Experimentation with different styles in an effort to define one's identity

- Better ability to handle multiple responsibilities
- Intense self-awareness and self-absorption
- Increasing dependence on friends for social activities
- Socializing with opposite sex, primarily in group activities
- Vulnerability to rejection by peers
- Less time spent with family, more time spent alone or with friends
- Possibly intensifying conflict with parents
- Development of one's own value system

Late Adolescence (16 to 18):

- Increasing cognitive abilities
- Ability to handle higher level cognitive functioning, such as advanced math concepts
- Development of strong preferences for certain activities
- Active involvement in and identification with a specific social group
- Less conflict with parents as comfort with self develops
- Consideration of long-term goals
- Dating and development of more mature or romantic relationships
- Possibly increased experimentation and testing of boundaries
- Possible use of alcohol, tobacco, and even drugs
- Ability to drive a car, hold a job, and take on other adult responsibilities

Young Adulthood (19 to 21):

- Physical maturity
- Well-developed cognitive abilities
- Well-established sexual identity
- Increasing idealism and philosophical approach
- More future orientation
- Development of well-thought-out plans and goals
- Choice of career and beginning moves toward attaining this goal
- Leaving home to attend college or join the military
- Handling one's own money
- Establishing more adult relationships with parents
- Less dependency on peer group for ideas and values
- Development of committed and long-term relationships
- Ability to participate in adult activities such as voting, drinking, gambling, and marriage

These developmental periods overlap and vary on the basis of an individual's physical growth, maturity level, and intellectual development. Teenagers' experiences with family, school, and peers help them develop these much needed characteristics, talents, and abilities. This book highlights how parenting style is instrumental to teens' acquisition of adult characteristics.

PART TWO

PARENTING STYLES

CHAPTER TWO

Parenting Style Self-Assessment

*Life affords no greater responsibility, no greater privilege, than the
raising of the next generation.*

—C. Everett Koop

Parenting style encompasses one's parental goals, expectations, responses, reactions, and behaviors. It is derived from one's family of origin, personal characteristics, emotional needs, and motivations. Parent behaviors may also be learned through a variety of sources and consciously applied to parent–teen interactions. Each parent has a specific parenting style, derived from his or her family background, personal characteristics, and motivations. Parents can also consciously learn and apply parenting behaviors. In addition, a teen's behavior and environmental factors affect parenting style. Parenting behaviors are complex and varied, but most parents use a fairly consistent style—and one that is similar to one of the five styles described in this book—in most of their interactions with their children.

The questionnaire that follows is not scientifically based, but simply a way to help you think about your parenting style and become more aware of the behaviors and responses associated with your parenting practices and their potential outcomes. First, you will answer a series of multiple-choice questions; next, you will read five sets of statements and choose the set that best describes your parenting style. Finally, you will interpret your answers to see which of the five parenting styles discussed in this book is closest to your own.

Section 1: Teen Scenarios and Parental Responses

The following multiple-choice questions present scenarios and general questions about parental responses. Each question has five possible responses. Choose the answer that most closely resembles how you would handle the situation. The more honest you can be, the more accurate and helpful the results will be, providing a good indication of your parenting style; there are no right or wrong answers. For now, ignore the letters in parentheses; you will come back to those later.

1. Your 16-year-old wants to go out on a Saturday night with friends and asks about curfew. What is your most likely response?

   - 10:30 P.M. No negotiation. (M)
   - It depends on the activity—usually between 11 and 12 P.M. (E)
   - I trust my teen to come home at a reasonable time. (C)
   - The question doesn't come up very often. My children are usually busy with a specific activity, and I am often involved in the activity with them. (L)
   - Midnight is okay, as long as we don't have to pick him or her up somewhere. (N)

2. How often do you check your teenager's social networking on sites like Facebook and MySpace?

   - Daily—I like to know everything I can about my teen's life. (L)
   - I just make periodic spot checks. (E)
   - I don't usually check; I'm too busy keeping up with my own e-mail. (N)
   - We are Facebook friends. I chat online or text my teen regularly. (C)
   - I monitor it closely for anything inappropriate. I also limit its use. (M)

3. Your 17-year-old comes home around midnight from a party and appears intoxicated. How are you likely to respond?

   - I'd let it go—it is probably just a little experimentation. (C)
   - I'd come down hard; suspicion is enough to warrant a response. (M)
   - I'm usually not awake when my teen comes in that late. I'd deal with it later. (N)
   - I would have my teen go on to bed, and we would talk about it the next day. (E)
   - I would insist on knowing where my teen has been and if he or she has been drinking, and I might also contact other parents to see if they knew about the drinking. (L)

4. How do you deal with your teenager's homework and school projects?

   - I am available to help with homework and school projects if needed. (E)
   - I'm actively involved in schoolwork and projects. We do most of them together. (L)
   - I let my teen take care of it; I have my own work to do. (N)
   - I expect my teen to do the work, but I monitor it. Poor grades would result in a consequence. (M)
   - I help out if I can. I may do some of it myself if my teen has a lot of work or has someplace to go. (C)

5. What is your primary reaction to most rule infractions?

   - I tend to yell, then let it go. (N)
   - Grounded for at least a week. (M)
   - We just talk it over; my teen usually has a good reason for the behavior. (C)
   - We're together most of the time, so my kids rarely engage in inappropriate behavior. (L)
   - We have a clear set of family rules with logical consequences for infractions. (E)

6. How do you handle your teen's choices in hairstyles and clothing?

   - I don't allow wild styles. I have to approve clothing and hairstyle choices. (M)
   - I let my teen make all his or her choices about hairstyle and clothes. (C)
   - I let my teen make the choices, but draw the line at any clothing that is inappropriate. (E)
   - We usually shop together; we like a lot of the same styles. (L)
   - I give my teen money to shop for him- or herself. (N)

7. Some of your teen's school grades have recently dropped from As and Bs to Cs. How would you respond?

   - I would tell my teen that he or she needs to pull the grades back up. (N)
   - I would explore with my teen what has changed in the school situation. Together we would develop a plan for pulling the grades back up. (E)
   - I would ground my teen until the grades were back up. (M)
   - I would contact the teachers to see what the problem is. (L)
   - I wouldn't worry about it. It's probably just that school has gotten harder. (C)

8. How do you feel about your 15-year-old's choice in music?

   - We enjoy the same music and often go to concerts together. (C)
   - I'm not all that familiar with my teen's music choices. I guess they are okay. (N)
   - I allow my teen to listen to anything as long as the lyrics are not inappropriate. (E)
   - I monitor all my teen's music; we often shop for CDs together. (L)
   - We often argue about my teen's music choices. (M)

9. How do you respond when your teen argues with you?

   - I hold my ground. My decisions are firm. (M)
   - I usually give in; I don't like it when my teen is angry with me. (C)
   - I wait for my teen to calm down and then may reconsider. (E)
   - I often give in. It's too much trouble to fight. (N)
   - I become upset; we are usually so close. (L)

10. How involved are you in your teen's extracurricular activities?

- I attend and am actively involved in all of my teen's practices and performances. I volunteer when parent helpers are needed. It's an important part of my life. (L)
- I try to make some of the games or performances if I can. (N)
- I support my teen's activities. I try to attend most of the games or performances and some of the practices as well. (E)
- I enjoy being involved in my teen's activities and try to go as often as I can. I find teen activities to be fun and interesting. (C)
- I attend all games and performances. I rarely attend practices. I often express an opinion on how well my teen performed. (M)

Section 2: Parenting Style Characteristics

The statements that follow are grouped together by parenting style. They are not intended to cover all possible parenting practices, and it's unlikely that any group will describe you perfectly. With that in mind, read each statement and then choose the group that most closely resembles your parenting style. Choose only one group. Again, the more honestly you evaluate yourself, the more useful this exercise will be in helping you get the most out of this book.

Group One

- I don't believe teens need a lot of rules; they can often make their own decisions.
- I enjoy being a friend to my teenager.
- I like my teen to be able to have friends over. My house is available for parties and sleepovers.
- I know that teens will experiment with alcohol, and I want to provide a safe environment for them to do this in.
- My teen knows that she or he can come to me at any time with an issue.

Group Two

- Authority is important in a home; teenagers need structure and rules.
- I insist upon knowing where my teen is at all times.
- I expect respect from my teenager and don't accept talking back.
- I monitor my teen's schoolwork and expect good grades.
- Punishment is the natural consequence for breaking rules.

Group Three

- My job keeps me from being able to participate in many of my teen's activities.
- I expect my teen to follow through on responsibilities without my having to monitor.

- I get frustrated when my time is interrupted by minor teen issues.
- I expect my teen to handle most of his or her own schoolwork.
- My teenager helps out with the housework. We all need to pitch in to take care of the house.

Group Four

- I provide my teen with structure but also believe that teens need to be involved in making decisions.
- Respect is important for all family members.
- My teen and I try to find time to have friendly chats on a regular basis.
- I am comfortable asking my teenager where he or she is going and with whom.
- I like to give my teenager second chances; teens need a chance to learn from their mistakes.

Group Five

- I like to be involved in my teen's activities.
- My teen is aware of my expectations.
- I often act as a strong advocate for my teen when he or she has a conflict with authority or is not being given an opportunity.
- I often help my teen with homework and school projects.
- My teen is often the main focus of my life.

Section 3: Find Your Parenting Style

Now, review your answers to find out which of the parenting styles described in the next chapters most closely resembles your own.

Teen Scenarios and Parental Responses

On the lines below, mark the letter corresponding to your answer to each multiple-choice question.

1. _____ 2. _____ 3. _____ 4. _____ 5. _____

6. _____ 7. _____ 8. _____ 9. _____ 10. _____

Note the total number of times you selected each letter.

M. _____ E. _____ L. _____ C. _____ N. _____

Parenting Style Characteristics

Next, note which group of statements you identified with most closely.

_____ Group One = C

_____ Group Two = M

_____ Group Three = N

_____ Group Four = E

_____ Group Five = L

Adding It All up to Find Your Style: Scoring Your Responses

Note the letter corresponding to your choice in Teen Scenarios and Parental Responses. Add five points to your total for that letter under Parenting Style Characteristics. (Example: You had 7 points under category M in the first section, and you chose Group Two, or M, in the second section, so you now have 7 + 5 = 12 points for category M.)

Note which category has the most points; this represents your parenting style on this list:

M = My House, My Rules
L = Your Life is My Life
C = Cool
N = Not Now, I'm Busy
E = Easygoing

Each of these corresponds to a parenting style described in one of the next five chapters. As you read on, keep in mind the style you identified as most like your own. Although most parents consistently exhibit one parenting style, certain life situations may result in changes. Keep in mind, too, that the goal is awareness, not judgment.

CHAPTER THREE

"My House, My Rules" Parents

If teenagers live with too many rules, they learn to get around them.

—Dorothy Nolte and Rachel Harris,
Teenagers Learn What They Live

Case Example

Tracy was a 16-year-old high school junior who came into therapy with her mother, Cyndy. Tracy lives with her mother, father, and younger sister. Her mother reported that she was bringing her daughter into treatment for lying. According to her mother, Tracy skipped swim practice and went to Starbucks with her friends and then lied about it. It was clear that the mother was quite angry with her daughter.

During the course of treatment, several important pieces of information came to light that helped clarify the context in which Tracy exhibited the problematic behavior. Tracy's parents, in particular her mother, had rigid ideas about how Tracy was to behave and what she should achieve. It was during the summer that Tracy had lied about going to swim practice. Tracy was remorseful about lying to her mother but felt that she had few options as she was allowed to spend very little time with her friends, even during summer vacation.

On the basis of her mom's rules, Tracy's summer consisted of swim practice, household chores, reading, and memorizing about 200 vocabulary words a week for the SAT. At the end of the week, Tracy's mother would quiz her on these words, and Tracy was expected to know the definitions of each. Mom's rationale was that Tracy was a bright student and she wanted to ensure that she scored well on the SAT and would be able to get into a prestigious university. In addition, mom pushed Tracy to be a "star" on the high school swim team and take all Advanced Placement classes.

Tracy was frustrated about being unable to spend time with her friends; her parents considered socialization to be unproductive. The parents' control extended to Tracy's friends, her outside activities, her clothes, and even her weight. Shortly after starting treatment, Tracy reported that she had gained a couple of pounds and that in response, her mother became upset, insisted that Tracy come downstairs every morning and weigh herself in front of mom, and gave Tracy two weeks to lose the extra weight. Tracy's mother, Cyndy, reported that she had quit work after her second child was born; it was clear that she resented giving up her personal life to care for her two daughters. Cyndy expected obedience from her daughters and showed little concern for their feelings or opinions. She would often tell Tracy, "I don't have to give you a reason—I'm your mother and this is my house."

Tracy was an intelligent, friendly, but incredibly sad teenager who felt helpless to deal with her mother's strong personality. For the most part, Tracy simply acquiesced to her mother's demands. A separate session with Tracy's father indicated that, although he was aware of (and not always comfortable with) his wife's level of control over his daughters, he was not willing to step in to make any changes. Tracy worked hard in therapy, but she was withdrawn early by her mother, who felt that the therapy was overriding her authority. To this day, I wonder how Tracy fared when she was finally able to leave home.

Parenting Style Characteristics

"My House, My Rules" parents' primary focus in parenting is on the need to have their teens conform to their expectations and to maintain the belief that they are in charge of their household. These parents are controlling by nature. They value conformity over individuality. Control, as it applies to these parents, includes any attempt by parents to influence their adolescent to carry out, or refrain from, an action—or to think or feel a certain way.

The controlling parenting style is probably the most frequently discussed in literature. Baumrind (1971, 1991), a research psychologist who has written extensively on parenting styles, identified two such styles that focus strongly on parental authority: the authoritative and the authoritarian. The more controlling parent is the authoritarian parent, whereas the authoritative parent provides more guidance and support. In *The Psychology of Parental Control*, Grolnick (2003) stated,

> The authoritarian parent attempts to shape, control, and evaluate the child using set standards. He or she values obedience first and foremost and uses forceful measures to inculcate desired behaviors. . . . This type of parent tends to enforce rules firmly, confronts and sanctions negative behavior on the part of the child, and discourages independence and individuality. (p. 5)

The primary focus for such parents is their need to be the authority figures in their home. Adolescents often challenge parental authority, and these parents often respond with increased emphasis on obedience.

Different Types of Control

Not all types of control are negative or unhealthy. Control that prevents a teenager from engaging in destructive behavior is necessary and healthy. There is a difference between being controlling and being in control. Parents who are in control provide structure and supervision for their teen, but in a way that is flexible and fair and encourages responsibility, maturity, and independence. Controlling parents, on the other hand, direct their teen's behavior with a strict set of expectations that are usually not negotiable, and the goal is compliance rather than independence.

Parental control can be achieved through positive interactions and rewards or through negative means. More often, parents invested in controlling their teens use negatives types of control. Control in these types of families entails limits not only on behavior, but also opinions, interests, food preferences, friends, choice of activities, music, clothes, hairstyles, and even emotions. Many Baby Boomers can remember the arguments that went on in certain households over young men's long hair in the 1960s. Although the issues change, the conflicts are similar. There are valid reasons to place limits on some adolescent choices, such as age-inappropriate movies and music with violent themes and vulgar language, but control that is based on parental preference without regard for current styles and interests can become excessive and unnecessary.

Parents attempt to maintain authority over their adolescents in a variety of ways, such as controlling their access to various privileges, limiting their contact with friends, withholding or withdrawing parental affection, imposing financial penalties, lecturing, and grounding. More extreme measures for control include inducing guilt, shaming, ridiculing, belittling, screaming, and physical punishment.

Positive types of control encourage adolescents to behave in preferred ways by providing incentives or rewards for their behavior. Positive incentives include financial compensation for good grades or completing chores, earning privileges for appropriate behavior or tasks completed, and receiving praise and affection for appropriate behavior. There are times when positive control is effective and has beneficial outcomes, as the parent feels in control and teens feel good about their behavior.

Although rewards and incentives are less harmful to the adolescent than punishments, they can have some of the same long-term effects when parents try to micromanage too many areas of the adolescent's life. Adolescents may feel that the only time they are acknowledged or appreciated is when they are performing in a way that pleases their parents. Further, when positive methods of control are used to excess, they can become detrimental or ineffective. For example, making every privilege at home contingent upon a specific grade in school can deprive teenagers of the opportunity to develop their own interests and feelings of accomplishment.

Parents who raise their children primarily through the use of control tend to share many similar characteristics. The following description is not exhaustive, and parents may exhibit some or all of these characteristics.

Issues with Authority

Most controlling parents have a strong need to maintain their authority with their children, and many believe it is in the child's best interest for them to do so. The parent's need to be in charge often overrides any other concern for the adolescent's developmental needs. Such parents' love for their child is often genuine and their parenting style is predicated on the need to raise their children in a manner that they believe will result in a well-behaved and respectful teenager. For other parents in this category, maintaining control is more important than their teens' needs, and their love is often conditional.

My House, My Rules parents set the rules, and their teens are expected to follow them. The rules are not always clearly delineated, but parents expect that the teen will know and abide by what is expected.. These rules include curfews, expectations for school grades, places they can go, friends they can have, household chores, and never talking back or disagreeing. In some households, the rules are spelled out, whereas in others they are arbitrary. Decisions are almost always at the discretion of the parent. Reasons for decisions may or may not be given. These are "if you live in my house, you will live under my rules" families.

Parents in this category often believe that their children owe them respect, love, and gratitude. Parenting does have many built-in rewards, but as adolescents attempt to separate from their parents, their childhood idealization drops away and they often act as if their parents' opinions and decisions are outdated and stupid. This does not sit well with controlling parents, who, as Neuharth (1998) said in *If You Had Controlling Parents*, "need, expect, even command their children to love, appreciate, admire, listen to, and reflect well on them. Because controlling parents believe they own their children, they feel justified in such expectations" (p. 134).

Respect seems to be a particularly strong expectation in homes where control is the primary method of parenting. Many parents demand respect, only to find out that they have created children who appear to respect them but in reality do not. Such parents often make statements like this: "If I had said that to my parents, I would have ended up on the floor." Control allows them to continue to feel loved and respected, even if their child's emotions are orchestrated by their demands.

High Expectations

Controlling parents often have very high expectations for their adolescents. They may expect their children to make all As, be the best players on the baseball team, be involved in school programs, and excel in other areas of their lives. Often, these parents' high expectations for their adolescents are connected to their own need to appear successful. They are often very proud of their child's accomplishments and brag to anybody who will listen. However, they often neglect to share how proud they are with their own children, choosing instead to focus on the small details that are less than perfect.

In such cases, it is the parents' need to have their child succeed or excel at a certain activity that leads to the controlling behavior. We might call these parents "stage moms" or "soccer dads"; they are the ones we often see berating their teen after a performance for failing to be the best. There have been several incidents in the past few years of violence breaking out during a children's sports event because of a parent's anger over something that happened during the game. Investigation into the parenting style of these perpetrators would probably show that they were controlling parents.

Overinvolvement

Another common characteristic of controlling parents is their need to get involved in the small details of their adolescent's life. These parents tend to micromanage their adolescents' schoolwork, friendships, dress, and even their opinions. They often ignore the adolescents' need for privacy and use any means necessary to remain informed of their activities, including reading their text messages, asking the teen's friends for detailed information, listening in on phone calls, and endless questioning.

Often these parents have trouble separating their children's lives from their own. To maintain closeness, they need to remain in control.

Emotional Manipulation

Another method that parents use to control their teens' behavior, and even their thoughts, is emotional manipulation. This may include emotional blackmail, guilt, long lectures, feigned distress or illness, verbal assaults on the adolescent's sense of self, and making the teen feel responsible for the parent's well-being. They control their teens through an aversive method—the need to avoid mom or dad's guilt or endless lectures—or other emotional unpleasantness.

Tina, a single mom, prided herself on being able to control her two teenagers with few consequences and without using physical punishment. Tina overreacted emotionally to her teens' behavior, stressing how disappointed she was in their behavior and inducing excessive guilt over minor infractions. Tina could go on for hours about the sacrifices that she made to give her children the best and how ungrateful they were. Her teenagers did their best to avoid her manipulation; as a result, they shared as little as possible with her.

Another emotional ploy is to exploit a weakness—such as back problems, migraines, heart problems, or even anxiety and depression—to control children by implying that if the child does not obey, the parent will become worse or even die. (Remember the father on the 1970s TV show *Sanford and Son*? He would pretend that he was having a heart attack every time his son disagreed with him.) Teenagers of such parents often have such an ingrained sense of responsibility for their parents' well-being that they would not even consider disagreeing with them. These teens often assume the role of caretaker for the parent and ignore their own social and emotional needs.

Emotional manipulation is a powerful form of control. Parents who control through manipulation tend to be emotionally needy and look to their children to meet their needs.

Methods of Control

My House, My Rules parents control their teens with excessive rules and harsh consequences. Some rules are well known to the teen, whereas others are made up on the spur of the moment. Most are established to allow the parents to feel like they have complete control over their teen's life. Curfews, for example, are standard in most homes; but in controlling families, the curfew can be arbitrarily changed and is often earlier than that of the teen's peers. Other rules are designed to control the teen's activities, companions, and schedules. Teens are expected to ask permission even for minor changes, and parents become angry if the teen deviates at all from the permitted activity.

Use of computers, cell phones, television, and music players is often subject to parental whim. Controlling parents tend to say "no" more often than they say "yes," even if there is no good reason to deny a request. "Because I said so" is enough of a reason for these parents.

Consequences in authoritarian homes are often harsh and excessive. These parents often resort to punishment as a way to control their children. Punishment can include withdrawal of privileges, yelling, threatening, and in some cases, physical violence. Teens may be grounded for weeks at a time. I have encountered many adults in my practice who talk bitterly about spending most of their teen years grounded for long periods. Most do not remember why. Consequences in these families are more about the parents' need to show their power than about helping the teen learn about life.

When Authority Is Questioned

One of the more common and harmful characteristics of My House, My Rules parents is their reaction when their adolescent rebels and argues with them. In some families, parents allow a certain amount of rebellion but then attempt to resume control over some small issue. This tends to result in erratic control being exerted; in response, the teen often becomes more angry and frustrated. In other families, controlling parents react strongly if their adolescent resists them, even on a minor issue. These parents often use terms such as "my house, my rules" or "if you don't like it, you can get out."

Controlling parents may also punish a teenager for not responding immediately or with the appropriate attitude. This can often lead to power struggles between the adolescent and the parent. Disagreement on the part of the adolescent is considered disrespectful, and parents often react angrily to the perceived disrespect.

Sam, a 14-year-old boy, came into therapy with his parents following a physical altercation with his father. What started out as a small disagreement over the volume of his music got physical when Sam's father became increasingly angry over Sam's sarcastic responses. Within minutes, Sam's father grabbed him and Sam pushed back. During the therapy session, Sam's father said he felt justified in his reaction, stressing how his son had disrespected him by not turning his music down when asked.

In many such cases, parents focus on the issue of respect and ignore the issue that the teen is concerned about.

Authoritarian parents often believe that the punishment must include some sort of pain, either physical or emotional. They become increasingly agitated and angry if their teenager defies them, which in turn often results in the adolescent responding physically as well. Most physical altercations are seen in families in which the parent is controlling and the adolescent is angry about the control. Bradley (2002) put it this way in *Yes, Your Teen Is Crazy*:

> Parents who use corporal punishment get small, conforming children who become large, aggressive adolescents. Teens with serious acting out problems usually come from parents with cold, demanding, inconsistent, and critical parenting styles. Kids can feel that these types of parents are really preoccupied with fulfilling their own needs for power and control, and are less concerned for their child's welfare. (p. 129)

Most controlling parents do not like their parenting methods to be questioned. These parents rarely seek out experts' advice on parenting and, if they do receive advice, tend to believe that the information does not pertain to them. Such parents need to appear competent. They staunchly defend their parenting style, even in the face of evidence that it has been ineffective. When the teenage children of controlling parents are brought into therapy, it is usually because the parents hope that the therapist will help them strengthen their control over the adolescent. These parents want their teen "fixed"; they do not want their style of parenting questioned. At times they even leave therapy and continue dealing with an out-of-control teen rather than face the possibility that their parenting methods need to change.

Parenting Style: Origins and Motivations

Parents adopt the My House, My Rules parenting style for four main reasons: family history, their own emotional issues, environment, and their teen's temperament and behavior. These four factors can interact or function independently. When they are combined, the result is often an increased need for control.

Family History

Most of our parenting choices come from our own childhood experiences: Simply put, we parent the way that we were parented. This pattern often surfaces especially in times of stress. Most My House, My Rules parents came from authoritarian families. They often use this experience as justification for their own controlling style, arguing that they "turned out all right" and their child will too. But further exploration usually identifies areas of distress or disturbance in their lives or personalities.

Many attempt to heal the trauma from their own childhood by becoming controlling themselves and thus convincing themselves that their parents acted out of love. Others adopt the authoritarian parent role as a way of finally becoming the good sons or daughters that they were never quite able to be, in their parents' eyes, during their own childhood. Other parents identify so closely with their own parents that they sincerely believe that their parenting style is appropriate and in the best interest of their child.

Controlling parents often come from homes that were highly structured or rigid. Maintaining the structure in the home was more important than an individual family member's needs. Other lifestyle influences—including the military, cultures in which parental control is the norm, cultlike groups, and certain religious sects—also stress parental authority.

Rheena was a 17-year-old girl who was born in India and moved to the United States with her family as a small child. Her parents, especially her father, were very controlling, and dating was forbidden until after high school. Rheena reported that many of her Indian friends dated in secret and covered for each other with their parents.

Rheena secretly began seeing an older man she met at her church and became pregnant. She stayed with relatives during her pregnancy and then gave the child up for adoption. Rheena came home depressed and eventually came into treatment with her father. Rheena's father was able to make some adjustments in his parenting style, and Rheena's depression improved. After graduating from high school, she was able to leave home and attend college. Prior to treatment, the expectation was that Rheena would live at home and attend a local college.

Another characteristic of controlling families is that punishment, especially physical punishment, is used to maintain the fear factor. This type of consequence intensifies the parent's position of power. It is well documented that children who were physically punished often become strict disciplinarians in their own homes.

Neuharth (1998) reported a high incidence of trauma in the lives of the parents interviewed for his research. This trauma included loss of a parent, sexual or physical abuse, having an alcoholic parent, or experiencing a chronic family trauma such as a severe illness or poverty. There is always a connection between parents' family history and the parenting style that they use with their own children.

Parents who stress obedience usually find this parenting style to be effective when their children are small, as children are likely to comply because they accept the parent's authority or fear punishment. However, parenting adolescents is a different experience, and blind obedience is not in teen nature. Leman (2002) put it succinctly in *Adolescence Isn't Terminal:*

> For about eight or nine years this parenting seems to work perfectly. They say "jump" and their son asks "how high?". . . . During the kids' adolescence, however, such a parenting style inevitably begins to fall apart. . . . You know what mistakes these parents made? They always thought of their kids as very obedient, when, in fact, they raise kids who were easily controlled. (p. 105)

Strict management of their teen allows many parents to feel a sense of control over their lives as a whole. When they can prevent their teenagers from questioning their decisions, parents can avoid having to look too closely at themselves. These parents believe that their approach is justified because it appears to result in well-behaved and safe children. Many would not consider themselves to be controlling but believe that they are providing a stable home environment for their children. It might be said that these parents take their responsibility as parents too seriously.

Bill came into therapy with his son John after numerous verbal confrontations. During the course of the treatment, it became clear that Bill had a strong need to be in control and that any disagreement from John would cause an excessively strong reaction from Bill. When it was suggested to Bill that his parenting style was too controlling, he became very defensive. However, when Bill's controlling nature was reframed as his taking his responsibility as a father too seriously, he was able to look at his parenting style and make the necessary adjustments in the way that he handled his son.

Personality Influences

The personality characteristics of controlling parents have a great deal of influence over their parenting style. Although it is not possible to detail every personality facet that can affect an individual's choice of parenting style, it can be safely said that some characteristics are more common in controlling parents than in noncontrolling parents.

Controlling parents are often rigid and have little tolerance for any situation or person that does not conform to their expectations. These parents like predictability, and although they cannot always control what goes on in the outside world, they do have a degree of control over what happens in their family. They often also have a low tolerance for stress. Stress is usually considered to have an external source; but for many, it comes from inside: their perceptions of the situation and their ability to handle it.

Teenagers by nature are impulsive, unpredictable, and emotional, which inevitably leads to a certain amount of chaos in a family. Parents whose children had dinner at 6:00 P.M., had their bath at 7:00, and were tucked in their beds by 8:30 suddenly discover that their teenager is still awake at midnight talking to friends on the phone. Teens are stressful! Insecurity is another common attribute of these parents, and they may try to control their own insecurity by controlling their children:

> Feeling flawed, controlling parents pretend they are perfect. Feeling small, they act big. Feeling afraid, they frighten others. Feeling bad about themselves, they shame others. Feeling wrong, they insist on being right. Feeling doubt, they confuse. Feeling deprived, they withhold. (Neuharth, 1998, pp. 147–148)

Teenagers in particular have a way of bringing out a parent's insecurities, which, in return, heightens parents' need to keep their teenager under control. Some parents need their children to meet their emotional needs, and control is one way that they try to ensure that the child will be available for them. Adolescents tend to be self-centered and more concerned with their peer group than their parents and, therefore, less available to meet a parent's needs.

Susan was raised by a critical and controlling father. When her own daughter reached adolescence and began to question some of Susan's decisions, Susan began to feel inadequate as a mother. To compensate for this sense of inadequacy, she became very rigid with her daughter, refusing to discuss most issues. Unconsciously, Susan was afraid that her daughter and other parents might find out that she was incompetent as a parent. In reality, she was not incompetent, just insecure and overwhelmed.

Parents may want to avoid having their child grow up and move away. One way to prevent this is to keep the child dependent on the parent for major decisions. These parents need their child to be dependent on them and need to have a sense of control over the child. This is a tricky undertaking with adolescents, who are working hard to separate and move on to adulthood. Controlled teens push harder and are more likely to look forward to leaving home.

Environmental Factors

Environmental factors clearly play a part in the etiology of parental control. Parents who live with a high degree of stress often need to control their environment in order to feel as if they are managing. There are a number of possible sources for the stress that parents and families experience. Stress can come from difficulties in the marital relationship, workplace problems, financial problems, or the responsibility of handling everyday family issues. Other stresses, though not common to every family, include chronic illness, emotional problems, substance abuse, poverty, and legal difficulties. Problems from the outside world—such as drugs, gangs, crime, terrorism threats, and natural disasters—can affect a family system.

Teens nowadays have instant access to others and to the outside world via cell phones and Internet sites such as MySpace, Facebook, and YouTube. This can create additional fear on the part of parents that there are dangers out in the world from which they cannot protect their child. In *The Good Teen* (2007), Lerner pointed out that

> as hard as it is to monitor teens as they live their actual lives, it gets even harder to monitor their virtual lives. And we all know that there are bad people out there who need to do harm; there are also crazy, hurtful ideas circulating every minute. But many teens don't realize this. (p. 121)

The need to protect teens from these outside dangers can increase parents' efforts to restrict and control their teen's behavior.

Parents may want not only to protect their children but also to protect the family from what the neighbors will think. There are times when parental control is related to a concern about how others will perceive their parenting skills. Teens, although very concerned about what their peers think, do not seem to care what other adults think about their clothes, hairstyles, and behavior. When parents are made aware of a teen's inappropriate behavior by an outside source—such as school staff, police, neighbors, or other parents—they react to regain a sense of control over the situation.

Parents are also aware that alcohol and drugs are a part of the adolescent world and do whatever they believe will keep their teen from using them. Even if parents themselves drank or used drugs as teenagers, they work to keep their own teen from doing the same. The drive to control teen alcohol or drug use may be especially strong if parents' own use led to negative consequences. There are a number of well-known symptoms of drug use in teens, but concerned parents may overreact to even minor behavior changes. Suspicious behavior on the part of the teen may invoke more control by the parent. Providing restrictions to curtail a teen's drug use is a parent's responsibility and can lead to an open and healthy parent–teen relationship.

Life Stressors

Work is a significant part of almost every adult's life. A job not only provides financial compensation but is also the primary source of an adult's sense of productivity and personal achievement. It is rare for anyone functioning in a work environment not to feel some stress, whether from his or her own internal pressure or from external forces such as a difficult supervisor, heavy workload, or pending deadline. This is the case whether a parent works in an office, is self-employed, or is a stay-at-home mom or dad. Stress in the work environment may result in parents becoming more authoritative at home, especially when they feel out of control at work. In *Life Matters,* Merrill and Merrill (2003) pointed out the following:

> All too often we tend to see work as a place to contribute and home as a place to crash. We come home from work exhausted, and we somehow expect that everything should be in order, everyone should be happy, and we should be able to simply recuperate from the efforts of the day. (p. 113)

Enter the teen with a less-than-pleasant attitude, and a parent's ability to respond calmly goes out the window. Further, when parents are unable to receive the satisfaction that they need from work or feel that their supervisors or colleagues are critical of them, they may compensate by becoming more controlling with their teens.

Gerald, 51, has been working at the same company for 20 years. He was recently hoping for a promotion, but a younger worker was promoted instead and became his new supervisor. Gerald's anger and frustration over this situation resulted in his becoming increasingly critical of his 16-year-old son's schoolwork and chores. Gerald's rationale was that he wanted his son to be able to handle the responsibilities and frustrations of the work environment.

The reality is that work and home both require our best efforts, and the rewards are not automatic or guaranteed. Many adults have an unrealistic expectation that home should be a place of peace and quiet, and frustration sets in when they encounter the chaos of home life, especially in homes with teenagers. It would certainly be in the best interest of parents and teens if parents gave their relationship with their adolescent higher priority than any work expectations. This does not mean that work should not be a significant part of an adult's life, but all areas of one's life should be kept in perspective. No one's headstone has ever said "beloved employee."

Financial stress can be a major factor in a parent's need to control the home environment. Teens may not always understand when a parent does not have the money to pay for something that the teen covets. Parents may also feel guilty when they are unable to provide something that their teen wants. Some of their controlling behavior may also be due to envy of the fun and freedom that their teens are able to experience. Limited financial resources can be a significant factor in a parent's need to be in control at home.

Poverty can affect the amount of time, energy, and patience that a parent has to devote to childrearing. Imposing rigid rules can seem easier and less time-consuming than dealing with individual issues on a case-by-case basis. Many low-income families also live in neighborhoods where drugs and gangs are a threat. Such environmental factors may result in parents being more controlling for the safety of their child rather than for their own need to be in charge.

Parents can also experience marital or relationship stress. Becoming parents adds significant stress to any marriage, but with the onset of the teenage years, the stress multiplies. In *The Good Enough Teen,* Sachs (2005) stated, "Raising adolescents can send even the most solid marriage into a tailspin that can take years to pull out of, if it's pulled out of at all, making the union feel much more like an ordeal than an ideal" (p. 246). Dissatisfaction in the marital relationship can lead parents to increase their focus on their teen's behavior. Controlling the teen's behavior may allow parents to feel more in control of their own lives, or it may be a way to delay the day when the teen moves away from home and leaves them alone with a partner they are dissatisfied with. The relationship of the roles of spouse and parent is intertwined and complex. The effect that the quality of the marital relationship has on parenting is discussed in other sections as well.

Changes Related to Adolescence

Some parents are not particularly controlling during their child's early years but become stricter when their child enters adolescence and starts to disagree with their decisions. Parents may do this for several reasons: They may fear the loss of control; they may be attempting to delay the child's growing up and separating from them; they may be afraid to lose the child's companionship; or they may need to maintain the sense that their child respects and idolizes them. Fear of losing the child to peers and adulthood may occur more in families where the parents' marriage is troubled or there is a single parent.

Some parents become My House, My Rules parents in reaction to their adolescent's behavior. They may have started out being more relaxed, but once the adolescent's behavior became problematic, especially if this came to their attention from outside sources, they try to control the behavior by whatever means possible. Maxym and York (2000) put it this way in *Teens in Turmoil:* "Often parents resort to trying to control their teen's behavior, attitude, and worldview in the vain hope that it would make their teen change, really change, and become once again the kid they used to know" (pp. 16–17). In fact, many books on adolescent behavioral problems encourage parents to regain control by asserting their authority.

Finally, the individual teen's personality, temperament, and behavior affect parents' reactions. Increased control may become necessary when teens are unable to keep themselves safe. Drug use, illegal activities, and truancy are some of the behaviors that a parent needs to respond to firmly. However, attempting to increase control after a teen is already out of control is difficult and may lead to more acting out.

There are also times when a teen's negative attitude becomes so frustrating for parents that they respond by becoming more controlling. This power struggle is more common between fathers and sons and mothers and daughters. Fathers often mistakenly believe that they need to be tough with their sons in order for them to become responsible men. For these fathers, being tough means maintaining control in the family, even if this requires threats and physical violence. Mothers, worried that they won't be able to maintain their authority with their sons, may become increasingly rigid in order to maintain the facade that they are in control.

Parents often become concerned about their teenage daughters when it becomes obvious that they have developed into sexual beings. When their teenage daughter begins to dress provocatively and spend more time in the company of boys, many parents attempt to prevent her from becoming sexually active by placing external controls on her activities.

Glenda was very concerned when her 14-year-old daughter started dressing in clothes she considered provocative and inappropriate. Glenda's sister had become pregnant at 16, and Glenda responded to her own daughter's budding sexuality by restricting her social events and continually accusing her of behaving inappropriately. In reality, Glenda's daughter had not become sexually active, but Glenda's overreaction eventually resulted in more sexual behavior by the daughter, not less.

Adolescent Reactions

By nature, teens are emotional and are often quick to react to issues. Adolescence is dominated by a search for identity, a need to separate from one's parents, and growing awareness that parents are not omnipotent. These three factors make it almost inevitable that the adolescent will react in some way to parental efforts at control. Some adolescents react by withdrawing emotionally and becoming outwardly obedient, others become compliant, and still others react in a negative and rebellious manner. Wolf (1991) made this comment in *Get Out of My Life, but First Could You Drive Me and Cheryl to the Mall?*:

When confronted by a rule they do not like teenagers will do all they can to get it changed, to somehow get around it, to confuse the issue, or where they feel they can safely contrive not to get caught, to disobey the rule altogether. They will tell half-truths, lies, whatever is necessary to accomplish their objective. (p. 97)

Rebellion

The first reaction of teenagers to parental authority they deem unreasonable is to become argumentative. In some cases, the teenager argues long enough that the parent either backs off or compromises. In other cases, the argument between teen and parent may escalate until the parent imposes additional punishment. Parents in these situations end up making absolute statements, such as "this is my house, and as long as you live in my house, you will follow my rules" and "if you don't like it, you can get out"—and the teen may opt to do just that. Some teenagers have left home and lived on the streets rather than deal with the rules and demands at home. Other teens escape by dissociating emotionally, using drugs or alcohol, isolating, or staying away from home with peers.

Raul and Maria came into therapy with their two teenage children. Both parents had a strong need for parental authority in the home, and both teenagers had responded by becoming increasingly rebellious. Arguments were a daily occurrence in the home. The more Raul and Maria tried to exert control, the more negative the teenagers' behavior became. The daughter started acting out sexually, and the son became involved in drug use. Both students' grades dropped. The teens' behavior was their way of making the point that they were not going to be controlled. Eventually, one teen moved out of the house and the other went to live with a relative.

Teenagers who feel that they are unable to change their parents' decisions through their arguments will often resort to passive–aggressive behavior. This includes engaging in the prohibited behavior without the parents' knowledge, being difficult and unpleasant during regular family events, sneaking around behind the parents' backs, and withdrawing affection. A particularly powerful way to respond passive–aggressively to controlling parents is to do poorly in areas that the parents cannot easily control, such as school grades. Teenage girls with controlling parents may become anorexic or promiscuous. Teenage boys may engage in impulsive behavior or bully others.

Teens often become less willing to be controlled as they get older. Frustration over limits can build for some teens, even those whose temperament is easygoing. Teens who are naturally quick to react may respond with little provocation—often with outright defiance, such as arguing, refusing to comply, or storming out of the room or house. Some teens even become physically aggressive in their defiance and punch holes in the wall, slam doors, throw things, or even push, grab, or hit their parents. Trying to get a teen to act reasonably once he or she has started behaving in an out-of-control manner is difficult, especially if the behavior began in reaction to parental controls.

John (whose case was described earlier) became increasingly confrontational with his father, Bill, arguing, storming out, or punching holes in the walls. Bill responded by trying to exert more control. The cycle escalated and caused damage to the entire family. Bill came into therapy with John when his wife threatened to move out and take John with her.

Compliance

Not all teenagers react to the My House, My Rules parenting style by becoming negative or angry. A number of adolescents become compliant and simply allow their parents to manage many of the details of their personal lives. They work hard to meet their parents' expectations and constantly elicit approval from their parents for their behavior and accomplishments. Often these teens become efficient at gauging their parents' reactions and behaving in a manner that fits with their parents' desires. Most were obedient as children and continue to be so as teenagers.

Other teenagers may initially try to argue but soon realize that they are not going to win the battle and simply give up and become compliant. Some submissive teens genuinely believe that their parents' rules and expectations are in their best interest and thus do not question them. In certain cultures, religions, and social groups, teenagers simply do not question parental authority. Some adolescents appear compliant but actually become adept at functioning under the radar and engaging in prohibited behaviors without their parents' knowledge.

Teenagers have a great deal of power in the family dynamics. In many cases, the teens can choose not to engage in power struggles with the parents. Parents will be less likely to exert control when teens are showing responsible behavior, such as performing well in school and doing their chores without complaining. Open communication by the teen, which allows parents to have some sense of awareness of what's going on in the teen's world, can often help relax a parent's fears, thus reducing the parent's need to exert control. Clearly, a combination of factors affects the amount of control exhibited in the home.

Negative and Unhealthy Teen Reactions

A small minority of teenagers who have difficulty dealing with their parents' control may react in ways that are harmful to themselves but that they view as a way to escape parental control. Some teens use drugs or alcohol. Others run away from home and live on the street. Others engage in promiscuity, anorexia, gang involvement, and a variety of illegal activities, including shoplifting and vandalism. For teenagers with the strongest reaction to parental controls, their personalities become formed as a negative reaction to the parent. A parent who stresses scholastic success may end up with a teenager who is a high school dropout, whereas a rigid and moralistic parent may end up with a teenager who is promiscuous. Forward and Buck (1989) wrote the following in *Toxic Parents:*

> The truth is, if we rebel in reaction to our parents, we are being controlled, just as surely as if we submit.... [We] call this "self-defeating" rebellion. It is the flip side of capitulation.... Self-defeating rebellion is a reaction against a controlling parent, an exercise in which the means attempt to justify an unsatisfactory end. (pp. 63, 65)

More harmful reactions to parental control include depression, anxiety, anorexia, and other emotional disorders. Adolescents who experience these strong emotional reactions are usually dealing with a combination of their own emotional capacity to handle situations and their parents' need to be in control. Many times, the type of control exhibited by these parents is excessive, punitive, and emotionally abusive. Control that is punctuated by negative assessments of the individual—including statements such as "you are so stupid," "you're worthless," and "you never get anything right"—take their toll on the teenager's sense of self. Even as adolescents are striving to develop their own sense of self, they are still very connected to their parents' opinions of them, and being "not good enough" will take its toll. This is not to imply that all teenagers who develop emotional difficulties have controlling parents, but when the teen's natural developmental goals are thwarted, some form of emotional reaction will occur.

Short- and Long-Term Outcomes

Adolescents who grow up in homes with My House, My Rules parents exhibit a number of personality traits or emotional difficulties as adults. Whether these characteristics are primarily positive or negative will depend on the teen's reactions. Studies have shown noticeable impact on academic achievement, identity development, personal relationships, and emotional problems associated with teenagers raised in controlling and rigid homes (Aquilino & Supple, 2001; Gonzalez, Greenwood, & Wen Hsu, 2001; Spera, 2005; Strage & Brandt, 1999). What happens when these controlled individuals grow up and need to set up their own household, but have never had the opportunity to set their own life rules?

Peer Pressure and Negative Behaviors

Negative peer influence is a concern for all parents. Teens who are controlled by their parents are often susceptible to control by their peers as well. This is especially true in romantic relationships. Teenagers who are used to being controlled and having their parents make most of their decisions for them are more likely to give in to peer pressure.

Nancy grew up with a controlling single mother who disliked every boy Nancy tried to date. In her early 20s, she married an older man who was her mother's coworker and friend, as she felt he was the only man her mother would approve of. Her husband became emotionally abusive, but Nancy lacked the emotional strength to stand up to him. She divorced him 20 years later; even then, her mother criticized her for her decision.

Many controlling parents are concerned about their teenagers becoming involved in negative and dangerous behaviors including drug abuse, sexual activity, and crime. Compliant "good kids" may not become involved in inappropriate behaviors out of fear of parental wrath, but this control is not always carried into their young adult life. Another possibility is that teenagers who wish to rebel against parental control may become involved in negative behaviors to get back at their parents or as a way of numbing the anger and frustration they feel about being controlled.

Emotional Issues

Teenagers are prone to emotional problems such as depression and anxiety when their home life is stressful because of high expectations and constant demands. They are also more likely to withdraw and numb their feelings. Darling (1999) reported that "children and adolescents from authoritarian families . . . have poorer social skills, lower self-esteem, and higher levels of depression" (p. 3). Such teens may turn to drugs or alcohol as a way of self-medicating these feelings of depression and anxiety. Even if their intention is to improve their teen, controlling parents tend to be critical rather than affirming, and the end result is a teenager or young adult with a low sense of self-worth and a poorly defined identity.

Academic Issues

According to a number of studies, the academic performance of adolescents from authoritarian homes tends to be somewhat lower than that of adolescents raised in more nurturing and democratic homes. Grolnick (2003) reviewed numerous studies that supported the hypothesis that parental control can lead to lower academic achievement:

> Evidence presented . . . showed that controlling styles are associated with lower levels of grades and achievement scores. . . . parental control can weaken children's intrinsic motivation to pursue a variety of activities, among them school activities. There is also evidence that parental control can undermine children's movement toward a greater valuing of and personal sense of responsibility for behaviors and activities that are not inherently interesting, thus keeping children tied to external contingencies. (pp. 118–119)

Teens need to feel they have a real stake in their schoolwork, in order to be able to use the knowledge they acquire later in life. In some cases, it may appear that adolescents are doing well at school, because they are compliant and work hard to make good grades, but they are only doing so in response to parental pressure. Grades made in order to please parents are less likely to have meaning for the teen and are unlikely to be viewed as important information to be retained.

Jason's grades had developed into a noticeable pattern. His three-week progress report would show disappointing grades, and his parents would react by grounding him until the next reporting period. At that time, his grades would show improvement, and then the pattern would repeat itself. Jason's parents were in a constant uproar over his grades, but Jason showed no sense of responsibility for his own schoolwork. The family worked in therapy to allow Jason to assume ownership of his schoolwork, and the pattern disappeared.

Such adolescents may do worse in college because they do not have the same structure and control to push them academically. It is not unheard of for high-achieving high school students to flunk out of freshman year at college. Parental involvement can have a positive effect as long as the adolescent also develops an enjoyment of and appreciation for education.

Identity Issues

As teenagers from controlling families grow into adults, they encounter a number of problems that can be directly linked to having been too controlled at home during adolescence. The primary task of adolescence is to develop a separate identity from that of one's parents; this is the task most likely to be affected by the type of parenting one experiences. Parents who make most of the decisions for their teen throughout high school prevent the teen from developing a clear-cut identity of his or her own. Forward and Buck (1989) concluded the following: "Adult children of controlling parents often have a very blurred sense of identity. They have trouble seeing themselves as separate beings from their parents. They can't distinguish their own needs from their parents' needs. They feel powerless" (p. 71).

Many teenagers, on reaching adulthood, develop an identity that is either in accordance with their parents' demands or a reaction against parental control. Adolescents from controlling families have difficulty making their own decisions, understanding their own emotions, and finding appropriate expressions for their feelings. Many try desperately to continue living up to parental expectations and demands.

Bruce was his parents' pride and joy, making good grades and getting admitted to his father's alma mater. School was strictly monitored in his family and anything less than an "A" was unacceptable. He earned a degree in electrical engineering, as was expected of him, even though he had no real interest in his major. Once he graduated from college and had to make his own decisions about a career and social life, he was at a total loss. After failing at several jobs, Bruce became depressed to the point of needing hospitalization.

Work and Career Issues

Authoritarian family styles can affect teens' ability to make career choices. As young adults, they often allow their parents' preferences to influence their career decisions:

> In recent studies conducted in my laboratory, my colleagues and I have shown that controlling parenting has ramifications for how young adults make the transition into the world of work. Young adults who perceive their parents as controlling are more external and less autonomous in their reasons for pursuing their careers. (Grolnick, 2003, p. 150)

Choice of career is not the only issue that these teens face in the adult world. Teens who were accustomed to being compliant as a way of making life easy at home tend to continue this behavior into adulthood. They are often submissive at work and in social relationships, abdicating their own interests and wishes. For many, this subservient position interferes with their chance for promotion. As adults, they may become resentful but have difficulty finding appropriate ways to express themselves. These adults may have difficulty asserting themselves as well.

Others may find that they are successful in work because they are very good at following workplace protocols, rules, and regulations. Careers in which compliance is expected may be suitable for such individuals. Many who lived under high expectations as adolescents become Type A personalities at work. They are perfectionists and push themselves to meet their own high expectations, some of which were developed by the stringent expectations of their parents. Such personalities are difficult to work for, as they have unrealistic expectations of others and can be very critical. In therapy, many of these adults, especially men, talk about the high demands placed on them by their fathers, who gave them very little approval and support.

Relationship Issues

Being raised in an authoritarian home also affects personal relationships—which, on the adult level, require a degree of independence, self-awareness, and comfort with expressing feelings. Individuals raised by My House, My Rules parents may struggle with these issues. Although they are not associated with one specific relationship type, some possibilities are more likely than others.

Teens from controlling homes may find themselves drawn to peers who are impulsive and rebellious. Others may avoid relationships for fear of not being able to handle the responsibility that love requires; for them, love is about meeting expectations. Many become controlling in their own relationships. Some may seek out strong personalities who continue the pattern of control, and even end up in abusive relationships.

Controlling parents may have difficulty letting their adult children leave home and may be critical of their partners. Grown children may have an ongoing sense of responsibility toward their parents that interferes with the functioning of their own family. Teenagers who depended on parental approval may, as adults, continue to seek approval from their parents and others. To have healthy relationships in adulthood, teenagers must successfully master the tasks of adolescence. This may not be possible in families where obedience is more important than the teen's developmental needs.

Teenagers from My House, My Rules families often become authoritarian parents themselves. The pattern may change slightly, but the issue of control continues to take center stage. As young adults, they may stay tied to their families of origin and continue to allow their parents to make many of their decisions. Others distance themselves from their parents, maintaining only a superficial relationship. Some stronger individuals work to establish separate lives and yet remain close to their parents, with appropriate boundaries.

Positive Outcomes

When parental control is limited to certain areas and allows adolescents to make decisions about other areas of their lives, such as clothing, friends, and music, there may be a positive outcome in terms of personality development. Many teenagers have a lot of stress from school and extracurricular activities, and a level of predictability and structure at home can allow them to focus on schoolwork or on developing a special talent. They may also learn to focus on what is important and downplay the smaller "drama" issues inherent in adolescents' social lives. They may grow into adults who are well organized and focused on their life goals. A teen from a controlling home may also develop a strong and decisive personality after finding a way to establish a separate identity while dealing with parental pressure.

Summary

The long-term consequences of growing up with My House, My Rules parents was summarized well by Grolnick (2003):

> What is at stake? A great deal. . . . Controlling parenting has been associated with lower levels of intrinsic motivation, less internalization of values and morals, poorer self-regulation, and higher levels of negative self-related affects. These issues relate not only to children's development and well-being but also to their success as happy, functioning adults during the course of their lives. (p. 150)

For many parents, controlling their adolescent is intended to create a well-behaved, responsible, and productive adult. However, when the need to maintain authority overrides the teen's developmental needs, the outcome is often less than intended, and can include high levels of parent–teen conflict and unhealthy levels of either rebellion or acquiescence.

CHAPTER FOUR

"Your Life Is My Life" Parents

If teens live with pressure, they learn to be stressed.

—Dorothy Nolte and Rachel Harris,
Teenagers Learn What They Live

Case Example

Claire, 15, came into therapy with her mother, Clarisa. Claire has a younger brother, age 11. Claire was 12 when her parents divorced. The first time I met with Claire and her mother, I noticed that they dressed alike. Both had long brown hair, wore heavy makeup, and were dressed in the latest teenage styles. The presenting problem was Claire's difficulty with her father.

During the initial sessions, it became clear that Claire and her mother were extremely close. Every morning Claire's mother would get up with Claire, help her pick out her clothes, and put her makeup on for her. Mom would then drive Claire and several of her friends to school. After school, Clarisa would take Claire and her friends out for a snack or anywhere the teenagers wanted to go. Weekends, and even some weeknights, the house was full of teenagers. Clarisa was always present and involved in these gatherings. She also allowed the teens to have coed sleepovers on the weekends. She would stay up late, laughing and joking with the teenagers in her house. She was also available any time one of Claire's friends needed a ride or a favor and bought expensive presents for the teenagers.

The closeness between Claire and her mother extended beyond daily activities and the constant parties at the house. Mom requested and received frequent updates via text message from Claire. During therapy sessions, Clarisa and Claire would read each other's text messages and giggle. Clarisa was always involved in her daughter's daily social activities. She would become extremely agitated and protective if she felt that anyone was making negative comments about Claire, even arguing with other parents over minor teen issues. Clarisa seemed to thrive on the drama of the teen world.

Clarisa made no attempt to impose any rules on Claire, except for an intense need for Claire to perform well in school. Conversations with Clarisa uncovered that, as a teen, she had been unpopular, and the only praise she received at home was for her grades. Although Clarisa made no overt attempt to set rules for Claire, she used a lot of subtle emotional manipulation to control Claire. She made a point of making Claire aware of her role as her mom's only companion. Clarisa did not date and had no adult friends.

Although Claire had regular visitation with her father, Clarisa discouraged the relationship. Clarisa maintained that her ex-husband did not have a good feel for what Claire liked or needed. The reality was that Clarisa did not like sharing her daughter with her ex-husband. The enmeshment between Claire and her mother made it extremely difficult for Claire to establish an identity separate from her mother.

Parenting Style Characteristics

"Your Life Is My Life" parents are enmeshed with their adolescent; the boundaries between parent and teen are weak or nonexistent. It is not the teen but the parents who are crossing the boundaries. These parents are involved in their child's life above and beyond the normal interest level of most parents. For these parents, "over" is the key term that can be used to describe their behaviors: They are overinvolved, overfocused, overprotective, overcontrolling, overly invested, overly perfectionistic, overly driven, and—often—overwhelmed. Many are completely invested in what their teens are doing and have high expectations for the individual that the teen is becoming. The majority of parents in this category exhibit some, if not most, of these characteristics.

There is a significant divergence of parental behaviors within this group. Some of these parents are overly demanding and push their teens relentlessly. Others think that their teen can do no wrong and inflate their teen's sense of entitlement. Others are so enamored of their offspring that they sacrifice their own lives to meet their teen's every little need. The underlying drive for these parents is the investment that they have in their teen's life. The teen's life literally becomes the primary focus of their life.

Overinvolvement

The strongest characteristic of these parents is their overinvolvement in their teens' lives. This obsession takes many forms, almost always related to the teen's life outside the home. These parents micromanage their teens' lives, including school, social activities, and sporting events. They read e-mails, listen in on phone calls, monitor Facebook accounts, search their teens' rooms, and question endlessly. Your Life Is My Life parents also ask teachers, coaches, and other parents for information. They lack a sense of boundaries when it comes to obtaining information about their teens. Such overinvolvement often works well with young children, but adolescents are different. They need and want a greater amount of separation from their parents as they mature.

Rachel, age 14, was adopted at birth, after her adoptive mother had spent years trying to conceive. Her mother considered Rachel her special gift and quit working after the adoption so that she could focus all of her attention on her daughter. This closeness worked well until Rachel entered adolescence. Mom went to great lengths to monitor her daughter's activities, reading all her text messages, asking for minute details about her friendships, checking her Facebook account on a daily basis, and going through her room. When mom was unsure about the information she was getting, she would contact Rachel's friends' mothers to find out further details. Rachel's mom could not understand why Rachel was angry about this. In mom's eyes, she was simply staying involved and being a proactive parent.

Parents of this childrearing style are enmeshed with their teenagers. They love the daily drama of their teen's world and become consumed by it. They are often dependent on their teens to meet their own emotional needs and to provide them with interpersonal interaction. They seldom take the time to develop their own social lives or interests. As Furedi (2002) put it in *Paranoid Parenting,* "adults construct their lives through and in interaction with their children. Adults do not simply live their lives through children but, in part, develop their identity through them" (p. 107). When these children move into the teen years, this enmeshment is no longer welcome. Many of these parents feel hurt and rejected when their teen starts to request that they back off.

Other parents who are overly involved in their children's lives are reliving their own adolescence through their child's. They want to be able to enjoy the fun stuff with their teens. Rosenfeld and Wise (2000) put it this way in *The Over-scheduled Child:*

> When highly intelligent people attempt to fill their heads with only the good things going on in their kids' lives—their clothing, interests, activities, schoolwork and social affairs—they end up paying far too much attention to small matters and too little to their own lives. (p. 211)

Rescuing

When Your Life Is My Life parents become aware of difficulties or problems their teens are experiencing, they will often swoop in to rescue them. These parents are often referred to as helicopter parents or fix-it parents. They not only rescue their children, they also often excuse any inappropriate behavior, insisting that "It's not my teen's fault" or "he is just being a boy." They blame the teacher if the teen receives a bad grade, drive their kids to school when they miss the bus, bring their homework to school when they leave it at home, and send an excuse if they don't complete a project. They may hire an attorney to fight a speeding ticket or shoplifting charge. They try to control the outside world, feeling that they need to protect their teens from any negative experiences, emotions, or consequences. The actual behavior of their teens is not as important as the need to rescue them.

Sam was a 17-year-old who came into therapy after being suspended from school for three days for punching another student. As requested, Sam's parents came with him to the first session. Sam's father insisted that the school was overreacting and that the fight was simply a guy thing and that Sam was defending himself. Sam's mother was more concerned with how Sam's suspension was going to affect his grades and what they were going to do with him while he was at home for the three days. It was clear that Sam's father did not consider Sam responsible for his actions. The parents hired an attorney to defend Sam against the "ridiculous charges" that were being pressed by the other teenager.

The Good Parent

Some parents with this parenting style are obsessed with being a good parent and believe that it means that they must anticipate and meet their teen's every need. They do not simply rescue their teens; they overindulge and overprotect them. These parents are afraid that their teenager might experience pain, disappointment, or unhappiness. In addition to providing for their teens' material needs, they try to shelter them from the dangers of the world. These dangers can include drugs, alcohol, and sex. However, the teen world is one of exploration and experimentation; complete protection is simply not possible:

> Here is a terrifying truth: your teens can do whatever they want to do. If they want to get drunk with their peers, they can. If they want to smoke dope, they can find a way. If they are absolutely determined to spray paint houses at midnight, there is very little parents can do to prevent them. . . . As much is this truth scares you, it is essential for you to come to grips with that for this reason: an overprotective parenting style is a prescription for disaster. (Leman, 2002, p. 121)

Expectations

Your Life Is My Life parents place high expectations on their teens: to take Advanced Placement classes and make As, to be captain of the football or cheerleading team, to be popular, and to meet any other parental expectation for success in the teenage years. These parents push hard because of their own need for their children to be successful. The teen's accomplishments are a reflection on the parent and feed the parent's need to be special. It is as if the teen's success becomes the parent's addiction.

Parents with high expectations tend to jump into high gear during the teenage years, because it is during this time that the teen's potential, personality, and future is on the line. This is the time in which the football player becomes the collegiate athlete and the good student gets into the Ivy League school. The movie *Friday Night Lights* (Grazer & Berg, 2004) features a father driven to have his son be the local football star. In the movie, the father confronts his son:

> You just ain't gettin' it. You don't understand. This is the only thing you're gonna have. Forever, it carries you forever. It's an ugly fact of life, Donnie, hell, it's the only fact of life. You got one year, one stinking year to make yourself some memories, son. That's all. It's gone after that. And I'll be damned if you're going to miss it.

In this fictional example, the father's demands on his son were connected to his own high school football career and subsequent dissatisfaction with life.

Appearances

Another common characteristic of parents who live their lives through their kids is the need to push the teen to meet their ideal of themselves. These parents are overly concerned with appearances and need their children to participate in a variety of activities in order to look good to the neighbors, the people at church, coworkers, anybody that the parent encounters. Having bragging rights is what matters. Did you ever listen to adults talking about their teens' accomplishments at a party or at the nail salon? It is often an issue of one-upmanship. They use their teen's activities and accomplishments to elevate their own sense of self. These parents are concerned with appearances, but often disregard their teen's internal emotional needs and personal preferences. For many parents, the title (honor student, Princeton graduate, baseball star) is the goal.

One of the biggest burdens placed on adolescents is their parents' need for them to do well in high school in order to get into a prestigious college. This means that the teens have to develop an impressive résumé. Most important, they need to take advanced classes and make good grades. This inspires all kinds of parenting actions and overreactions. Progress reports and report cards become screaming events. Tutors are hired. SAT prep courses are taken. Some parents even try to have their teens placed on ADD medication to enhance performance.

An extreme example is the mother, a school secretary at her daughter's high school in Pennsylvania, who was arrested in June 2009 for hacking into the school computer and changing her daughter's grades to improve her class rank. The mother also lowered the scores of several other students ("Pa. Mom Charged," 2009).

Besides pushing academics, these parents push their teens to volunteer, have a part-time job, and take part in any other activity that they believe will help them to be selected for the right school. Most of the time, such parents are far less interested in developing the teen's interest in school than in the teen's grades and academic standing.

Joseph was a bright but shy adolescent whose mother was adamant about his attending an Ivy League school. Joseph's mother constantly monitored his grades and pushed him to become more socially active, insisting that he join several school clubs to make his résumé look good. None of the clubs were of interest to Joseph, so he decided to start his own club for shortwave radio users. As it came closer to the time for Joseph to apply to colleges, his mother became more adamant about his attending an Ivy League school. She told him that she would only pay for an Ivy League school and would not support him if he went anywhere else.

Joe made all of the arrangements for college by himself, seeking out scholarships so that he could attend the college of his choice. When it was time to leave for school, his friends helped him move out of his mother's house. Joseph's mother's pressure resulted in her not only losing her dream but her relationship with her son as well.

Parents and College

Overinvolved parents are a relatively new phenomenon at the college level. Parents are stepping into areas that were previously the domain of college students themselves. A 2006 article in the *Washington Post*, aptly titled "Putting Parents in Their Place: Outside Class" (Strauss, 2006), addressed some of the issues that colleges are now encountering with these parents. Although it is not unusual for parents to help their children fill out college applications, overinvolved parents completely take over the process, even rewriting their teen's essays.

Stories abound about mothers and fathers calling and requesting roommate changes, coming in to clean dorm rooms and do laundry, and calling to complain about little disputes between roommates. Intrusive parents demand that their teen be allowed to take a specific class and complain about the course curriculum. Parents now are requesting daily updates from their teens, and some parents even go so far as to install Webcams in their teen's dorm room. One has to wonder when and where this all will end.

Parenting Style: Origins and Motivations

Not all Your Life Is My Life parents are alike; parents in this category may have a number of different characteristics. Some are overly involved because of their intense need to be perfect parents and produce perfect children who will attend a prestigious college. Others are so enamored of their children that they are unable to let them experience any of life's difficulties. Yet others are attempting to resolve their own childhood trauma. These parents are often responding to their own family history or seeking to meet personal or social needs. Whatever the reason, these parents tend to overprotect, rescue, overindulge, and overpressure their adolescents.

Family History

Family dynamics create patterns of behavior and set up styles of dealing with one's children, and often parents are not consciously aware of these ingrained patterns. Every parent has probably experienced a moment of realization that an action or statement came directly from memories of his or her own parents. "I sound just like my mother" and "you are just like your father" are rarely meant as a compliment. Sometimes parents recreate childhood experiences with the unconscious hope of repairing old wounds. Books on adult emotional disorders are replete with references to the traumas experienced in childhood.

A predominant reason for parents' overinvolvement is a need to give their children what they believe they were denied. Often, such parents came from economically disadvantaged or dysfunctional families and have a strong need to make sure that their children do not experience the pain that they experienced growing up. Some parents in this category came from extremely unhealthy and even abusive homes and did not receive the love and attention they needed. In reaction, they tend to be overly loving and concerned with their own children. Those who feel that they were never cared about as children often have a strong desire to never let their children feel unloved, unnoticed, or unwanted. They are motivated by what was missing or painful in their own childhood, not by what they learned or experienced.

In *When Parents Love Too Much*, Ashner and Meyerson (1990) told the story of a mother who, having grown up in a dysfunctional and abusive family, overcompensated by indulging her son: "Being a perfect parent was supposed to heal her of her perceived shortcomings and faults and take away the pain of her abusive childhood" (p. 211). Too often, parents try to heal the wounds of their own difficult pasts by providing their perfect ideal of a completely happy childhood and adolescence for their own children. What they fail to take into account is the possible negative effect of this overindulgence. To give what they were denied meets the parents' needs more than those of the adolescent.

Expectations

Current life stressors and expectations can also influence this parenting style. For many years, the media has extolled the importance of making one's children everything that they can be:

> American parents have been persuaded that average, typical or even "normal" is no longer good enough. Every article and news report reinforces that. To prepare children adequately for the impossibly competitive new millennium, parents are exhorted to give them an edge over the competition. The media uses strong active verbs to convince parents that they not only can but should work hard at helping a child excel. (Rosenfeld & Wise, 2000, p. xxi)

On the other side of the coin are parents who push their children to succeed so as to match their own high expectations of themselves. Years ago, it was common practice for fathers to raise their sons to join them at work and eventually take over the family business. Although it is now accepted that adolescents will grow up and pursue their own careers, many company executives are unwilling to accept a son's desire to major in art rather than business. They have developed a certain, career-dependent lifestyle and expect their teens to show respect for it by choosing equally prestigious career paths.

This attitude occurs at every socioeconomic level. A father who has made his living working with his hands may be uncomfortable with his children's academic pursuits and encourage them to be realistic and develop a viable work skill. Such parents have set ideas about the adult that their child needs to become and fail to take into account his or her individual interests and personality. In essence, they wish to mold their children to meet the highest expectation that they have of themselves.

Another common motivation for these parents is their own need to feel successful in the parenting arena. To them, parenting is a test of their self-worth. They need their teen to be happy, because unhappiness or anger may mean they are not being good parents. This may be especially the case if they struggled with their parents during their own teen years. They may also be afraid that without their help and support, their teens will not succeed. Some parents see it as their sacred responsibility to make sure that their children excel. After all, the media today is replete with messages that stress the importance of the role parents play in their teenager's success both academically and socially. As Rosenfeld and Wise (2000) pointed out,

> as a generation, we contemporary parents desperately want to do right by our kids. We buy into this message for the best reasons . . . committed to letting their children know how important they are to them; these parents sacrifice adult interests to make their kids' lives central. . . . We all want the best for our children. More often than not, we put their happiness ahead of our own—way ahead in fact. We become heavily invested in their childhood at the expense of our own lives—and that isn't healthy, for them or us. . . . Our hyper-parenting is born of best intentions. (pp. xvii–xix)

Parents who strive to be the perfect parents believe that they know their child's needs better than anyone else. They are the ones who raised and provided for their child and have an insider's knowledge about what the child likes and doesn't like. Adolescents, however, are a whole different ball game. Teens' tastes change dramatically during these years, making it almost impossible for parents to make the right selections for their child. Just try bringing home clothes for your teenager and see how close your choices are to their actual preferences. When teens develop their own interests and sense of taste, overinvolved parents still believe that they have a better idea of what will make their child happy. They cannot let go of the need to be involved in their teen's everyday choices and activities.

Social Needs

Some Your Life Is My Life parents grew up feeling like an outsider. Perhaps they were teased at school or never made it into the popular group. Now they need to see their teen become a cheerleader or a football star. Adults who did not do well in school may push their teen to make the honor roll. Unfortunately, many of these parents simply want their teens to appear successful because they think that, by looking good to the outside world, they can finally accomplish their own unfulfilled needs. The thought of "my son the football hero" goes a long way to erase the pain of being an outcast in high school. These parents are particularly enmeshed and ruthless when their teen is being ostracized or pushed out of the limelight. Remember the 1991 Texas cheerleader mom? She tried to hire someone to kill the mother of her daughter's cheerleading rival in order for her daughter to have a better chance at making the cheer squad (Maier, 1992).

Another reason parents become overly involved in their teen's social activities is that their own social lives revolve around their teens' activities, and they are afraid of losing their closeness with them. They are often cheerleader moms or football dads.

My son's high school band had an active parent booster club. For some parents, this activity became their whole lives. They attended every practice and competition; they volunteered to clean uniforms and bring snacks for the kids. Outside of their involvement with the high school band, they had few other social contacts. What happens to such parents when their high-schoolers graduate and leave for college? Teens, by nature, are driven to develop their own social and emotional lives and then to move out, whether it is for college, the military, or their own apartment and a job. This is particularly scary for parents who cannot handle the idea of being alone—especially if they are also in a difficult marital situation or are single parents.

Other parents in this category may feel inadequate in their own social arena and find that being with their children is an easier and more rewarding experience. They need to maintain the closeness that they had with their children when they were little and become overly involved in the social activities of their teen. These are the parents who volunteer at school, attend all games, and chaperone dances. They want to have their teen's friends over and be in the middle of what's going on; they read text messages and have their own Facebook account. They do anything they can do to maintain their closeness to their teen. But this can prevent teens from developing their own social skills. The example of Claire at the beginning of this chapter is a good representation of this parenting behavior.

Parental Loss

In a small number of cases, parents have lost a previous child to a miscarriage or early death and compensate for this loss by overinvolvement and disproportionate attachment to the living child. In other situations, the child may have been very ill as a small child, and the fear of losing that child underlies parents' excessive attachment. Adolescence, during which time the child starts to pull away from the parent, may trigger this fear of loss and increase the parent's need to be connected. Along the same lines, a parent who feels uncared for by his or her spouse may unconsciously treat the teen as a substitute for the emotionally absent spouse. This may also be the case if one parent feels the need to make up for the absence of the other, whether the other parent works a lot, travels, is alcoholic, or simply is not involved. Unhappy marriages result in more stressful home environments for teens, and some unhappy marriages result in overindulged teens and overly enmeshed parent–teen relationships.

Adolescent Reactions

A key task of adolescence is to gradually separate from parents and transition to peer-group relationships. This process is likely to create some stress in even the most normal household. For teenagers whose parents are overly enmeshed, this process is more difficult and can take a variety of forms.

As a small boy, Robert would cling to his mother's legs and cry when she tried to leave him. As he got older, Robert was Mom's little pal, and he was always asking her to play with him. Mom was present at every one of his games, read stories to him nightly, and generally paid him lots of attention. "Watch me, Mom, watch me!" was his favorite request. But then Robert became a teenager, and suddenly Mom's involvement and constant attention were unwelcome.

Teens react to Your Life Is My Life parenting in different ways. Most of their reactions depend on the type of enmeshment parents exhibit and whether the teens feel as if they can function comfortably with it. This particular parenting style includes a wide range of behaviors, and different teen reactions occur most commonly with different parent behaviors.

Rebellion

Although children under the age of 12 usually enjoy having their parents at their side, teenagers generally want more distance. A few teens continue to be comfortable with their parents' constant presence in their lives and find effective ways to incorporate this presence while still undertaking the tasks of adolescence, such as individuating, developing peer relationships, and pursuing personal interests.

However, most adolescents react to parental overinvolvement by attempting to create more distance. Many react strongly at some point. They don't want mom or dad involved in all of their activities; they don't want mom reading all their cell phone texts or searching their room. They want some control over their personal lives. In order to achieve it, most teens react instinctively rather than with a well-thought-out plan. They may begin to argue and fight over every little issue to make their point. They may plead and scream for mom or dad to leave them alone and stay out of their lives. Make no mistake—teens will find a way of separating from their parents. The only question is whether they achieve this through minor scuffles or major wars:

> Some parents struggle too hard against their teens' demand for separateness, creating an atmosphere of toxic enmeshment that suffocates their offspring and precludes growth. Because there is so little room for the adolescent to carve out individual space, extreme, extraordinary, and sometimes even dangerous measures have to be invoked. (Sachs, 2005, p. 191)

Although most teens don't go to extremes, teenagers by nature are highly emotional and reactive. For most teens, the tighter that parents hold on, the harder they fight. Adolescents whose parents overpressure and micromanage them respond in different ways. Some willingly and successfully live up to their parents' expectations. But most rebel against the pressure and push back against the high expectations. They often sabotage the very things that the parents have tried to accomplish. So parents who demand good grades get poor students, and their beautiful little blonde child turns gothic and dyes her hair black. During this time, many teenagers drop out of sports; most say that their reason for quitting has more to do with the pressure, especially parental pressure, than with their feelings about the game.

Darryl really enjoyed playing baseball and had shown potential ever since he was in Little League. During his sophomore year, he made his high school junior varsity team, and his father was ecstatic. However, every game became a nightmare for Darryl, because his father would sit on the sidelines, screaming at him to play better, and would spend hours after the game berating him for every little mistake. Free time was spent batting and catching at the local park with his father. Darryl dropped out of baseball during his junior year. He reported that his father was angry and disappointed but that the constant pressure was off. Darryl also noticed that his father paid a lot less attention to him once it was clear he would not meet his father's expectation for him to be a great baseball player.

Reacting to Parents' Expectations

During adolescence, children become acutely aware that the expectations being placed on them are their parents' idea of what they should be. Some teens meet their parents' basic expectations just to keep them off their backs. They learn to look successful and become good at hiding their imperfections. For other teens, striving to meet their parents' expectations becomes a painful requirement of their place in the family.

Another teen reaction to parents' high expectations is to strive to meet them. They push themselves relentlessly to make good grades, get involved in all the right activities, and maintain an acceptable social position within their peer group. For some teens, this is acceptable and becomes a part of their personality:

> These teens strive to be not only the best at everything but also truly "perfect." They need to be the best dressed, have the best body, be the most popular, and seem completely in control of everything in their lives. (Maxym & York, 2000, p. 22)

Living up to parents' expectations can result in unhealthy teen behaviors. They may neglect their own health, especially their need for sleep, in order to keep up with all their activities. It is not uncommon for a teen to sleep less than six hours a night, but most teens need eight hours. Teens involved in sports have early morning or late afternoon practice sessions, followed by homework. Other teens have part-time jobs or volunteer commitments. These teens must also find time to engage in social activities and complete household chores. It is not unusual for teens to tell me that they are frequently up till midnight or 1:00 A.M. doing homework or talking to friends online. Many teens do not take the time to eat healthy meals, or they limit their food intake to remain thin.

Some teens try desperately to meet their parents' high expectations, but still end up feeling like a failure. To avoid this, they may go to more extreme methods to do well. They may cheat on a test, have a friend do their homework, or lie to their parents. When they are unable to meet parental demands, they may resort to blaming others, including parents, siblings, friends, and teachers. When they do so, they are developing a way of getting through life that includes lying, cheating, and misrepresentation.

Teens who find that they cannot meet parental requirements, or who get tired of trying so hard, may simply stop trying:

> The pressures involved in being the best of the best . . . is enough to convince some kids that giving up altogether is much better, or at least a more achievable goal. After all that striving, finding themselves unhappy and unfulfilled anyway is devastating. Feeling betrayed, feeling they cannot be the best of the best, they become overtly resentful. Some kids then choose instead to be the worst of the worst. (Maxym & York, 2000, p. 23)

These teens are building an identity that is not based on their own strengths and weaknesses but on their reaction to the expectations placed on them.

Entitlement

Teens with overindulgent and overly devoted parents often develop an inflated and superficial sense of self and a feeling of entitlement. Teens growing up with a sense of entitlement may have more difficulty outside of the home. (This is not to imply that they do not also encounter difficulties at home.) They don't expect that they should have to follow the rules in the same way that others do. When privileges are not granted, when teachers do not respond to their requests, and when classmates expect them to do their share of the work on a school project, they react negatively. These high-maintenance adolescents typify the idea of a spoiled brat. They develop an expectation that they should get whatever they want, especially material possessions.

For these teens, their wants become their rights—even if they want a $35,000 car at age 16 and all the latest electronic gadgets. One teen that I worked with had two iPhones in case one phone's batteries died. This phenomenon is not confined to the wealthy; some parents sacrifice their own needs to make sure their teen has the latest fashion or electronic device. The problem occurs when the teen's demands override the family's resources. As children get older, the price of their toys increases significantly.

When these teens' demands are not met, they can become quite angry. They do not know how to handle the word "no," and in extreme cases, they use inappropriate or illegal means to obtain their desires. If they believe that they deserve an A on a project, they may have no qualms about buying a paper off the Internet or paying someone else to write it for them. The end result is more important than the process.

What happens when these teenagers internalize their parents' philosophy and believe that they should get everything that they want, because, after all, they are special? They let this philosophy become a part of their personality and expect the world to treat them accordingly. They become egocentric and often fail to consider others' needs. They often develop superficial relationships, with the goal being to attain more for themselves.

Social Skills

Parents who are overly present in their teens' lives make it difficult for the teens to have individual time with their own social group. Because of this, some teens may have difficulty developing the social skills necessary to be successful at this stage of life, whereas others may have trouble being alone and may constantly seek interaction and attention. Some teenagers may spend an inordinate amount of time playing video games, because this is the one area in which parents typically do not get involved. Playing video games may be the only time that the teens feel that they are in control, can make their own decisions, and can be involved in a world in which they are the sole creators.

The term "helicopter parents" has been used to describe parents who swoop in and rescue their children from any perceived discomfort or danger. At first glance, it would appear that teenagers would enjoy being rescued, if only because it would allow them to behave irresponsibly without having to pay the consequences. For some teens, this is exactly what happens. Sam, whose case was discussed earlier, was so accustomed to his parents rescuing him that he did not give a lot of thought to his actions. Teens whose parents rescue them quickly adjust to having their own personal servants and have no trouble calling mom or dad to bring their homework to school, give them a ride if they missed the bus, pay for a friend's item that they lost, or compensate for any other irresponsible action. Some teens escalate their negative behavior because they do not feel any responsibility for their actions.

Other teens become frustrated with their parents' constant attempts to rescue them and become better at hiding their problems and mistakes. These teens cannot simply bring an issue or problem to their parents without the parent feeling the need to solve it for them. In *The Self-Esteem Trap*, Young-Eisendrath (2008) expressed concern over the effect of parental rescue: "We rush in and sweep up the gravel on Life's road and eliminate any opportunity for our children to work through difficulty and come out the other side, knowing they have solved a problem and can do it again" (p. 60). For some teenagers, this creates a stronger desire to solve their own problems and to keep their parents from interfering in their lives.

Sue was a 15-year-old whose mother had always been active and involved in her life. Sue's mother read all of her text messages, questioned her extensively about every outing she had with her friends, contacted teachers and other parents for information about Sue, and routinely went through her room. Sue found her mother's involvement overwhelming and started avoiding her questions. When Sue expressed frustration with her mother's overinvolvement, her mother became angry, sometimes punishing Sue for disrespect, talking back, and uncooperativeness. Sue learned how to hide things from her mother in various ways, including lying and sneaking around. Sue's mother meant well, but did not realize that her overinvolvement had become a form of control and was having an adverse impact on Sue's behavior and emotional development.

Negative and Harmful Reactions

The most harmful consequence of parental overinvolvement, especially the pressure to meet high expectations, is that some teens use drugs or alcohol to deal with the resulting stress. One young lady I worked with was a high school valedictorian and student council president and smoked pot regularly to relieve her stress. It is not uncommon for college students, once away from home, to engage in a certain amount of acting out, including excessive drinking. Most college students say that the teens who do the most acting out and drinking are typically the ones who came from families that were rigid and controlling or had high expectations for them.

Some teens seek out Ritalin and similar drugs because they believe they will help them to deal with their stress and exhaustion. Depression and anxiety are also possible outcomes for teens who don't have a sense of control over their own lives. These teens feel inadequate to deal with the strong emotions that can develop as a result of the pressure to be someone else's ideal, especially if that someone is your parent.

Short- and Long-Term Outcomes

The Your Life Is My Life parenting style has a wider range of behaviors than some of the other categories and therefore a wider variety off consequences. This parenting style can affect a teen's academic life, college experience, and future career. It also has an impact on the development of the teen's personality and subsequently the adult that teen becomes. Interpersonal relationships are also significantly affected.

Academic Impact: High School

Many of these teens have been living with a high level of expectation for their academic success, especially those teenagers who are expected to develop a prestigious résumé in order to get into a college acceptable to their parents. Some do very well, because they are bright, have a genuine stake in their own education, and are supported and praised for their academic success without being made to feel as if it's a requirement of their position in the family. Other teens are expected to do well and get into a good college because that will please mom and dad. Many teens who are pushed too hard fail to develop an intrinsic love of learning, so parents should ease up as their teenagers progress through high school and allow them to take more ownership of their academic success. Support and pressure are not the same thing:

> Pressure, even in the form of rewards or evaluation, leads children to take a particular stance toward learning. When children learn under these conditions, the locus of their attention is on the outcome, the test, or getting the reward. Because of this, their attention is narrowed—their focus is on the details or the path to the easiest solution. This kind of orientation is at odds with conceptual understanding of material or problem solving, because both

of these types of learning require flexibility, openness, and a broadening of perspective. (Grolnick, 2003, p. 120)

Teens who do well in school because of outside pressure also tend to be less spontaneous and less creative and have less cognitive flexibility. They are concerned with the end result, not the process.

The same can usually be said for teens with a special talent or ability that the parents pressure them to make the most of. This may be in an area such as music, dance, gymnastics, tennis, or art. Some people with talent have been fortunate to have parents who teach them to love their art, sport, or other activity. But some teens find that their special talent has become the primary domain of the parent and not a gift that the teen gets to explore. Such teens often develop excellent technique but may lack an emotional connection to their talent. Whether a talent is academic, musical, or athletic, parental pressure to perform can diminish a teen's ownership and enjoyment of his or her ability.

Frank was an 18-year-old with a talent for tennis. Starting when he was five, his father spent hours on the court with him, pushing him to be the best. During his teen years, his father arranged for home schooling to give Frank more practice time. Frank had very little time for friends or other activities. To deal with the pressure, he began smoking pot. Frank's grades started to slip, but his father was unconcerned. Despite Frank's natural talent, he did not play well enough to compete at the college level, as he had no passion left for the sport by the time he finished high school. Frank ended up at the local community college with no idea what he wanted to do with his life.

For teens whose parents are overinvolved or overindulgent, the school experience may have a different outcome. Adolescents in this category typically do not perform as well in high school and often depend on their parents to complete their projects and make excuses for them with their teachers. They often do not learn to value education or to take responsibility for their work:

> For many kids who grow up believing mom or dad can and will bail them out of life's scrapes, when they have to start producing on their own, life becomes too challenging . . . when diligence, perseverance and some maturity need to be brought to the table as the work in high school becomes more demanding, they don't know what to do because they have no experience to guide them. (Maxym & York, 2000, p. 20)

Academic Impact: College

Teens who achieve because of high parental expectations often do very well in high school, confirming their parents' belief that what they're doing is in the best interest of their children. But success does not always follow such teens to college, where they often have difficulty making the transition. Accustomed to having external structure and control, they may have a hard time motivating themselves and can easily become procrastinators.

It is not unusual for teens from pressured environments to have difficulty picking a major; they may even change their major several times. Many teens simply pick the major that their parents recommend and continue their college years under their parents' watchful eyes. It is very difficult for parents whose lives have been tied up in their child's academic achievements to simply back away. "Helicopter parents" have become a problem even at the college level. In reality, this is often a difficult position to maintain, as college life encourages more and more independence.

Rescuing teens during the college years can interfere with the important life learning that should take place then. For teenagers whose parents made excuses for them, rescued them, and otherwise smoothed the way, college can be a real shock. College professors do not care if a student's father sends a note explaining why he or she didn't get a project done, and mom cannot bring homework to class when the school is a three-hour drive away. College means independence and responsibility. For many of these teens, the first year of college is difficult; they have to learn very quickly to stand on their own, or they may end up back home.

Pressured teens also often have difficulty working in groups. They can become highly competitive and usually retain this trait throughout high school and into college. Guthrie (2002) talked about this in *The Trouble with Perfect*: "A spirit of competition fostered by parents can corrode the social atmosphere and force teens to behave more like lone wolves than the pack animals they long to be" (p. 158). Teens growing up with this parental philosophy tend to regard peers as competitors rather than friends and supporters. A successful and fulfilling college experience requires interacting with and depending on peers.

Career

What happens when these pressured teens enter the workforce? Sometimes they continue to function as if everything is a competition. These individuals become classic Type A personalities. Others become disillusioned with the reality of work. They still expect to be praised and held in high esteem. They need the reinforcement of others to assure them that they are doing a good job, since they did not develop the ability to realistically evaluate themselves.

In addition, they may fear success or failure, because nothing they do comes without a price. If they fail, they disappoint their parents or someone else. But success sets a standard that they must maintain—a salesperson who makes the top sales for the month must reach or exceed that same goal month after month. Real life is not so straightforward: It has ups and downs, successes and failures. I have worked with young adults who had difficulty adjusting to the routine and mundane aspects of the job. I have to remind them that everybody needs to be the "regular" person in a job before becoming the manager or the CEO. Entry-level jobs rarely give As, and you're lucky if you get two weeks' vacation.

What are the expectations and experiences of overindulged teens going into the work world? Some teens' expectations are distorted by having grown up treated as if they were special. As Littwin (1986) said in *The Postponed Generation*,

They feel entitled to interesting, fulfilling work without supervision or menial tasks. They feel that work should have meaning. And yet they don't seem to have any realistic notion of how to get these extraordinary privileges. They simply expect them. (p. 58)

Adjustment to the work world can be difficult for teens who grew up being pampered and feeling entitled.

Teens who grow up believing that they should come out on top, and that the result is more important than the process, may not have developed a strong sense of ethics. Is it not possible that these teens may become adults who are more concerned with their own success than with the method that they use to get there? Bernard Madoff, the infamous financier who misused billions of dollars of other people's money for his own benefit, comes to mind as an example of the sort of individual who may have grown up believing that his success and wealth were more important than the people who trusted him.

Financial Concerns

How do overinvolved parents affect their children's ability to handle money? When teenagers grow up being overindulged, rescued from mistakes, and made to feel that they should expect only the best for themselves, they are unlikely to develop healthy attitudes about handling money. During the teen years, they come to expect to possess whatever material item they want, and do not stop to think about where mom or dad is getting the money to pay for it. When they become adults, they still believe that if they want something, they should have it. If the money no longer comes from mom or dad, it can come from plastic. Entitled teens often become indebted adults. They do not develop the ability to delay gratification, and finding out that they can't get the car or the vacation they want is terribly disappointing. Adults who don't make it in the job market or end up drowning in debt often end up asking mom or dad for help.

Marla, age 32, came into treatment because she was feeling increasingly unhappy with her marriage to Tom. Marla reported that her husband was unemployed; in the 10 years since his graduation from college, he had had a variety of jobs. He quit some of them because they weren't interesting enough and was fired from others for failing to meet basic requirements. The couple was now living off money given to them by his parents. Every time the couple had encountered financial difficulty, Tom had simply gone to his parents to be bailed out. Further discussion revealed that Tom had grown up "spoiled," especially by his mother, whom he still called daily. Marla expressed frustration over the close relationship between Tom and his mother, reporting that Tom's mother still bought his underwear and socks. Marla appreciated the help from Tom's parents but felt that they would be better off if there were more separation between them.

Teens who were raised with high expectations often continue to believe, as young adults, that they must have the best of everything, resulting in unhealthy patterns of spending. Their focus is on appearing to be successful, and this often means a house in a nice neighborhood, an expensive car, and luxurious vacations. One young adult that I worked with was struggling with his monthly expenses and worried about getting laid off from his job. Within the same conversation, he mentioned that he and his wife had recently bought four flat-screen TVs for their house.

Personality Development

Whether Your Life Is My Life parents lean more toward setting high expectations or overindulging their teens, the effect can be similar on their adolescents' personality development and interactions with others.

Much of the literature about teens with overinvolved parents clearly indicates that this type of parenting harms the teen's ability to develop a separate identity. This key adolescent task is a struggle for teens whose parents are too enmeshed in their lives and who grow up with high expectations and the belief that their job is to please mom and dad:

> A pushed child has more difficulty finding who he is—what really interests him, what gives him pleasure—because he has been so undermined, consciously or unconsciously, by parents who have been working hard to produce the child they want or need rather than the child they have. These pushed adolescents have a kind of partial identity formation. This incomplete identity will be a source of unhappiness as they struggle to become autonomous adults. Like houses built on sand, they lack the very things their parents would wish for them: solid identities and the strength to meet new challenges. (Guthrie, 2002, pp. 157–158)

Teens put on pedestals, or constantly hovered over and rescued, develop a false sense of their own specialness that interferes with their development of an identity as a regular person. Teens with an inflated sense of self have a much harder time interacting in the world. These indulged teens often end up being knocked off their pedestals by reality.

Teens whose parents make most of their decisions, solve their problems, and rescue them from their mistakes, grow up with the message they are not capable of handling their own lives. This affects their sense of competence and self-confidence. Adults who don't feel competent tend to be less willing to explore new situations, have trouble making decisions, and constantly second-guess themselves. Parents who constantly rescue their teens are actually giving them the message that they are not capable of taking care of themselves and undermining their willingness to undertake challenges.

Sense of Entitlement

Adolescents who grow up praised, protected, and privileged develop an unhealthy sense of entitlement. As adults, they go out into the world expecting that everything should come easily for them, and are often thrown off balance when they find out that the wider world is not as forgiving as their parents. These entitled adults often expect too much of themselves, their friends, and the world. When everything they do or have is not of excellent quality, they may become terribly disappointed or give up. They may also end up feeling betrayed by their parents, who made them believe that the world was their oyster, when in reality all they are getting are fish sticks.

As adults, children of overinvolved parents may either become perfectionists or be inconsistent in their follow-through on projects. Those who were raised with parental pressure to be the best have trouble accepting anything less than perfection from themselves. Fear of being less than perfect can make them procrastinate or work inconsistently. They may have trouble following through on projects because they get stuck in the details and often wait for guidance from others. They are usually not self-starters:

> It's no mystery that we come to expect that things would be magically taken care for us. We start projects and wait for this genie who never comes anymore. . . . Procrastination became our downfall when we internalized a message that we could not accomplish anything very well on our own and needed to be constantly protected. Or it happened when we internalized such high expectations that any task began to seem like a set up for failure. (Ashner & Meyerson, 1990, p. 30)

These characteristics may extend into many areas of the young adult's life.

Nicole came in, shortly after marrying for the second time, with feelings of anxiety. Nicole had two children, and her new husband had custody of his two children. During the course of treatment, it was revealed that Nicole's mother was a controlling perfectionist who demanded the same from Nicole. Nicole was trying, unsuccessfully, to be perfect in every area of her new life and was unable to meet her own unrealistic standards. She was eventually able to understand the power of her mother's expectations and start to be less demanding of perfection in her own home.

Relationships

As mentioned before, establishing an individual identity is particularly difficult for teens with Your Life Is My Life parents. These parents may fear losing the closeness that they have with their teen and discourage their teen from developing peer relationships. Or they may see time that the teens spend with peers as neglect of their primary responsibilities. Because of the strength of the bond between parent and child in these families, the struggle to separate is especially intense.

Healthy relationships require give and take, and teens with overinvolved parents experience extremes in this area. Teens with high-expectation parents constantly feel the need to meet their parents' goals. Their job is to make mom and dad proud. Teens with rescuing and overindulgent parents are accustomed to being provided for. Either way, they are likely to have difficulty with the emotional intimacy and give and take that are necessary for healthy relationships, especially love relationships.

Teens with overinvolved parents are often too self-focused or too entangled with their parents to establish healthy intimate relationships with peers. For many, peer relationships are simply a means to an end. They seek friends who will help them with schoolwork, admire them or their latest electronic gadgets, and generally place their needs first—like the popular "queen bee" and her followers.

As adults, they often have a continued need for others to praise, indulge, and rescue them. Although most healthy adult relationships provide some of that, it is often not enough to satiate these young adults. When they become involved in serious relationships, and when they marry, they often expect to be catered to and have difficulty adapting to another person's needs or admitting that they were wrong.

When young adults have a difficult and painful time loosening their ties to their families of origin and beginning to establish their own relationships and place in the world, they often develop emotional problems such as depression and anxiety. Those who were "loved too much" as teens may later have a hard time feeling like others care about them and may constantly look to others to satisfy the empty feeling inside them that comes from no longer being able to be the best of the best or the prince or princess.

Positive Outcomes

Teenagers who are able to differentiate from their parents during adolescence may incorporate some of the positive aspects of this parenting style into their adult personalities. It is highly probable that teens who are able to function independently despite parental enmeshment were strong individuals to begin with. These teens develop a positive sense of self while being pragmatic about the world. As adults, they may continue to have high expectations of themselves, but these expectations are realistic. These teens learn to delay gratification and have reasonable and healthy goals. For some teens, the grandiosity of adolescence becomes the healthy self-confidence of adulthood.

Summary

Parents who are overly enmeshed with their teenagers are often attempting to meet their own needs. These needs may have resulted from a childhood of deprivation or a desire for their own or their teen's success. These parental needs can also be socially or emotionally motivated or aimed at maintaining the family status. Whether the Your Life Is My Life parenting style involves excessive demands or excessive indulgence, it is more about the parent than the teen. Teens brought up in this way often have distinct behaviors and reactions, many of which are unhealthy. Some push back and rebel, whereas others internalize the belief that they are special. What is of concern is the lengths to which these teens will go to maintain their elevated status or meet parental expectations. Although some teens simply go along with their parents' expectations, most fight to develop their own identity. After all, this is the primary task of adolescence.

The Your Life Is My Life approach backfires. Parents want their children to feel special and excel. However, the transition from childhood to adulthood is an individual journey, and no matter how well-meaning parents are, they cannot craft an adult in their image or shelter their adolescent from all pain and disappointment. Overinvolved parents would do more for their kids if they let them realize that life isn't easy and that the basis for happiness and success is hard work, resilience, determination, and the ability to be ordinary.

CHAPTER FIVE

"Cool" Parents

If teenagers live with too few rules, they learn to ignore the needs of others.

—Dorothy Nolte and Rachel Harris,
Teenagers Learn What They Live

Case Example

Eighteen-year-old Donnie and his parents had a great life. He was the only child of two working parents, and there was always plenty of money for whatever activities the family wanted to engage in. From his earliest years, he traveled, stayed in the best hotels, had designer clothes, and bought the newest electronics. When he wasn't traveling with his parents, usually during the school year, he was cared for by a series of nannies who eventually either resigned or were fired if Donnie expressed any unhappiness with them.

Donnie attended private school. He was intelligent but usually underperformed in school because of behavioral problems. Many of his friends lived similar lifestyles. Home life was relatively conflict free, as his parents had few expectations regarding maturity, self-control, or responsibility.

When Donnie was 16, his parents bought him a muscle car; soon thereafter, he got a ticket for going 25 miles over the speed limit. His parents hired an attorney to get him out of the ticket, bought him a radar detector, and had a brief conversation with him about being more careful in watching out for cops. At 17, he was arrested for shoplifting; again, an attorney got him out of trouble.

Donnie and his parents had great parties; his parents allowed him to drink, under their supervision, starting at age 16. By the time he was 17, his house was one of his friends' favorite places for parties, and his parents would provide the alcohol. Their idea of chaperoning was to close themselves off in their room while the teenagers partied in the family room.

Donnie graduated from high school in the lower half of his class and was admitted to a university with a reputation as a party school. During his fall semester, he was arrested for selling a large quantity of cocaine. Donnie immediately contacted his parents, asking that they get him out of this situation. Donnie's parents were devastated and unable to understand how he could be involved in selling drugs. After all, they had provided him with the best of everything. His parents brought him into therapy in an attempt to show the court he was working on his issues.

Parenting Style Characteristics

"Cool" parents are a relatively new phenomenon. These are the parents who would rather be seen as their teen's friend than provide structure and discipline. Cool parents tend to be permissive, indulgent, and lax in setting rules and expectations. They need to be liked and approved of by their teen and their teen's friends. They provide a wide range of freedoms for their teens. The Cool parenting style is similar to the permissive parenting style identified by Baumrind (1971, 1991), which others (Lamborn, Mounts, Steinberg, & Dornbusch, 1991) have further divided into indulgent permissive and neglectful permissive. These parents strive to be perceived favorably at the expense of their parental responsibilities, which is not actually "cool."

Cool parents allow their teens to have parties at their house and even provide the alcohol. Many are willing to sacrifice the parent role in order to appear cool to their teens. Often they are uncomfortable with the role of disciplinarian. Not all Cool parents provide unsafe environments for their children and friends. Many wish to provide their teenagers with an opportunity to develop their own personality and style without excessive limitations, demands, or expectations. They may genuinely believe that their teens have the maturity to make decisions for themselves.

Cool parents are often indulgent, tending to respond more to their teen's demands rather than to make demands themselves. Discipline is rare, and these parents often have low expectations of maturity and self-control. Cool parents are rarely indifferent; they usually have a genuine love for and interest in their teenagers.

Few Rules, Lax Enforcement

The first rule of most Cool parents is that there are very few rules. They are usually laid-back, undemanding, and lax in enforcing the limits that they do set. The rules they establish are provided for the safety of their teenager or in accordance with societal expectations. They may allow their teen to dress outrageously but ask that he or she dress appropriately for family functions or church events. Some may set limits but relent as soon as their teen pushes against the boundaries. For some, enforcing limits requires too much time and energy. Others don't want to risk their relationship with their teen. In many of these homes, permission may be given for activities that can be unhealthy or even dangerous, such as attending unchaperoned parties, having coed sleepovers, and smoking.

Friends, Not Parents

Cool parents prefer to be a friend to their teenager rather than a parent. Enjoying the feeling of being popular, at least among teenagers, they encourage their teens and their teen's friends to spend social time at their house, and strive to be part of the group, joining in the teens' activities. They provide video games, movies, refreshments, and very little supervision.

For some parents, the Cool parenting style is driven by their need to have their own second adolescence. These parents enjoy, actively and vicariously, the adventures of their teens, and may even encourage reckless behavior and experimentation. Often lacking emotional maturity themselves, they find their teenager's adolescent years to be an opportunity to reengage in fun and immature behaviors that they may feel they missed in their own teenage years. These parents play video games and buy sports cars or motorcycles for their teenagers. Mothers may begin to dress in teen fashions and show interest in attending concerts with their teenagers.

These parents often share their own youthful escapades with their teens, savoring the opportunity to impress their teens with their own wild behavior. Many engage in a type of competition with their teenagers. A few parents openly engage in illegal or unethical activities. Dogan, Conger, Kim, and Masyn (2007) cited a 1995 report by David P. Farrington indicating that "parents of delinquent youth were not only more likely to be delinquent themselves but also tended to use inept parenting practices. . . . They were also lax in enforcing rules and supervised their children poorly" (p. 337). For these Cool parents, the goal is enjoyment rather than active parenting.

Mary came into therapy stating that her marriage had recently become more strained. She and her husband, James, had a 14-year-old son, Simon, and a 9-year-old daughter. James was a 32-year-old office manager, and Mary worked as a bank teller. The couple married at age 18 after Mary became pregnant. Mary complained that ever since Simon became a teenager, James had become increasingly involved in his son's activities. He started dressing more like his son, listening to his son's music, hanging around with Simon and his friends, and spending hours playing video games. James also seemed overly inquisitive about Simon's growing interest in girls.

Mary also complained that James was starting to treat her like a parent, telling her to "back off his case" and to "chill out." James had also stopped disciplining the kids because he didn't want to make his "best bud" angry. Simon was starting to complain that his father was intruding in his life and trying to too hard to act cool with his friends.

It was clear that James was trying to relive his own adolescence, which was cut short by the responsibility of parenthood. However, in doing so, James was preventing his son from having his own adolescent experiences and was creating distance in his marriage.

Parents and Parties

One characteristic of Cool parenting that has received a lot of press recently is the willingness of some parents to provide the alcohol for their teenager's parties. Many such parents insist that the purpose is to provide a safe environment for their teens to drink in, and they rationalize that teens are going to drink anyway and that by taking the teens' car keys they are protecting them. These parents reassure themselves that they are limiting the amount of alcohol that the teenagers will consume by providing a supervised environment. The reality is that most adolescents do drive when they leave the party, especially when they need to be home for curfew. Others become drunk to the point of throwing up in the front yard. A 2006 *Washington Post* article described the case of Silvia Johnson, a mom from Colorado

> who entertained high school kids at weekly parties with Jack Daniels, Barcardi rum, and peppermint schnapps. Johnson provided the liquor, did shots with the 15- and 16-year-olds, supplied the methamphetamines and joined the kids in taking them. And she sexually serviced at least five boys, right there at her parties. She did this, she told police, to be the "cool mom." (Fisher, 2006)

An all-too-obvious outcome when alcohol and teenagers mix is the possibility of sexual behavior. Although it may be difficult to prevent teenagers from becoming sexually active, providing lax supervision in the home exponentially increases the chance that they will do so. Permissive parents are also more likely to provide teenagers with contraception and tacitly approve their sexual activities. Boys are given their first box of condoms, and girls are put on birth control, just in case. A recent study found that "at high levels of permissiveness girls reported more sexual risk taking than boys, and girls were more likely than boys to report having sex while using drugs and alcohol and having sex without a condom" (Donenberg, Wilson, Emerson, & Bryant, 2002, p. 138).

Cool parents may also be less than particular about the type of friends their teen chooses. Uncomfortable establishing limits, they may also allow teenage girls to date boys who are considerably older. A 15-year-old girl dating an 18-year-old boy will have difficulty setting boundaries for herself.

Even parents who do not provide their teens with alcohol may knowingly allow them to attend parties where alcohol is available. Some ignore obvious signs of their teen's intoxication. All too often, parents leave teenagers home alone while they go out of town, half-heartedly admonishing them not to have any parties while they are gone.

Linda, 16, had recently moved in with her father and stepmother. Linda was clearly having difficulty adjusting to this arrangement and had come into therapy to help her adjust. Although Linda came home clearly intoxicated several times, the parents went away for the weekend leaving Linda home alone. Linda promptly called a few friends to come over for the evening. These friends then texted several other friends, and the word spread. Linda lost control of the situation, and soon there were more than 50 teenagers at her house, many of whom had brought alcohol. After neighbors called the police, Linda became extremely agitated and subsequently took a number of Tylenol. She had to be hospitalized for several days.

Other Questionable Activities

Alcohol and drug use and sexual activity are not the only behaviors allowed by Cool parents. Many allow teenagers, even young teenagers, to watch R-rated movies, listen to music with inappropriate lyrics, have undersupervised coed sleepovers, and access dangerous and inappropriate Web sites. These parents also allow other peoples' children to engage in these behaviors in their home. When other parents complain, Cool parents may react negatively and accuse the protective parents of being unrealistic about the world in which today's teenagers live.

Many Cool parents allow unsafe behavior under the guise of being laid-back or encouraging their teen's activities and interests. A particularly extreme case occurred in Pennsylvania when a mother bought several guns for her teenage son:

> A troubled teenager accused of plotting a school attack built up a stash of weapons with the help of his mother, authorities said. . . . The parents were indulging the boy's interest because he was unhappy, not knowingly aiding the school assault, Montgomery County District Attorney Bruce Castor said Friday. The parent didn't know of the teen's plans, but "by virtue of her indulgence, she enabled him to get in this position" Caster said. (Associated Press, 2007)

The mother was subsequently charged with several violations, including endangering a child and purchasing illegal guns. In addition, the father, a convicted felon, was sentenced to house arrest after he lied about his criminal record in an effort to buy a rifle for his son.

Nontraditional Values

Some Cool parents may be permissive or lax in their parenting because they genuinely value creativity and self-expression in their teens. These parents tend to be nontraditional and place more value on self-expression and personal development than on obedience. They genuinely believe that their teens are capable of making major decisions for themselves and that imposing too many restrictions would undermine their personal development. They tend to trust their teens and would rather be a resource than a disciplinarian.

In most cases, these parents intervene in, or at least advise against, any behavior they feel is unhealthy or unsafe, but for the most part, they allow teens to make their own decisions about many issues, including curfew, style of dress, choice of music, and friends. Some even allow the use of alcohol and drugs under the tenet of allowing normal teen experimentation.

These parents practice a more relaxed and teen-centered style of childrearing and encourage a close and open relationship with their teen. Most parents in this category decide how much freedom to allow the teen on the basis of the teen's age and level of maturity. They are supportive and rarely place restrictions, except for safety and health reasons. These parents are rarely neglectful and do not see themselves as abdicating their parental role.

Fifteen-year-old Emma was the only child of Carl and Eddi. Eddi was an art teacher, and Carl was a photographer. Emma was bright and creative, and her parents took a laissez-faire approach to parenting. Academically and behaviorally, Emma was functioning well. Household decisions were made in a family meeting. Affection between family members was the norm. Emma's maternal grandparents had lived in a commune in the 1960s, and their own approach to parenting Emma's mother had been indulgent and permissive. This philosophical approach to parenting has held across generations for Emma's family and has shown success.

Belief in the Adolescent's Maturity

Many parents adopt a Cool parenting style once their teens have reached high school, mistakenly believing that they are capable of making most decisions for themselves and monitoring their own behavior. They allow their teens to be responsible for their own schoolwork and make their own choices about social activities. These Cool parents encourage their teens to participate in most decisions and believe that their children are capable of learning from their mistakes. They treat the teens as equals in the family and encourage joint decision making, even if the issues pertain to the parents alone.

This shift in parenting style usually occurs during the early adolescent years but becomes more pronounced as the teen enters high school. These parents are emotionally warm and responsive and have a great deal of trust in their teens' ability to manage their own lives. They are often popular parents, especially with their teen's friends whose own parents are more restrictive.

Avoidance of Responsibility

Other Cool parents have difficulty with their own authority: They simply do not like to say "no." They may be insecure in their role as parents and find it easier to simply back away, especially during the teen years. They are uncomfortable with conflict and controversy, which are unavoidable in homes with teenagers. For these adults, arguments with teens are to be avoided, and therefore they offer little resistance to their teen's demands. They are Cool parents by default.

Other parents may not discipline or set boundaries for fear of losing their position as friend to the teen or as the Cool parent. They are more concerned with being likable than with setting limits. These parents abdicate their role as disciplinarian in favor of being the teen's best friend. Eventually, they may find themselves having to maintain their position as friend by indulging the teen. These Cool parents are always driving their kids somewhere, financing their activities, and keeping them supplied with the latest teen fashions or gadgets. Demands are usually given in to. Their most common expressions are "sure, go ahead" and "why not?" Their teens often consider them cool, but frequently they end up being prisoners of their teens' demands.

Parenting Style: Origins and Motivations

As with the other parenting styles, parents adopt the Cool style for a number of different reasons, including family history, personal needs, and philosophical beliefs. Cool parents are permissive, indulgent, or lax in response to their needs rather than the teen's. They often neglect some of their parental responsibilities so as to be viewed as fun or likable or to avoid conflict. What these parents gain in comfort and flattering self-image often becomes a loss for the teen. When the parenting actions are based on a philosophical belief, the outcome is more likely to be positive for the teen.

Family History

For many Cool parents, their parenting style is a reaction to the home environment they experienced as children. Many were raised in strict and rigid homes in which they felt stifled and did not thrive and choose to parent their own children in a dramatically different way. Some experienced an abusive upbringing, making it difficult for them to feel comfortable in the role of disciplinarian or to know what an appropriate response to teenage misbehavior is. Parents from overly strict or abusive homes may also fear their own anger or be concerned that they may repeat their parents' mistakes; therefore, they simply abdicate the disciplinarian role.

Other Cool parents grew up with indulgent or permissive parents, and this environment worked well for them. These parents have fond memories of their own childhood and want to provide the same atmosphere for their own children. Many parents' families of origin may not have been as permissive or laid-back as they recall, but they selectively remember the enjoyable parts of their childhood and try to recreate them in their own families.

Other Cool parents were raised in homes in which material goods and opportunities were lacking, whether for financial, cultural, or religious reasons. They may have been required to work to help support the family and may not have been financially able to participate in some of the social activities that other teenagers enjoyed. As adults they may feel a strong need to provide their own children with the opportunities and material goods that were not available to them.

Susan and Frank were raising three teenagers, two boys in high school and a daughter in middle school. Frank was employed as an engineer with a major oil company, and his job required regular travel. Susan was a stay-at-home mom. Her background was one of significant deprivation and dysfunction, with an alcoholic mother and a father who was often out of work. In reaction, her own parenting style was overly lax and indulgent. All three children were demanding and showed her very little respect. Whenever Frank was out of town, the boys openly disregarded her requests. Susan felt out of control but did not feel strong enough to enforce any limits when Frank was not available to back her up. Susan came into therapy when she realized that her family situation was beginning to be dysfunctional as well.

Personal Needs

Another basic reason that parents become Cool is that they have a strong need to be liked by their children and their children's friends. These parents are often somewhat uncomfortable or insecure with the authoritarian role and thrive on the positive regard of their teens. They may also enjoy being considered cool by their teen's friends, and this may override the discipline needs of the teen. Often they do not discipline for fear of losing their position as the Cool parents. They need their teens to meet their own social and emotional needs, and they become more involved in their teens' lives rather than developing their own.

Cool parents may see themselves as their teens' friends and allies rather than as their parents. There are a number of reasons for this, including difficulties encountered during their own adolescence. These adults were often misunderstood as teens, maybe even ostracized, and now have a second chance to be accepted in the teenage world. Other Cool parents simply use their teenager's adolescence as an opportunity to relive their own teenage years.

In the case of Silvia Johnson (mentioned earlier), the mother was arrested and, in talking with the police, stated, "I fell in love with being a part of the group in a way 'cause that was never something I was part of growing up. I was never in the popular group. I was never cool. Here, I was considered the cool mom" (Fisher, 2006). This was her justification for providing alcohol, drugs, and sex to teenage children. This was clearly not in the best interest of the adolescents but met her personal need to be accepted.

Parents Who Can't Say No

Some parents are permissive simply because they are extremely busy and do not have the time or energy to establish structure and discipline for their teens. They differ somewhat from truly uninvolved parents because they would like to be involved and to provide a good home environment for their teens, but are simply unable to find the time. Many prefer to spend the time that they do have with their teens in enjoyable activities and harmonious interactions rather than dealing with unpleasant behavioral issues. Having an enjoyable afternoon at the mall with their daughter becomes more important than dealing with the fact that she came in an hour late for curfew the night before. Some of these parents give their children material items and freedom because they feel guilty about being too busy to give them much time. This can be especially true for parents who frequently travel for work or pleasure.

Other laissez-faire parents simply have no ability to deal with confrontation. They are uncomfortable saying no, or just don't know how, and find it easier to give in to their teen's demands. Adolescents are quick to figure out their parents' limits and often push to see how far the line will move. As their teens' demands increase and become even more inappropriate (such as allowing alcohol use), these parents have even more trouble setting limits and following through on them. Many are permissive only because they do not have the strength to battle with their teens.

This may be particularly true for parents who were intimidated in their own families. Some even become somewhat fearful of their teen's anger and find it easier not to engage in confrontation. This may be especially true for single parents. Many insecure parents are easily manipulated and easily worn down. When conflict begins early in the child's life, insecure and conflict-avoidant parents are more likely to become permissive and nonconfrontational.

Evan was a 17-year-old who lived with his mother. His father moved out of state after the parents divorced when Evan was four years old. Evan rarely saw his father and, for most of his life, his mother had been single, though she remarried briefly when Evan was seven. Evan was a heavyset adolescent, and his mother was rather petite. Evan was referred for therapy by his school after several behavioral issues on campus. In discussing his family, he reported that his mother was cool and allowed him to do pretty much what he wanted. When his mother came in for a session, she admitted that she was not a good disciplinarian and shared that she was afraid of her son and that Evan's father had been quite intimidating during their marriage. The mother felt like she had no control over her son and just hoped he would be able to finish high school.

Parental Expectations

Some Cool parents believe that their teens are sufficiently mature to make their own life decisions. Many have a misunderstanding of what their teens are really capable of handling. They do not have a good feel for the structure and support adolescents still need and sincerely believe that 16- and 17-year-olds are ready to take on much more responsibility than they probably really are. Teens who are highly intelligent and verbal often appear more emotionally mature than they are.

Similarly, some parents believe that the developmental stage of adolescence requires them to step back and allow their teenager to find his or her own identity and path in life. These parents stress independence and believe their teen will become responsible and self-sufficient through experience. In most cases, these are the parents of teenagers who have been able to function with very little guidance. This is their philosophical belief and not an attempt to avoid responsibility for their children. Most such parents are affectionate, warm, responsive to the teen's requests, and available as trusted advisers.

Adolescent Reactions

At first glance, it would seem that teenagers would love to have Cool parents and would be the envy of their peer group. Their house usually becomes a center of social activities. As such, they have a built-in set of friends (although many of them are most likely coming around for the benefits). However, being the teen with the Cool parent is not always a positive experience.

Adolescents' reactions to this parenting style vary depending on the teen's personality, the extent of the permissiveness, and the activities allowed by the parents. Another significant factor is the amount of warmth, responsiveness, and support the parent provides the teen. In general, adolescents who come from homes in which the ideological basis of parenting is a sincere interest in developing the teen's independence and unique personality are likely to develop healthier and more positive reactions. Teens whose parents are more focused on partying and avoiding responsibility are more likely to react in negative and unhealthy ways.

Separation and Individuation

A key developmental task of adolescence is separating from parents and developing one's own unique personality. A certain amount of parent–teen conflict is common during this transition, but contrary to popular belief, it is not inevitable and does not have to involve significant turmoil. Adolescents typically develop their sense of self and identity in two primary ways: trying on various styles, and differentiating themselves from their parents. For the latter to work, it is usually necessary that the adolescent have parental expectations to push against. Permissive parenting can either make individuation more difficult, if teens aren't challenged enough, or easier, if parents encourage perseverance and independence.

Cool parents who are supportive and whose parenting philosophy is centered on allowing the adolescent sufficient freedom, encouragement, and support to develop his or her own identity may sidestep parent–teen conflict issues and provide their teen with the opportunity to mature in a relaxed environment. This allows for an easier transition to adulthood. In such families, teens enjoy a comfortable, affectionate, and healthy relationship with their parents. They mature sooner and tend to have a more comfortable and confident self-image. Many do not feel the need to rebel or engage in excessive or outrageous behavior in order to differentiate. Like other teens, they may try on different styles, peer groups, and behaviors, but they feel less compelled to hold onto these styles when parental conflict is not an issue.

Relationships with Parents

Parenting style has an impact on parent–teen interactions and relationships. Teens whose parents are comfortable and relaxed in their role are able to share a close bond with open and honest communication. However, this can become problematic when teenagers begin to confide information that puts the parent in the position of having to make an uncomfortable judgment call. For example, teens may share that they have been involved in dangerous or illegal activities, or they may share troubling information about a friend. Then parents must decide whether to take action on the information and possibly risk their Cool status. This can also be an uncomfortable situation for the teenager, as most teenagers want to have a parent they can confide in but need this individual to be a parent, not another friend.

Inappropriate Behavior

Parents' socially inappropriate actions—such as providing alcohol or drugs, disregarding traffic laws, and paying to keep their teens out of trouble—may create ethical dilemmas for teenagers concerning socially appropriate behavior. Inappropriate social activities may create negative reactions from peers and may also put teens at odds with their friends' parents. These teens become the "bad influences" that peers' parents won't let them hang out with. Many adolescents adopt their parents' distorted thinking about what acceptable activities are. In addition, teenagers tend to be defensive about their parents' behavior. This question was posted to the *Yahoo! Answers* Web site: "Is it ok to let teens drink alcohol?" One response was this:

> Yes. Not being funny but me and my brothers drink (ages 16, 17, 18, 13, 13 not much). She says as long as you don't get yourself into trouble and be responsible with it then fine. . . . Most people call it bad parenting but it isn't like she makes us have 20 cans of beer she only gives us like a glass or two a week. (*Yahoo! Answers*, n.d.)

Acting Out

Teens need and want limits from their parents; if they don't get them, they may push the limits and exaggerate their negative behaviors in order to get noticed. For many teens, boundaries and structure provide security, and when that security is not available, they have difficulty setting limits on their own behavior. Therefore, adolescents with parents who are too permissive often end up with more significant behavioral problems. Many of these teens feel out of control and overwhelmed, a phenomenon that I have seen in many of the more conduct-disordered teenagers with whom I have worked. Behavioral difficulties can range from minor mischief to serious criminal behavior. Teens from overly permissive homes may skip school, sneak out at night, shoplift, or commit other crimes. Others smoke, abuse drugs or alcohol, become promiscuous, or use excessive and inappropriate language.

Some teens may disregard safety; many sneak out at night, taking the family car. In a 2007 incident in Houston, four teenagers were killed in an accident after a 15-year-old stole a car and six teens went joyriding late at night. The driver survived, and felony murder charges were filed against him. His brother was one of the teens who died (Wrigley, 2007). Although there is no indication of parenting style in the report, it does offer an example of teen impulsive behavior, which is more likely in permissive families.

There is clearly a downside for teens whose parents are more focused on being cool than on providing behavioral limits. When parents do not set clear limits, the only deterrent is the teen's own internal self-control. Some teens in these types of homes do develop self-control, but often only after a number of painful mistakes.

Lack of Self-Control

Teens with Cool parents often lack self-control, as they have never been expected to manage their impulses, emotions, and behavior. A three-year-old who receives cookies in response to temper tantrums will probably still be throwing tantrums when he or she is 13. These teens are often disrespectful to adults at home, at school, and in public. They are very more likely to be argumentative and engage in power struggles. With an exaggerated sense of their own power, they have difficulty accepting authority, as their family environment provides them with very little opportunity to learn more appropriate interaction styles. As they are not accustomed to hearing the word "no," they often overreact to even minor limits. They may become disrespectful and belligerent with teachers who attempt to set limits. It is not unusual nowadays for teens to call their teachers inappropriate names and even to become physically violent with them. These teens have difficulty learning that life has (and needs) rules even if their own homes do not.

Paula was 13 and the second of three children. As a child, she was emotional and demanding. She was famous for her wild temper tantrums as a toddler. Her parents were concerned that disciplining her would break her independence and spirit and assumed that she would grow out of it. At 13, she continued to make demands and resort to loud emotional outbursts to get what she wanted. The most recent incident involved her screaming and stomping in a store after mom declined to buy her a pair of $100 jeans. Mom admitted that giving in to Paula was easier and that neither she nor her husband was very good at setting limits. But they were concerned now, as Paula's behavior had become so out of control.

Often these teens have poor decision-making and problem-solving skills. They are self-centered, feel entitled, and may expect others outside of the home to cater to their whims. When parents cater to a teen's fluctuating demands, the teen has difficulty learning how to function cooperatively with others.

Anger

Anger is a primary emotion felt by all individuals, especially adolescents. In families where the Cool parenting style is practiced, the issue of anger takes on several different characteristics. Although it might be expected that teenagers in a lenient home would have little reason to become angry, they do in fact experience anger. They may have difficulty knowing how to handle being angry at someone who seems to always be focused on granting your wishes and making you happy. The need to separate and individuate from these friend-parents may create intense anger. These teens often angrily overreact to small issues, in part because they have not been required to control their emotions. Other teens may feel guilty for being angry at their indulgent parents and may express their anger in sneaky or passive–aggressive ways. Many teens find themselves angry that their parents are not providing them with the structure and guidelines that they need to feel safe as they work through the difficult tasks of adolescence. They may even exaggerate their anger as a way of getting their parents to pay attention. Adolescents with inadequate control at home may be unable to control their anger and aggressiveness in the outside world, leading to delinquent behavior.

Chad, 17, had Cool parents. Dad worked in construction but was often out of work. Mom worked the evening shift at a local delivery company and was often tired or sleeping when Chad was home. Dad smoked pot and even gave some to Chad and his friends. Chad's house was the one where everyone liked to hang out. However, Chad was beginning to question his home environment. He noticed that some of his friends' parents were more concerned about school and did things together as a family. Suddenly, Chad was tired of sharing his friends and smoking pot with his out-of-work dad. He became angry and critical of his parents, often engaging in screaming fights with his dad, who resented his "snotty little son" judging him. The family environment deteriorated, and Chad left to live with his girlfriend's family.

Social Relationships

Teens whose parents' primary focus is providing a social environment for teenagers tend to be less involved in school activities and more involved in social and leisure activities. Teens with Cool parents may also seek out peers who engage in impulsive and negative behaviors because they have, in essence, been given permission to develop friendships with these types of people. For teens whose parents allow parties and serve alcohol, the majority of their friends are likely to be adolescents who drink alcohol and are sexually active. If their parents are primarily interested in having fun and throwing teenage parties, it is difficult for teens not to become involved with more destructive peer groups, leading to increased behavioral problems.

In many cases, the parents of other teenagers limit or forbid interaction between the Cool parent's teenager and their own teenagers, thus further limiting the social groups that the teen can become involved with. The teen is also dealing with parental role models that suggest that drinking, partying, and disobeying the law are acceptable behaviors. Numerous studies have shown that teens with parents who drink or allow their teens to drink are much more likely to use alcohol and drugs (Jacob & Johnson, 1997; Montgomery, Fisk, & Craig, 2008).

Academics

Adolescents in homes with limited structure and lax control may have more difficulty performing well in school. Many Cool parents are not interested in spending time on homework and school activities. Whether this is because the parents need to let their teenagers forge their own way in the academic world or because they are too busy focusing on social activities, these teens do not receive adequate encouragement and support to do well in school. They often struggle with completing assignments, show low persistence when faced with challenges, and have less interest in getting good grades. They may also engage in more problematic behaviors at school because they are not accustomed to following rules that they don't like. Lamborn et al. (1991) found that "these adolescents are relatively disengaged from school and show a higher frequency of involvement in certain deviant behaviors, including drug and alcohol use and school misconduct" (p. 1062).

Adolescents from permissive homes can do well in school if they have family support and are internally motivated. Academically successful teens depend on their personal drive, intelligence, and self-control. They may not require external support, as they receive their positive feelings from their success. However, teens with parents who support their interest in school grades and activities are likely to do better.

Positive Responses

Adolescents who respond positively to parental permissiveness may learn to make their own decisions, learn from their mistakes, and benefit from the fact that their parents do not react as negatively as some parents to normal adolescent behavior. When their teens make mistakes, they simply allow them to learn from the natural consequences. In response, these teens can correct their mistakes and move on without feeling guilty or inadequate. This can be a positive experience for teens, especially when they feel that their parent is supportive and available.

For shy or introverted teens, a parent's relaxed approach to parenting can take some of the pressure off of the expectations of adolescence. When parents allow their home to be open to other teenagers and social activities, it may provide the teenager with an opportunity to develop social skills and friendships. Not all Cool parents allow alcohol, drugs, or inappropriate sexual behavior in their homes. Many simply allow adolescents to enjoy themselves in healthy ways. Problems arise when they fail to provide adequate supervision and limits.

In these relaxed and socially open home environments, teens can learn to enjoy themselves and their friends and become socially competent. Many take on leadership roles. A review of several studies found that the "low-control-but-high-supportiveness . . . parenting group was associated with children who were prosocial, competent, and psychologically adjusted" (Weiss & Schwarz, 1996, p. 2111). What appears to be the distinguishing factor is the level of supportiveness provided by the parents rather than the lack of control. Teens are likely to respond positively to permissive parenting styles that are based on philosophical beliefs rather than on the desire to have a good time.

Some teens with Cool parents are able to develop healthy attributes. They show appropriate emotional and behavioral self-control. They become self-reliant and seek out suitable peers and activities. Healthy teens may seek out other role models such as teachers, clergy, or friends' parents. These teens are self-starters; they learn from their mistakes and make good decisions.

Short- and Long-Term Outcomes

Outcomes for teens with Cool parents depend on several variables: the home environment; the degree and type of permissiveness practiced by the parent; the amount of warmth, support, and supervision shown by the parent; and the teen's personality. Parenting style usually influences the teen's personality more than the teen's personality affects parenting style. Short- and long-term outcomes for the Cool parenting style are mixed. Many teens, especially those whose parents abdicate their parental responsibilities, experience significant negative long-term outcomes. Teens with parents who base their parenting style on specific beliefs and provide support and guidance have the most favorable outcomes. Teens with parents who allow or ignore negative and self-destructive behaviors are more likely to have long-term difficulties.

Participation in Activities

Encouraging teens' interests can have positive results, as when teens develop long-term involvement in healthy activities, or negative results, as in the cases of the mother who bought guns for her son and parents who encourage drinking or promiscuity.

Studies have consistently shown that teens who are allowed to drink during adolescence tend to drink more, become alcoholic earlier, and have more long-term difficulties with alcohol. The same holds true for cigarette smoking and other unhealthy behaviors. Parents can reinforce antisocial behavior either by modeling it or giving it tacit approval. Parents who excuse their teens' delinquent behavior or help them avoid the consequences of it may be setting the stage for future criminal activities. A study on parental transmission of antisocial behavior concluded the following:

> Antisocial behavior may be interpreted by the child as less wrong if the parent models the activities. Taken together, the research evidence suggests that perceptions of parental behavior may be particularly salient predictors of adolescent subsequent activities, thus helping to explain the connection between parent and adolescent antisocial behavior. (Dogan et al., 2007, p. 336)

Direct or indirect parental permission for sexual activity may also cause teens long-term sexual difficulties. Adults who engaged in sexually promiscuous behavior during adolescence are likely to have more difficulty with their sexuality. Some may continue to be promiscuous and have difficulty equating sex with a committed relationship, whereas others may feel guilty and ashamed of their early sexual behavior. On the other hand, teenagers who engaged in sexual activity in the context of a committed relationship are often able to develop healthy adult sexual relationships as well.

High School, College, and Career

Academic accomplishment is often associated with parental involvement, support, and encouragement. As discussed in earlier chapters, too much parental pressure can result in negative outcomes. However, the danger with the Cool parenting style is that the teens will lack sufficient encouragement and challenge during the high school years. Grolnick (2003) reported that "adolescents from nondirective homes were low in achievement orientation, competence and self-regulation" (p. 7).

There will always be exceptional students who excel despite a lack of parental structure or guidance, but most teenagers require some degree of parental involvement. Teenagers whose parents are more involved in their social lives than in their academic lives often show the most difficulty in school, getting poor grades and possibly even dropping out. Another distinct possibility is that these teenagers will not be achievement oriented and will seek out jobs that give them just enough money to meet their basic needs and allow them to continue their party lifestyle. When these teenagers decide to attend college, they may have difficulty selecting a major and a career. They may spend too much time on social activities, jeopardizing their ability to graduate. The fact that they are not used to working hard for what they want can make college and career a distinct challenge.

Adolescents with Cool parents may find some unique challenges once they move into the job market. The first challenge may be dealing with authority and rules. Working for someone who tells them when to be there, what to wear, and what to do can be a significant change for these young adults. They may have difficulty behaving professionally with coworkers, as much of their adolescence was spent partying and acting irresponsibly.

At the other end of the Cool spectrum are those parents who value creativity and individuality and provide their teenagers with acceptance and support for their interests and goals. As adults, these teens may feel confident and comfortable with pursuing their dreams. They may show exceptional drive to meet their goals and may not expect others to provide for them. However, young adults whose parents were too indulgent may struggle with accepting the limitations that the real world brings.

Identity and Self-Concept

Identity is the sum total of one's characteristics, that which sets one apart from others. Self-concept is one's perception and judgment of the various aspects of one's personality. Many characteristics developed during adolescence carry into adulthood. Teens who are allowed to behave immaturely and irresponsibly will have difficulty developing a strong identity and a healthy self-concept. Many of these teens have not learned to be responsible and to exhibit socially appropriate behavior. A lack of limits and boundaries may result in poor impulse control, immaturity, and poorly regulated emotions. These young adults may have difficulty delaying gratification and may have a sense of entitlement. They can also be easily stressed and may have trouble with self-confidence in the face of adversity. Unless they are challenged, many of these teen personality traits will continue through the adult years.

Parents should provide structure and control for an adolescent's impulsive behaviors. When parents allow, and even participate in, these behaviors, they can inhibit their children's development of identity and autonomy. As young adults, these children may remain dependent on their parents and caught up in the partying lifestyle. They may continue to live at home and may be late in developing their independence and self-sufficiency.

Liam, 21, came into therapy at the insistence of his mother and stepfather. Liam was unemployed and lived at home with his parents. He had made several attempts to go to community college but did not follow through on attending classes and turning in the work. Liam had had several jobs in the last few years, but none had lasted more than six months. He had been a poor student and had smoked marijuana on a regular basis with his friends. Liam's parents excused much of his behavior as typical teenage escapades and assumed he would grow out of it. In talking about his situation, Liam acknowledged, "I never really pushed myself in school, and my parents seemed okay with that. I really don't know how to make myself accomplish anything."

Social and Intimate Relationships

During adolescence and young adulthood, social relationships come to the forefront, and teenagers have a chance to develop appropriate interactional styles as well as to separate from their family of origin and begin taking steps toward developing their own family. Social skills are developed through a variety of activities, including athletic events, school social activities, social outings, part-time jobs, church youth groups, and volunteer experiences. Adolescent social activities should provide healthy ways of having fun. During these activities, teens learn to interact and connect with peers. When the majority of the interactions one has during adolescence include free-flowing beer, the social lessons are distorted. Adults need to know more than how to behave at a drinking party. Individuals who grew up in a permissive, party-oriented environment may feel awkward, out of place, and socially incompetent in mature social situations.

Teenagers who grew up in open, democratic, and accepting homes also may consider their parents cool, but have learned more appropriate social interactional styles. Teens who are given freedom to interact with peers are likely to be more social and place a higher value on friendship. They may become confident adults, have a strong sense of self, and feel comfortable in a variety of situations.

One of the main aspirations of adulthood is to develop intimate romantic relationships. Parents are role models for sexual identity, adult relationships, and marriage. Within the family, one learns how to communicate, deal with conflict, and consider the needs of others. Indulgent parenting may prevent some of these lessons, such as sharing and compassion, from being learned. Party parents may teach party games but not life's important lessons. Relationships require give and take, empathy, consideration, and affection—all traits that may be distorted in homes where teens are overly indulged.

Party Skills and Life Skills

Parents should supervise—not participate in—teenage parties. Cool parents who provide the alcohol for parties, and especially those who participate with their teens in alcohol and drug use, are giving their teens an unhealthy message: that having fun and using drugs are more important life goals than hard work and accomplishment. Although it is possible and even likely that teenagers will engage in drinking and drug use, parental disapproval indicates that this is not a desired behavior and reinforces the message that excessive drinking is unhealthy. Being the life of the party should not be a life goal.

Life Control and Satisfaction

How an adult handles his or her life depends, in large part, on the successful accomplishment of adolescent developmental tasks. When a teen is able to develop a distinct and separate identity, achieve self-confidence, and become responsible and self-sufficient, he or she is likely to experience more success and satisfaction. Adolescents whose parents were focused on being their teen's friend, rather than on setting limits and applying consequences for inappropriate behavior, may have a harder time handling their own adult life. As adults, they may make poor and impulsive choices and have difficulty making decisions. Poor choices can lead to financial problems.

Many teens raised in the Cool parenting style are constantly given acceptance and approval; as adults, they may continue to be dependent on the approval of others. Some, especially those from families that engaged in inappropriate and illegal activities, may adopt poor core values and morals. These individuals are rarely satisfied with their lives. As parents themselves, they are likely to struggle with providing discipline and structure for their own children.

Positive Outcomes

Teens who receive support during adolescence, even if they aren't given limits, often are able to develop healthy life skills. Some develop resilience, self-reliance, confidence, and the ability to solve problems. In most cases, their parents were supportive of their endeavors and individuation. As young adults, they are often creative, intelligent, and self-motivated, and they are usually psychologically healthy, with good life satisfaction. They are also more likely to continue having a healthy relationship with their parents. They often raise their own children in a relaxed, supportive, and permissive manner but may provide a little more structure.

Summary

Cool parents are fun parents. They are more invested in being their teen's friend than in being an active parent. Parents who host teenage parties and provide alcohol for them are in this category. Some permissive parents are simply opposed to or insecure about asserting their authority. Adolescents may assume that having Cool parents is a good thing, but many teenagers with Cool parents go to great lengths to get their parents to provide them with the attention and structure they need. Teens from permissive families engage in some of the most problematic behaviors, including alcohol and drug abuse and antisocial behavior. They often have difficulty making the transition to responsible and self-sufficient adulthood. Parents whose permissiveness is based on philosophical beliefs tend to provide some structure for their teens and have more positive outcomes.

CHAPTER SIX

"Not Now, I'm Busy" Parents

If teenagers live with rejection, they learn to feel lost.

—Dorothy Nolte and Rachel Harris,
Teenagers Learn What They Live

Case Example

Mason, 16, was admitted to a psychiatric facility for drug rehabilitation. The precipitating event for his admission was a minor car accident that Mason caused while intoxicated on alcohol and Valium. Mason's parents insisted on his admission to the hospital after he was ticketed for failure to control his vehicle. The police officer who responded to the accident declined to charge him with driving while intoxicated, but merely contacted his parents. At the time of his admission, he acknowledged regular use of alcohol, marijuana, Ecstasy, and various prescription medications that he found in his parents' medicine cabinet. Mason stated that he started using alcohol at age 13, and by age 15 was regularly using a variety of drugs.

Mason was an only child, and his mother was 38 years old when he was born. She reported that she and her husband were career-oriented individuals and agreed to delay parenthood until their careers were established. Both parents were high-powered executives in the oil and gas industry, and their positions often required travel. Although Mason's parents tried to avoid being out of town at the same time, this was not always possible, and when they were both gone, their housekeeper stayed overnight to supervise Mason.

Prior to this event, Mason had appeared to be doing well. His grades were acceptable and he had no behavioral problems at school. Free time was often spent alone in his room or out with friends. The family made an effort to go out for a nice dinner every two weeks. Although Mason's parents had established a number of rules concerning school and outside activities, they often did not have the time to respond to infractions. The parents denied being aware that Mason was heavily involved in alcohol and drug use, although both admitted having caught him coming home late in an inebriated state. His parents wrote these events off as normal adolescent experimental behavior. Mason reported that he had been coming home drunk since he was 13 and that his parents did not notice. Mason also admitted that he began to smoke marijuana in his room and stole alcohol and prescription pills from his parents, but all this went unnoticed by his parents.

During the course of therapy, Mason acknowledged that he was making an effort to get noticed by his parents and that his drug and alcohol abuse was a cry for help. Mason's parents were devastated when they realized how many warning signs they had failed to notice.

Parenting Style Characteristics

The "Not Now, I'm Busy" parenting style characterizes those parents who are not fully invested in parenting their adolescents for a variety of reasons. This parenting style encompasses a wide range of motivations and behaviors, from regretfully unavailable to emotionally and physically neglectful. The majority of Not Now, I'm Busy parents fall in the middle of this range. They are often overextended, uninvolved, disinterested, discouraged, indifferent, or otherwise unavailable. Their households tend to be parent centered rather than teen centered.

The majority of Not Now, I'm Busy parents are dealing with life circumstances that prevent them from being as active in their teen's life as they would like to be. Other parents in this category do not wish to spend the energy it takes to parent a teenager. Some simply do not seem to care and find parenting an unwanted responsibility. The end result is neglect of parental responsibilities. Most of these parents love and care about their adolescents; unfortunately, many do not have sufficient resources or opportunities to focus on their teens. Others mistakenly believe that a small amount of high-quality interaction makes up for a lack of quantity.

Work and Obligations

On one end of the spectrum are those parents whose lives prevent them from spending a lot of interactional time with their teen. They often have busy work schedules and may even hold more than one job in order to support their families. Their careers may require late hours or travel, which significantly limits the amount of time they spend with their teens. Certain occupations—for example, offshore work and firefighting—require absence from home for days or even weeks, followed by several days off. Often, these workers have trouble fitting into the family routine when they are home, and some work second jobs. Ministers and physicians are often on call for others at the expense of their own family. Single parents who have no choice but to work often have limited time available to spend with their teens. They often struggle to balance work and home and may feel guilty about the lack of attention they give to their teens.

Many Not Now, I'm Busy parents cite work obligations as the reason they cannot attend an event with their teen: "I'm sorry, I can't make it to your game today. I have to work late." Some parents do not actually need to spend as much time as they do at work, but they find their jobs to be more compelling than their teens' activities. They may show up at a game half an hour late, spend part of the time talking on their cell phones, and leave early. Many of these parents see their attendance at the event more as coming to see their teen perform for them rather than being there to support their child. These parents rarely attend practice, only important games or performances. They often depend on other parents to help out with their teens. They may also talk on their cell phone during dinner or while driving their teen to practice or school rather than talking with their teen.

Clearly, some parents have no choice but to work and do not have control over their work schedule. Many parents struggle emotionally with their inability to be in two places at once. They make a concerted effort to be available to their teen and are able to find other solutions for remaining connected with him or her—for example, by calling regularly from work or setting aside time in the evening.

Other parents choose their career over parenthood. These parents find the work environment to be much more satisfying than parenthood, particularly during the difficult years of adolescence. They have little time for interruptions and often find that they have more important tasks to attend to than responding to their teen's need at the moment. These are the "can't it wait? I'm busy right now" parents. They may promise to get back to the teen, but often they do not.

Wealthy and socially active parents also sometimes neglect their teenagers, leaving them with a series of nannies or other caretakers. They often provide material items—expensive cars, electronic gadgets, and trips—as replacements for their time and attention. They may place their teens in boarding school and rarely visit them.

Janis was a 16-year-old who attended a prestigious private school in New England. Her father was a wealthy banker, and her mother was a socialite. Janis's parents traveled extensively, and she was cared for by a series of nannies and housekeepers over the years. The only expectations that her parents had for her were that she do well in school and present herself properly in public.

Janis came into therapy following a half-hearted suicide attempt. When they heard about it, her parents declined to return from their trip but requested a report from her doctor. She was depressed and lonely and had few true friends. As she got older, her attachment to her family became more an issue of keeping her trust fund and meeting family obligations. Janis also struggled with being genuine and tended to view others in terms of their usefulness.

Limited Involvement

Many Not Now, I'm Busy parents are task oriented rather than relationship oriented. They view their parental responsibility as providing structure, financial support, and meals. These parents rarely help with homework or include the teenager in family-oriented discussions or decisions. They often have high expectations for mature behavior. They do not want to be brought into the adolescent's personal issues and are uncomfortable with the emotional aspects of parenthood. They don't know how to deal with teen drama or don't have the patience to listen to their teen's issues. Many avoid unpleasant information.

These are "don't ask, don't know" or "don't ask, don't worry" parents. Many of these parents believe that by providing a home, food, clothes, and a few basic (often inflexible) rules, they are fulfilling their parental responsibilities. They may say, "I work hard and long to provide for my family" and see this as the way they express their love for their family.

Some Not Now, I'm Busy parents are simply not interested in their teens' lives. They find adolescent angst too difficult and time-consuming to deal with. They use a variety of excuses to avoid interaction or responsibility. Some focus on their household responsibilities, such as the parent who would rather vacuum the living room than sit through a softball practice. Many were also underinvolved in their children's lives during the early years. Stay-at-home parents may become focused on housework or social or volunteer activities. Working parents may come home from work, sit on the couch, watch TV, and demand not be interrupted.

Teen requests are treated as an imposition. These parents will respond with comments such as, "Do you really need me to do that right now?" or "Can't you see I'm busy?" The care provided by these parents is often unpredictable, inconsistent, or overly reactive. They can become screamers if they have to deal with the teen's unacceptable behavior and are particularly angered if they are called at work or have to make a trip to the school.

Phillip, age 17, had been an exemplary student and active in football throughout high school. One afternoon, he ended up in a fight with another boy who had been disrespectful to Phillip's girlfriend. The school, which had a zero-tolerance policy on fighting, called his mother, and Phillip was suspended for three days. As Phillip and his mother were leaving the school, his mother was overheard screaming at him about how furious she was that she had been called at work and had to leave her job to deal with him. "Do you think I had nothing better to do than deal with you?"

Unrealistic Expectations

Not Now, I'm Busy parents often have an unrealistic expectation that the adolescent can take care of him- or herself. Teens are expected to get themselves ready for school, keep up with their schoolwork and schedules, keep their room and bathroom clean, do their laundry, and in many cases, get a job in order to pay for their own clothes and entertainment. Such parents may also expect their teens to take on household chores such as cooking dinner and caring for younger siblings. These parents want and expect their teens to monitor their own behavior and not to engage in any activity or behavior that would require parental time and involvement.

Some parents mistake physical size and verbal ability for maturity and assume their teens are ready to take over primary responsibility for themselves. Others view the later adolescent years as the welcome end of their parental responsibilities. In many cases, parents pass their responsibilities over to teens who are not quite ready to assume them. These parents often say that the adolescent is living at home out of the goodness of the parent's heart and can be asked to leave at any time. In this sense, the teenager is prematurely ejected from the family. In other families, even if the parents would prefer otherwise, a family crisis may create a situation in which the teenager is required to take over responsibility for the household. Many times, even after the crisis has subsided, the new responsibilities remain in place.

Stressful Life Circumstances

Some, Not Now, I'm Busy parents are struggling to meet multiple responsibilities. They may work two jobs or have to care for their own elderly parents. Other parents are unavailable due, in part, to the needs of a disabled sibling or other family member. Unfortunately, in this situation, teens often receive the least focus.

When a parent takes on the care of his or her aging parent, teenagers are often expected to make significant changes in order to accommodate the needs of their grandparent, who may spend a significant amount of time at the home or move in permanently. Teens may have to give up their room and share with a sibling. They may not be able to have friends over as often and may have to be quieter. They may be expected to help more with household responsibilities and with the grandparent's care. If the elderly family member is hospitalized, the teen's parent may be absent from home for significant periods. This situation causes significant stress and can lead to changes in how the family functions and the home environment. For example, dinners are not prepared and homework assistance is not available.

Families with a disabled child (or other family member) may find their resources and time stretched thin. The extra responsibilities inherent in dealing with a disabled child often mean that the teen must make allowances for the sibling's needs. Most children who have a disabled sibling adapt very well, but they almost always must sacrifice some activities and one-on-one time with their parents.

Neglect

At the other end of the spectrum are parents who are outright neglectful of their adolescents. They are not interested in being parents and may have had children accidentally or for the wrong reasons. Psychological problems may influence their neglectful parenting style. They are nonresponsive and emotionally distant and may also be physically neglectful. They show very little interest in their teens and make very few demands on them. Most behavioral expectations are established on the spur of the moment, and usually relate more to the parent's needs or comfort level than to the teen's situation. They may become disproportionately angry with the adolescent.

In studying the association between parental psychopathology and conduct disorder in adolescents, Marmorstein and Iacono (2004) reported the following:

> The family environments of children exhibiting delinquent behavior have been shown to be less warm and affectionate, less accepting, less emotionally supportive, and including less supervision. . . . Parents of conduct disorder youth tend not to clearly set out expectations regarding acceptable and unacceptable behavior, not to provide consistent discipline following antisocial behavior, to inadequately monitor and supervise their children and to use ineffective family problem-solving strategies. (p. 378)

Some neglect may be the result of a parent's dislike of their child. These parents may have enjoyed the cute-little-kid stage but are disdainful of the adolescent their child turns into. This may also be the case when a stepparent has primary responsibility for the care of the adolescent. In other situations, the neglect may come from noncustodial parents, who make court-ordered visits out of a sense of obligation but have little emotional connection with the teen.

When a parent lacks affection and interest in an adolescent, the end result is often indifference and neglect. These parents or stepparents do not monitor the teen's whereabouts or keep up to date on events in the teen's life. Often this neglect is obvious to the adolescent, whose self-esteem and behavior can be strongly affected; teens experience parent figures as models for how they perceive themselves.

Substance-abusing parents are especially likely to neglect their teens. They may disappear for hours or days on end, or lock themselves in their room and parent through a door. Substance abuse probably leads to the most neglectful parenting style.

Parenting Style: Origins and Motivations

Family history, life circumstances, illness, and personal issues all can play a role in parents' adopting the Not Now, I'm Busy style. Some may have grown up in neglectful or abusive families that did not prepare them for parental responsibilities. For others, life circumstances can be overwhelming, or personal issues can result in inadequate parenting skills. Medical or psychiatric issues can interfere with parental responsibilities. Some adults are simply too self-absorbed to consider their teen's needs.

Family History

Parents who are disengaged from their adolescents were often raised in families in which they got little attention. Their own parents may have been neglectful, preoccupied, or indifferent. They may have been raised in the "children should be seen but not heard" philosophy and may never have had healthy parental role models.

Growing up in a family in which most personal interactions were painful can create parents who are devoid of parental emotions. The presence of a great degree of conflict or abuse, including spousal abuse, in the home can result in emotional numbness and a lack of connection between family members and can produce a new generation of inadequate and neglectful parents. This process is clearly seen in the movie *Precious* (Daniels, 2009), the story of a teenage girl, Precious, who has been made pregnant twice by her stepfather in a home where poverty and abuse are everyday occurrences. Her mother cruelly tells her, "You are a dummy, don't nobody want you, don't nobody need you. Schooling ain't gonna help you none." Here the cycle of neglect, poverty, and abuse is portrayed as an inevitable outcome for Precious.

Not Now, I'm Busy parents may come from families in which there was significant financial or material deprivation. This may drive them to become adults who are overly focused on their own life rather than their parenting responsibilities. Many of these adults become driven workaholics whose focus on making money and having material items supersedes family relationships. They may provide their teens with all the latest gadgets but not with attention and supervision.

Life Circumstances

In a small number of cases, family circumstances interfere with the parent–teen bond. For example, a parent may travel to another country to find work, and it may take years before he or she is sufficiently established to send for the rest of the family. Or children may be raised initially by grandparents or other family members and then returned in late childhood or early adolescence to parents with whom they do not have a strong family bond. There may be an unrealistic expectation of what being together will be like; the fantasy of a family is often much more ideal than the reality. Adolescence is a particularly difficult time, and although a parent may be comfortable providing a home environment, the emotional relationship is not as easily established. The teen may be angry and detached from the parent, which may cause the parent to withdraw or become angry that the teen is not more grateful for the sacrifices that he or she has made. The teen may respond with more anger, and this negative cycle may persist.

More often, parenting style is influenced by circumstances in present-day life that limit parents' availability to their teens. Parents may be less involved because of circumstances, not choice. They are often loving and caring but exhausted.

Work requirements and financial needs may dictate long periods of time being spent away from the family. Single parents, who are often the sole providers and primary caretakers, are at a special disadvantage. Overburdened parents may choose to focus on providing the basics: housekeeping, laundry, and meals.

Parents may have to take on responsibility for the care of their own aging parents, which can involve frequent medical appointments and visits and, in some cases, the grandparent moving in with the family. A sibling or other family member who needs special care because of developmental disabilities, physical illness, or emotional problems may take up the parent's time, energy, and resources. In such cases, teenagers may be asked to take on the responsibility for many of their own needs, to forgo certain social activities because of financial or other issues, and to help care for the family member. However, these realities do not lessen a teen's need for parental attention.

Single parents may become overwhelmed, especially if they are caring for a number of children with little outside support. Parents who are single because of the death of a spouse also have to deal with grief, which often leads to emotional numbing or withdrawal, leaving teens to fend for themselves at a time when they are in significant pain. Other single parents may still be dealing with the pain of divorce and focused on developing a new life. A contentious divorce and custody battle can leave teens on the losing end. Relationship issues can interfere with parents' focus on their adolescent. They may abdicate their caretaking role in order to make their own lives easier.

Providing for the family's basic needs may be all that single parents can handle. With little support, they may be unable to handle their teenagers. They may be unhappy, lonely, frustrated, and exhausted. In families with several children, teenagers may have to take care of the house and younger children.

Gina had four children, ages 5, 8, 11, and 14. A year before, her husband had died suddenly of a heart attack. There was no life insurance, and Gina had to go back to work as a teacher at the local elementary school. Her grief was overwhelming, and she was becoming depressed because of the stress. Her 14-year-old son, Vince, reacted to his father's death by becoming increasingly angry and rebellious. The angrier he became, the more Gina withdrew, and by the time Gina brought Vince into therapy, the relationship between the two of them was almost nonexistent. In reality, Vince's anger and grief terrified Gina, and when she withdrew, Vince felt like he had lost not only his father but also his mother.

Remarriage is another situation in which parenting styles can significantly change. In newly created families, teens are often neglected in favor of the new spouse. Stepparents often find it difficult to bond with teenagers and may be unwilling to put forth the effort it would take to develop a close relationship, especially with those teens who only visit on alternate weekends. Stepparents may also find teens to be unpleasant to deal with and resent the time that their new spouse spends with them. (Issues of divorce and remarriage are discussed in more detail in chapter 8.)

Physical Illness and Psychiatric Disorders

Physical illness and psychiatric disorders can significantly affect a parent's availability. A mother or father fighting cancer has little time or energy to parent and may become absorbed in his or her own struggles. Depression, bipolar disorder, and other mental illnesses severely limit parenting abilities—sometimes only briefly, but sometimes for a long time. Not all psychiatric disorders result in neglectful or uninvolved parenting, but they can be so debilitating that teens are left to fend for themselves.

Emotional issues can be the root cause of parenting styles that are less than adequate to meet the needs of teenage children. Adult attention deficit disorder (ADD) can result in the parent being scattered, easily overwhelmed, and unreliable. More often than not, the child of an ADD parent is also ADD, resulting in a more chaotic and disorganized home. ADD teens need more structure and emotional support, which ADD parents may be unable to provide, especially if their ADD is undiagnosed and untreated. Homes that are overly cluttered and provide very inconsistent discipline are functionally neglectful. Parents who are anxious or unable to handle stress may withdraw from parenting responsibilities as a way of avoiding stress.

Alexis was a married 42-year-old mother of two teenagers—Tony, 12, and Sydney, 14. Alexis worked part-time at the high school as an attendance clerk, and her husband worked on offshore oil rigs with a two-week-on schedule. Both teens were involved in after-school activities. Alexis came into treatment feeling overwhelmed and showing signs of depression. Further exploration revealed that she was feeling stressed and inadequate. She reported that her home was a mess, she was often late in picking up her kids from practice, and had recently been written up at work for mistakes. Of considerable concern for her were the recent problems she had with her teens' increased disrespect; she acknowledged that she often resented their demands on her. As therapy progressed, Alexis was diagnosed with adult attention deficit disorder and started on medication. Therapy helped her become more organized, and she was able to set aside more time for her children.

Another characteristic that can affect parent–teen interactions is a parent's difficulty with attachment, which relates to an individual's capacity to emotionally connect with another:

> The link between attachment difficulties and neglect lies in the parenting styles and patterns of family functioning. . . . A parent with an avoidant attachment style may respond to emotional and practical demands by failing to acknowledge their legitimacy and by becoming psychologically unavailable. . . . Ambivalent attachment can result in the parent being preoccupied with their own emotional needs to the extent that they are unable to respond adequately and/ or sensitively to the child. Parenting can be unpredictable and uncertain, with the parent finding it difficult to reliably hold the child in mind when they are themselves under pressure. (Turney & Tanner, 2001, p. 197)

In a similar manner, parents with a personality disorder, such as narcissistic personality disorder or borderline personality disorder, have trouble putting aside their own needs in order to parent their teenagers. Neglectful or uninvolved parents are often very self-centered, a hallmark of many personality disorders.

Alcohol and substance abuse can result in some of the most neglectful and abusive parenting. Substance abusers can experience sudden rage, often focused on their children. At other times, the alcohol or substance misuse creates an unhealthy and inappropriate parent–teen relationship. (Physical illness, psychiatric disorder, and substance abuse and their effect on parenting style are discussed in more detail in chapter 9.)

Indifference or Early Withdrawal

Some parents have no real interest in being parents. They may have had children when they were very young or in response to the demands and expectations of their spouse or other family members. Some parents enjoy their children, and are fairly good parents, as long as the children are young, but find the challenge of parenting an adolescent unenjoyable or simply too difficult. Parents with teenagers who are intensely rebellious and disrespectful may withdraw from the responsibility of parenting, feeling ill-equipped to handle the adolescent years. Mothers may be uncomfortable or fearful of their sons' growing masculinity, whereas fathers may be unable to handle their daughters' developing sexuality. Other parents withdraw from active parenting when their teenagers are old enough to start assuming more responsibility for themselves, mistakenly assuming that their adolescent is ready for independence at 16 or 17.

Adolescent Reactions

Studies have consistently shown that adolescents with uninvolved or neglectful parents exhibit the most emotional and behavioral problems (Lee, Daniels, & Kissinger, 2006; L. Steinberg, Lamborn, Darling, Mounts, & Dornbusch, 1994; Weiss & Schwarz, 1996). Teen reactions to the Not Now, I'm Busy parenting style vary on the basis of the degree of parental involvement and the emotional connections between parent and teen. The greater the neglect or indifference perceived by the teen, the greater the negative reaction is likely to be. Although separation from the family is a necessary step toward adulthood, closeness to and support from parents is still of great importance to adolescents.

Attention Seeking

Most teenagers say that they wish their parents were less involved in their lives, but teenagers with parents in the Not Now, I'm Busy category usually make a concerted effort to engage their parents. Attention seeking may take several different forms. The most obvious is acting out, which is designed to get a reaction from the parent. This can include dressing in outrageous styles, getting inconsistent or poor grades, running away, or using alcohol or drugs. Most of the time, the acting out relates to something that matters to the parent—a teenager from a socially prominent family may sport tattoos and body piercings, whereas a teacher's child may fail classes. Disrespectful comments or emotional outbursts can be attention-seeking actions. When teens feel like their behavior is not resulting in a parental response, they often up the ante. Of course, most teens deny that their behavior springs from a need for attention.

Finding an Alternate Home

When home does not provide them with security, support, and attention, teenagers eventually seek to fill these needs elsewhere. Peer group affiliation is much stronger in teens from neglectful families, who quickly learn not to depend on their parents for attention and approval but to turn to their friends or other adults. Healthier teens will find other adults, perhaps teachers or extended family members, to function as role models.

Lack of attention and supervision makes teenagers, especially girls, susceptible to those who prey upon young adolescents. Gangs are another temptation for teens seeking a replacement family. The sense of kinship, identity, and companionship that a peer group provides may persuade teenagers to rationalize or excuse any dangerous or illegal activity in which it engages. Other teens leave home prematurely or get pregnant in order to create their own family. Adolescence is a period of identity formation, and adolescents need a family or group that they can incorporate into their sense of self. If parents don't provide it, teens will create their own.

Tenisha, 15, came into therapy with her mother after it was discovered that Tenisha had become sexually involved with an older boy. Tenisha's parents reported that she had recently started hanging out with a negative group of teens in their neighborhood. Both parents worked; an older brother, Greg (19), still lived at home. Exploration of the family dynamics revealed that Greg received a lot of the parents' focus, as he had had behavioral problems since childhood. Many of the family interactions involved loud and long arguments with Greg, and Tenisha dealt with these by hiding out in her room. As she got older, she started sneaking out and spending more time with some of the more problematic neighborhood teenage boys. Tenisha's parents were loving and concerned and had not realized that Tenisha was struggling with a need for more attention and less chaos in her family.

Failing or Excelling in School

The literature has clearly shown that academic behavior is connected to parental support and encouragement. Uninvolved or indifferent parents do not consistently monitor academic accomplishment, and their teens' grades reflect this. Lee et al. (2006) found that "children with this parenting profile . . . had lower math and reading scores" (p. 257). Poor grades and disruptive behavior can be a teen's passive—aggressive way of expressing anger. Even busy parents will usually react to a bad report card.

Some adolescents find school to be a place where they get approval and acceptance and therefore become very good students. When getting good grades is the only way they can get attention from their parents, they may work harder at school. Academics can be a way out of poverty. Some such adolescents place too much emphasis on academic accomplishment and become overachievers and perfectionists. Unfortunately, academic success may come at the price of other emotional difficulties.

Emotional Repercussions

Teens in indifferent or neglectful homes often show lower levels of psychosocial adjustment:

The children who had the lowest achievement scores and were the least adjusted were from Unengaged homes. . . . Children from Unengaged homes had the most extreme, low scores on Agreeableness and Openness to Experience . . . were significantly more nonconforming, maladjusted, dominating and unoriginal and had a higher consumption of alcohol than children from most other homes. (Weiss & Schwarz, 1996, pp. 2101–2110)

Adolescents with parents who are emotionally unresponsive and provide inadequate supervision tend to be emotionally unhealthy and needy. They struggle with low self-esteem, insecurity, loneliness, and impulsivity. They may have poor decision-making skills, have difficulty following through on tasks, lack self-confidence, and become easily frustrated. Without encouragement, they may give up quickly. They may develop superficial identities at the expense of a solid and secure sense of self-worth. Individuality and autonomy may be rushed and incomplete. They may develop a negative self-image, and many suffer from depression.

Anger

Anger can be a particularly difficult emotion for adolescents to handle and express. They may become uncooperative, disrespectful, and argumentative with their parents. Neglected teens may bait their parents, hoping to get a response. They may blow up with little provocation because they have little self-control. They often scream, curse, slam doors, and storm out. They may play out their anger in antisocial, delinquent, or criminal behavior. Teens with parents who are too busy to interact with them on a consistent basis feel rejected and unloved. When teens feel ignored, they often become even more difficult to control. They often express their anger with statements such as "I don't care what you think" and "get out of my life" (when they really mean "get back into my life"). Without caring adults, they do not learn how to modulate intense emotions.

Behavioral Difficulties

Adolescents from homes in which supervision is inconsistent or nonexistent usually exhibit increased behavioral problems. These behaviors can range from being uncooperative to serious antisocial activity:

Inadequate parenting, which is characterized by lack of affection and/or high levels of criticism and hostility, lax or inconsistent discipline and supervision and general lack of involvement, provides the foundation for the development of an aggressive, antisocial behavior pattern. . . . Over time, and with ongoing parenting difficulties, noncompliance evolves into a behavior pattern characterized by early peer rejection, poor academic performance, delinquency, AOD [alcohol or other drugs] abuse, and association with deviant peers. (Jacob & Johnson, 1997, p. 206)

The behavioral problems that begin in adolescence may continue well into adulthood.

Alcohol, Drugs, and Sex

Alcohol and drug use is more common among adolescents with Not Now, I'm Busy parents than in any other group. It can be a part of adolescent experimentation, or it can signify that the teen is experiencing emotional problems. Parents may themselves be abusing alcohol or drugs or may fail to notice that their teens are doing so. Often alcohol or drugs are used to deal with emotional difficulties, such as feelings of insecurity or rejection, which are more likely among teens of neglectful parents. These behaviors can quickly escalate into addiction. In addition, these teens are more likely to become involved with harder drugs such as inhalants and cocaine (Montgomery et al., 2008; R. A. Turner, Irwin, & Millstein, 1991). Numerous studies have shown that alcoholism and drug abuse that begins in adolescence is highly likely to become a long-term problem (Jacob & Johnson, 1997).

Sexual behavior, which also may be part of adolescent experimentation, can also become an unhealthy way of trying to satisfy unmet emotional needs. Sex can be a means of connecting emotionally to another person, being a part of a peer group, numbing sadness, or feeling lovable. Some teens try to become pregnant because they believe that having a child will ensure that there is someone in the world who loves them. Pregnancy might also be a way of creating a family of one's own. Adolescent girls who are unsupervised and feel unloved have a high probability of becoming sexually active. They are particularly vulnerable if they are allowed to associate with older males. Many become promiscuous and end up in a pattern from which they do not know how to extract themselves. This can also lead to problems with sex and love addiction.

Serena, 16, became pregnant after a brief relationship with an older man she met online. Serena was a quiet, awkward teenager with few friends. Her parents were divorced and she saw very little of her father, who had remarried and lived out of state. Serena's mother worked evenings as a waitress and had very little time to spend with her daughter. When Serena's mother found out about the pregnancy, she insisted that Serena get an abortion. Serena complied, and the situation was never discussed again. Serena grieved the loss of her unborn child alone and continued to seek male companionship as a way of alleviating her feelings of loneliness and insecurity. Serena's mother brought her into therapy at the recommendation of the school counselor, after she reportedly cut herself. However, after only two visits, the mother discontinued therapy, stating that it was too much trouble to bring Serena for her sessions.

Short- and Long-Term Outcomes

Many of the behavioral and emotional difficulties that begin in adolescence carry through to adulthood. Most teenagers are able to work through their adolescent difficulties with support and guidance from their parents, but teenagers with Not Now, I'm Busy parents may not have this opportunity. Clearly, there is a wide spectrum of behaviors and degrees of involvement in this parenting style as in the other parenting styles. However, research has shown that teens from unengaged families have the worst long-term prognosis (Aquilino & Supple, 2001; Slicker, 1998; Weiss & Schwarz, 1996).

Academics and Work

To succeed academically, an adolescent must attend school regularly, do homework, show respect for authority, and develop self-motivation and long-term aspirations. Teens with uninvolved parents often do not have enough support and encouragement from their parents to succeed at school. Further, cognitive functioning has been shown to be negatively affected by a disengaged parenting style (Lee et al., 2006; Spera, 2005). Therefore, Not Now, I'm Busy parenting decreases the likelihood that these teens will be successful or even graduate. This parenting style is most likely to produce high school dropouts, and proportionately fewer teens from this group attend college. Many of these teens are uncertain about their interests and career goals. In many cases, their first priority may be to find a quick way out of their family system and an opportunity to stand on their own financially. They often think in terms of quick money rather than long-term career satisfaction.

When neglected teens become adults and begin college or enter the workplace, they may bring with them certain characteristics that diminish their work ethic and make them less likely to be hired or promoted. They may have difficulty working with others, be overly competitive or attention hungry, have difficulty following through on projects, or lack appropriate respect for authority. They may also have difficulty with decision making, have poor problem-solving skills, and make only halfhearted attempts to work through difficult situations. They may also have trouble being punctual and lack good time management.

At the other end of the spectrum, adolescents with workaholic parents may adopt many of their parents' workaholic traits:

> Children of workaholics often grow into adults who are envied by everyone: responsible, achievement oriented, able to successfully take charge of any situation—at least, that's how they appear to the outside world. Inside, they often feel like little children who never do anything right, while holding themselves up to standards of perfection without mercy, judging themselves harshly for the most minor flaws. (Robinson & Kelley, 1998, p. 234)

These adults are also prone to anxiety and depression, but their high standards for themselves often prevent them from receiving support or treatment.

Adult Behavioral Issues

Adults who grew up in a Not Now, I'm Busy home may continue to exhibit behavioral problems, many of which began in adolescence. They did not grow up with a consistent set of rules and expectations and, therefore, may not have developed a set of values and morals by which to guide themselves. Attention-seeking behavior that was tolerable when they were adolescents may persist as inappropriate adult behavior. They may have poor impulse control and may not set appropriate behavioral limits on themselves. If they engaged in delinquent behaviors as adolescents, they may continue to be involved in criminal activities. Gang affiliation may continue and escalate. Sexual promiscuity interferes with healthy adult relationships and can result in sexual and love addiction issues.

Cognitive and Emotional Difficulties

Adults from neglectful families can develop serious emotional and cognitive difficulties. At the very least, they experience a number of emotional problems that can affect their functioning and life satisfaction. Numerous studies have found a link between neglectful parenting and lack of emotional well-being:

> Failure to provide structure and adequate supervision during adolescence, specifically, may affect ER [emotional regulation] such that increases in behavior problems due to lack of supervision are linked to emotional dysregulation, particularly problems in anger regulation. . . . Moreover, neglectful and uninvolved parenting likely puts adolescents at greatest risk for ER problems as these adolescents have the fewest boundaries and experience the highest levels of adjustment difficulties. (Morris, Silk, Steinberg, Myers, & Robinson, 2007, p. 377)

When adolescents fail to learn how to appropriately handle their emotions, they carry with them lifelong consequences. In addition to problems in regulating their emotions, these adults also have difficulty with insecurity and low self-worth and are often anxious and unsure of themselves in social situations. When parents do not question or correct adolescents' ideas, they have difficulty seeing others' point of view and may question their own perceptions. They may exhibit rigid thinking, have difficulty seeing options, and have trouble compromising. As adults, they seek validation and may become quite competitive and driven. They can easily become perfectionists in an effort to get noticed or to validate themselves through their accomplishments. McArdle (2009) found that "low parental involvement significantly predicted maladaptive cognitions associated with perfectionism" (p. 609). Many adults in therapy tell me that they never feel good enough.

Adults' emotional and cognitive difficulties can often be linked to growing up with parents who did not help them learn to solve problems, deal with their emotions, or validate their feelings. Feelings of insecurity, poor self-confidence, and low self-esteem are the byproducts of inattention and lack of praise at home. Lack of emotional connection with parents may lead to feelings of loneliness and depression.

Relationship Issues

Adults who grow up with insufficient parental involvement and nurturing will undoubtedly have issues in their interpersonal relationships. As teenagers, they probably craved attention and approval and found a variety of ways to replace the sense of family that they lacked in their own home. As adults, these issues are replicated with spouses and friends. These individuals may constantly seek love and acknowledgment, or they may become emotionally numb and avoid close relationships. When they become involved in a relationship, they have difficulty trusting that their feelings are real and are often insecure and jealous. Attachment difficulties are common, and these adults may have difficulty with commitment. Since they did not feel loyalty from their parents, they may have difficulty with fidelity and mistrust. When they do become involved in a committed relationship, they may become overly dependent or codependent. If the relationship doesn't work out, they are devastated. Other friendships and associations may take on the same characteristics and difficulties.

In the long run, these adults will always be the least connected to their families of origin. Growing up feeling like they were a burden will most likely lead them to detachment rather than healthy separation. Premature separation from the family, in the form of emotional detachment, may lead to incomplete identity formation. In essence, these individuals become adults before they can complete the adolescent developmental tasks. Completion of these tasks takes place within the context of adult interpersonal relationships that may not have the strength and stability to handle it.

They often lack the necessary skills to be good parents themselves. After all, their role models were often too busy for them. Hendrix and Hunt (1997) described them as "minimizer parents":

> Without contact with her own needs, she became insensitive to the needs of others, thus copying the parent who was the source of her greatest pain and becoming in adulthood a minimizer parent herself. . . . She's not warm and seems to be incapable of empathy. Whatever feelings she has, she keeps to herself. . . . She shares little of her thoughts or experiences with her children and she doesn't ask about theirs. She is a loner who usually does not share her space with her children. Her boundaries are rigid. (pp. 63–64)

This passage highlights the legacy of emotional neglect. Parents without emotional connection fail to develop the ability to share themselves with their own children.

Other parents who grew up neglected may become overly involved or controlling in an effort to get as far away as possible from the parenting style they experienced. They try to repair their own childhood wounds and may not be aware of the impact their parenting has on their children. They have no guidebook for their parenting and often feel insecure and inadequate as parents.

Positive Outcomes

In spite of the challenges of growing up in a Not Now, I'm Busy home, some adolescents make a healthy adjustment to adulthood. Teens whose parents tried to make up for the times they were unavailable are usually more capable of working through their reactions. The primary forces behind their ability to become emotionally healthy, independent, successful, and happy are their own personality, temperament, and drive. We have all heard stories of individuals who overcome dysfunctional family environments. They are usually intelligent, have good self-control, value academics, and seek alternative role models. As adults, they continue to depend on themselves for what they achieve in life. Many take advantage of resources outside the home in order to achieve their goals. For some, psychotherapy has been helpful in allowing them to overcome problems they experienced in their family of origin.

The movie *The Blind Side* (Netter & Hancock, 2009) told the story of Michael Oher, a teenage boy who came from a poor and neglectful home and went on to become an All American football player. Michael was the son of a negligent and drug-addicted mother and an absent father. He was essentially homeless when, as a teenager, he was taken in by a wealthy family, the Tuohys. In a poignant scene, Leigh Anne Tuohy offered Michael a room of his own in their home:

Michael: It's nice, I never had one.
Leigh Anne: What, a room?
Michael: A bed.

After hearing this, the usually tough Leigh Anne is overwhelmed with tears.

Michael, with the love and support of the Tuohy family, graduated from high school, received a college football scholarship, and went on to become an NFL draft pick. The movie highlighted the ability of an individual to overcome a neglectful childhood with the guidance and support of adults who take the time to be there for him.

Summary

Most teens in this parenting style category come from families where the lack of involvement and supervision is due to difficult life situations. Often these parents feel guilty about their lack of attention. Workaholic parents will choose work over time with their teens, often because they find more satisfaction in their job. Parents may neglect their teen when the responsibilities are too emotionally taxing or they want to avoid dealing with confrontation. Many need to make more of an effort to be involved. Any amount of inattention can create problems for adolescents.

Adolescents from disengaged and neglectful homes struggle with numerous emotional and behavioral problems and often feel inadequate and unsatisfied with their lives. They often seek out others who can provide them with the love and attention they lacked at home. As adults, they often continue to be insecure and needy. When they become involved in unhealthy relationships, they may continue to exhibit emotional and behavioral problems. When they are able to connect with other healthy adults, they are often capable of overcoming their difficult start in life.

CHAPTER SEVEN

"Easygoing" Parents

If teenagers live with support, they learn to feel good about themselves.

—Dorothy Nolte and Rachel Harris,
Teenagers Learn What They Live

Case Example

Laura and Nathan Hartford had been married for 21 years and had two teenage children, Luke, 14, and Nora, 18. Nathan was an engineer and Laura worked part-time. Both teenagers attended private school. Recently, Laura asked that her son have an opportunity to talk with someone about the difficulty he was having at school. Luke was initially reluctant but agreed to come. He asked that his mom sit in with him during the first session.

According to his mother, Luke was enrolled in a private school that was his father's alma mater. His sister was a senior at the same private school and was doing very well. Mom described Luke as a good student, a bit shy, who had a little difficulty with the workload at the private school. Luke was also involved in Little League, and for most of the spring session had attended after-school practice, followed by homework, which he considered too time-consuming. Luke shared that he felt pressure at school to perform well, as the school had a reputation for high-achieving kids. In addition, most of the kids that Luke hung out with on weekends were from his neighborhood. The option of attending another school had been brought up in the family, but both parents had concerns about the neighborhood public school, which had a reputation for drugs and gang activity.

In an individual session, Luke shared that he felt out of place at the private school, found the academic expectations to be stressful, and did not feel very connected to the other students. Luke voiced concern that he might disappoint his father if he left his father's alma mater. He was concerned about competing with his sister, who had performed extremely well academically and would soon graduate. Both parents believed that the private school would give Luke an advantage in applying for college.

In a family session, Luke was able to talk with his parents about his discomfort at the private school. Although dad did express his admiration for the school and his reasons for wanting his son to attend, he also gave Luke unconditional permission to make up his own mind about the situation. However, both parents voiced concern about the neighborhood school and suggested that they look at other alternatives for Luke. Luke eventually decided to go to another smaller private school, a decision his parents supported.

Family members' mutual respect was evident. Although the parents maintained their parental role and provided Luke with rational explanations for their preference that he attend private school, they also gave him an opportunity to share his feelings. It was clear during the discussion that the parents were very aware of the personality differences between their two children and encouraged individuality. The Hartfords were an excellent example of Easygoing parents, as they found a way to balance their teenager's individual needs and their parental expectations in a warm family atmosphere.

Parenting Style Characteristics

"Easygoing" parents are nurturing and supportive and provide appropriate supervision during their child's adolescent years. They often approach parenting in a relaxed, confident, and flexible manner. They do not expect to be perfect or have all the answers. These parents adapt their parenting style to the needs of the teen and the situation. Easygoing parents are comfortable with the adolescent developmental period and allow their teens to make the necessary changes in themselves in order to individuate and separate from the family.

This parent style is probably the most researched and discussed in the literature on adolescent development and corresponds to the authoritative parenting style identified by Baumrind. The authoritative parenting style is characterized as nurturing with clear expectations. Baumrind (1971, 1991) distinguished between authoritarian parents, who are more controlling and less emotionally responsive, and authoritative parents, who are responsive and warm but also provide structure, expectations, and supervision. However, the similarity of the two terms is often confusing for parents. Easygoing parents are more aligned with the authoritative parenting style and other healthy parenting styles identified in the literature.

Other labels associated with this parenting style include balanced, engaged, and healthy parenting. Henry, Robinson, Neal, and Huey (2006) investigated adolescents' perceptions of their family's overall functioning; they reported that balanced families

> provide a family emotional climate where parents foster a balance between
> separateness and connectedness. . . . Further, balanced family systems allow
> flexibility in family rules and roles as the needs of the overall family system,
> subsystems, and or individual family members change. . . . Balanced families

tend to create a warm, flexible atmosphere in the overall family system that facilitates adolescent perceptions of parental support. (pp. 320–321)

Warmth

The most important characteristic of Easygoing parents is the level of warmth that they exhibit. These parents are warm, accepting, and playful with their adolescent. Even when the adolescent is being standoffish or difficult, the parent is able to convey a feeling of affection for the teen. For these parents, this fondness is genuine. The warmth felt for the teen comes from the parent's ability to see through the emotional difficulties that the adolescent may be experiencing at the moment.

Some parents are clearly more demonstrative and openly affectionate, whereas other parents are more reserved. These parents respect that adolescents may become less comfortable with physical affection as they age, especially with the parent of the opposite sex. Healthy parents, who understand these changes and differences, find other more appropriate ways to show their affection. They may offer a light pat on the back, playfully tease, or ruffle their teen's hair. In public, these parents may walk in close proximity to their teen while allowing the teen to feel that his or her personal space is respected. They offer verbal affection with comments such as "you are a really great kid" or "I love you." These parents let their teens know that they are loved by casually saying so over the phone, as they walk out the door or as they say goodnight. Warmth and affection are openly shared between the parents as well.

Support and Encouragement

Easygoing parents provide an environment in which their teen feels safe and secure. With this sense of security, the teen is able to make the transition from childhood to adulthood. These parents are aware that teens need to try on different behaviors and identities in order to establish their sense of self. They encourage their interests and allow them to have their own ideas and opinions. Even if teens' interests seem a little unrealistic, these parents will let them experiment within reasonable limits. So the teenage boy who thinks he's going to be a rock star and wants to start a band in the garage is encouraged to do so, and the parents may foot the bill for guitar lessons. These parents realize that from adolescent interests, career choices may come. Bill Gates, for instance, started as a teenager fooling around with computers in his garage.

Parental Interest

Easygoing parents show an interest in their teenagers and actually find their teens interesting and enjoyable to be around. They laugh and chat with their teens during dinner. One evening, while dining out with my own two teenage children, I observed a family of four at a nearby table: two parents, a boy who looked about 15, and a younger child. Throughout the course of the meal, the parents interacted with the teenage boy only once when he made a brief comment. The father gave a short response and didn't even bother to look at his son. My limited observation made me sad for the teenager, who appeared lonely even in the company of his parents. Easygoing parents engage in conversations that elicit information about what's going on in their teen's world without coming across like interrogators. Often these conversations occur while driving, over dinner, or when they make a point of seeking out their teen at home. Open communication is important in these families.

Easygoing parents show interest in and may even participate in their teens' extracurricular activities. They attend not only the major events but also some of the practices. They often chaperone or become involved in their teen's after-school activities.

Easygoing parents often make a concerted effort to spend time with their teen in a mutually enjoyable activity. This may be watching a movie at home, shopping, having lunch, or working on a special project together. They make spending time with their teens a relaxed and enjoyable experience. Teens often do not react well if forced into activities with their parents, but they often enjoy spur-of-the-moment interactions. For example, a father might go outside and help his son wash the car, or a mother might take her daughter with her to get a manicure. These parents actually feel interested in what their teen is involved in and do not push the teen to participate in activities that meet the parents' needs rather than the teen's. Parents make an effort to understand the activities that the teen finds important; this shows validation and acceptance to the teen.

The Wallaces were a typical family with two teenage children, Johnny, 17, and Sarah, 13. Over the years, the family had made a practice of going out to dinner together on Thursday nights and using that time to interact on an informal and relaxed basis. However, now that Johnny was a senior in high school, they were allowing him the freedom to make his own decision about attending the Thursday night dinners. After several weeks of Thursday dinners without Johnny, the Wallaces realized that they missed spending that time with their son. The next Thursday, they suggested going out to dinner together, but Johnny declined, saying that he was going to be working on his friend's car. When it was time for dinner, the Wallaces drove over to Johnny's friend's house, opened the door, and encouraged Johnny to get in and come to dinner. They had an enjoyable evening and shared with Johnny that they missed his company during these dinners. Johnny acknowledged that he also enjoyed the evening and wanted to make more of an effort to come along to Thursday night dinners.

Supervision

Allowing adolescents to go through this important developmental stage without supervision is like letting them drive a car without having had driving lessons. Teenagers need parents who pay attention to where they are going, what they are doing, and who they are associating with. Supervision not only pertains to social activities but also to Internet use, movies, TV, music choices, and other influential activities. Easygoing parents are able to accomplish this without the teenager feeling overly restricted or controlled.

In these homes, there is an understanding that activities outside of the home require sufficient information for the parent to feel comfortable that the activity is a safe one. Most of the time this simply means that the parent asks for information about the teen's plans, including the time frame and who else will be participating. Parental supervision of Internet use may include locating the computer in a family-accessible room, monitoring browser history, and spot checking social networking sites. As parents become comfortable with the adolescent's friends and activities, they may need less detailed information. In addition, parents will be more observant and inquisitive about a younger teen's activities than those of older teens who have already proven that they can handle themselves socially. Easygoing parents are comfortable with their monitoring responsibilities and try to ensure that discussions about their teen's activities and requests remain calm interactions rather than tense interrogations.

Ginny, a 16-year-old, lived at home with her parents and younger brother. She had an open and comfortable relationship with her parents. Ginny was a junior in high school and had recently started dating a boy in her class. She had an active social life with a group of friends that she had known for several years, all of whom her parents had met more than once. Except for a few occasions, Ginny had been good about keeping her curfew of 11:30 P.M. and openly shared her evening plans with her parents. The parents recently met Ginny's new boyfriend when he came over to visit Ginny.

Ginny asked to go out Saturday night with her boyfriend; he has his own car. Her parents asked for basic information about their plans (a movie and ice cream) and set a curfew of 11:30 P.M. Ginny came home on time, and the family talked casually about the date during breakfast the next day.

Clear Expectations and Rules

Expectations refers not just to rules and structure but also to the family norms that guide behavior. Expectations give the adolescent a sense of what is acceptable within the family and out in the world. For example, families may have the expectation that the property of other people—family members and others—is to be respected. Although some expectations can be clear-cut, others are more of an understanding based on family history and behavior. An example of a more clear-cut expectation is that teens will attend school and do their homework, whereas one based on family history is that the teenager will attend a four-year college. Expectations may not be explicitly stated but are the end result of family interactions, parental comments, role modeling, and other methods of sharing familial beliefs and personal values. When parents model kindness and respect to a waitress while the family is out to dinner, they instill in their teen an appropriate way to treat others. Teens need someone to look up to, and they tend to mirror the behavior of their parents.

Other expectations may be clarified in a more direct manner, such as a clearly stated rule like "you need to be home by 11:00" that specifies the consequences for failure to comply. When such rules include an explanation of the reasons and purpose behind them, they can have a positive impact on teenagers' ability to think for themselves and solve problems.

Easygoing parents rarely have difficulty making clear their expectations about unhealthy or dangerous behaviors. These include admonishments against drinking, using drugs, smoking, and early and unhealthy sexual activity. In these situations, parents often have an open and direct discussion about their expectations (for example: "Smoking is unhealthy, and I do not want you to smoke"). They may also make clear statements about the consequences of breaking these rules (for example: "Alcohol use is unacceptable, and if I find out that you have been drinking, you will be grounded for two weeks. Enjoy the party"). Not only do these parents set expectations clearly, they often give their teen a reasonable and informative explanation as to why they have established a rule. The parents might explain their concerns about teenage drinking, the legal ramifications, and perhaps even the alcohol-related problems that members of the extended family have experienced.

Easygoing parents also encourage teens to engage in a discussion about the expectation or rule. They listen with interest and respect to the teen's opinion, clarify any misconceptions they believe the teen has, and if necessary, assert their authority in establishing the rule. Providing explanations allows the teen to observe how the parents process information and make decisions.

Parents in this category are comfortable setting rules, and their rules are usually age appropriate and fair. These parents strive to be consistent. They often include their teenager in discussions of house rules while maintaining their own authority. Authority, in these homes, is connected to mutual respect between the teen and parent and does not involve threats or intimidation. In healthy homes, parents understand that, although teens may have the right to make requests and present their reasons and opinions, the parent has the ultimate veto on any actions that the teen wishes to undertake. Consequences are applied logically and fairly, with an explanation. Easygoing parents do not engage in long, drawn-out lectures, nor do they personalize a teen's behavior. An important aspect of this style is that these parents treat the behavior as an infraction, offering information the teen needs in order to understand, apply a consequence, and then move on. Moving on is important; these parents do not carry on about the misbehavior or bring it up for days, nor do they bring up every past misdeed that the teen has ever committed.

Focus on the Behavior, Not the Person

Easygoing parents are able to differentiate between the teenager and his or her action. They do not attack the adolescent personally but stay focused on the issue or the behavior. Negative attitudes and impulsive behaviors are not unexpected during this time, and healthy parents are able to distinguish between normal and what is inappropriate adolescent behavior. Although these parents are not above getting angry, they avoid belittlement and overreaction. They are able to put the adolescent's actions in context.

When parents are comfortable with their expectations and rules, and have a good relationship with their teen, they are able to deal with issues without excessive anger and conflict. Easygoing parents do not scream, lecture, try to induce guilt, or threaten as a way of controlling behavior, nor do they withdraw their love as a punishment. When confronted with unacceptable behavior, they make an effort to stay calm and discuss the situation rationally. The consequences they attach to unacceptable behaviors are logical and appropriate.

Teaching Responsibility

Developing responsibility is one of the important goals that parents have for their teenage children. Easygoing parents provide various opportunities for teenagers to learn responsibility by allowing them to make certain decisions for themselves. They assign age-appropriate chores that help adolescents to become more self-sufficient—for example, doing their own laundry or cleaning their own room—and chores that benefit the family as a whole. Requiring adolescents to take ownership of their schoolwork increases their sense of responsibility and self-efficacy. Parents may also allow or encourage their teen to become involved in community volunteer activities or take on a part-time job. When adolescents are able to earn their own money and are required to budget it, they learn fiscal responsibility.

Thoughtfulness

Easygoing parents are thoughtful parents. They parent with a plan and have distinct goals in mind that guide their parenting behavior and parent–teen interactions. They are aware of the different developmental stages that their children go through and make an effort to adjust their actions and decisions to their child's age and level of maturity. They discuss concerns with each other or with the family as a whole.

Easygoing parents make it clear, through their actions and words, that they are available as a resource for the teen. They offer advice and support, not judgment. When they say "you can talk to us about anything," they genuinely mean it. Even when the topic that the teen wants to bring up is extremely uncomfortable for the parents, they try to make the conversation as open and easy as possible. Sexual issues may be among the uncomfortable topics that the teen needs to discuss. Other teens may want to talk about relationship issues or other personal feelings. Teens are often aware that their parents will intervene if they believe that the teens are getting into a situation they cannot handle. Adolescents need to be able to depend on their parents to provide a safety net for them and protect them from dangerous or unhealthy situations.

Easygoing parents keep their teenager in mind when they make decisions and set guidelines. They allow one successful activity or well-handled privilege to serve as the foundation for the next. They may permit their 13-year-old go to the mall for a few hours with friends; when he or she is 14, they may allow evening movies with other teenagers. Parents often allow a teen to date unchaperoned at age 16. As the teen matures and shows responsibility, parents broaden the boundaries and allow more privileges with fewer restrictions. Responsible teens are encouraged to start making some significant decisions for themselves. Younger teens may be able to choose their own hair or clothing styles, whereas older adolescents may be allowed more freedom to choose their own activities and friends. Older adolescents may be given access to a car and can go out evenings with friends, without having to be specific as to their hour-by-hour plans.

Recognizing Mistakes

Easygoing parents make mistakes and are able to admit that they do not always make the best decisions or handle situations correctly. They are willing to question whether their reaction or decision is in the best interest of the adolescent. This provides for a more relaxed and less stressful parenting experience. These parents also acknowledge that they do not know everything about parenting and seek information from literature, members of their extended family, or friends. They seek therapeutic help if needed. In seeking information, they keep in mind their teen's need for respect and privacy and do not share information unnecessarily.

When Easygoing parents make an error in judgment, they do their best to rectify the situation, even offering an apology to the teenager if the situation warrants it. "The most powerful weapon in your arsenal of adolescent parenting is the one I see used the least: the apology" (Bradley, 2002, p. 185). Easygoing parents also expect and require their teens to be respectful of their feelings and teach them to acknowledge and show empathy for others.

Parents and Imperfection

Easygoing parents are able to find a balance between emotional warmth and healthy control. They accept that they are imperfect and readily acknowledge that sometimes they're in a bad mood, that they overreact, and that they are sometimes too busy or tired to spend time with their teen. Many struggle to balance work and family responsibilities. Easygoing parents find ways to increase their interactional time with their teens. They may briefly chat by phone from work, spend extra time over dinner, or set up special outings, such as Saturday lunches.

Like most parents, they worry and are sometimes overly cautious. Perhaps this is one of the characteristics that make them healthy; they are aware of the types of issues that the teen may encounter and are realistically concerned. These parents ask questions and explain dangers. Many of their rules and expectations are designed to protect their teens from alcohol, drugs, and Internet predators. They are also realistic that they cannot protect their teens from every situation and realize that the best option is to provide their teen with a safe and supportive home.

Easygoing parents share themselves with their teens—not in detail, but enough to allow teens to realize that their parents are people and deserve to be treated as such. They talk about their day, express opinions without insisting that the teens accept these opinions as their own, and are not ashamed or afraid to show emotion when appropriate. They share tears and laughter. The difference between them and Cool parents is that Easygoing parents remain on an adult level in their interactions and do not encourage or participate in inappropriate social activities.

Balanced Households

Easygoing parents make their homes about everyone in the family. Theirs are not parent-centered homes or child-centered homes but family-centered homes. Respect and individuality are the norm in their homes. These parents believe that all family members should have equal access to the benefits of the home and that each individual in the home should have a space of his or her own in which privacy is respected. For teens, this is usually their room, although some homes also have a designated children's game room. These parents knock on their teen's door and wait to be acknowledged and expect the same in return. They don't make statements such as "this is my house and you can get out if you don't like it" or "not in my house!" The home is for the security and enjoyment of all family members.

Parenting Style: Origin and Motivations

Parents usually adopt the Easygoing style because of their family history, ideological perspective, and personal issues. They have the least complicated family history and are often close to their extended families. Philosophically, they value individuality, respect, and family connection.

Family History

Parenting style is primarily learned from one's own family. Most Easygoing parents come from families that are emotionally healthy and provide appropriate levels of support and supervision. Healthy and well-adjusted adults usually remain connected to their own parents and often include their own extended family in their children's lives. These families continue to take care of each other for each member's lifetime. Many Easygoing parents enjoyed their childhoods and have fond memories of parent–child interactions. They recall their own adolescence as being handled with fairness and respect. Their families were close and the importance of family was stressed.

Some Easygoing parents did not have a family home environment like the one that they are trying to provide for their own children. Many adults who feel that their childhood was unsatisfying make a determined effort to parent their own children in a different way. They remember saying that they would never do "that" to their children and, in this case, they meant it. Parents who are able to make the transition from a difficult family situation to a healthy adult life usually use a different parenting style than that under which they were raised. Adults whose family of origin was abusive or neglectful may find the transition particularly difficult. Those who are able to successfully parent in a balanced and healthy manner truly enjoy the parenting experience and find that it is emotionally cathartic for them.

Parental Philosophy

Parents with a strong belief in the importance of parenting make a consistent effort to parent in a way that is in the best interests of their children. These informed parents are likely to read books, search the Web for information, or take parenting classes. Easygoing parents take their job as parents seriously, yet strive to enjoy the experience and find emotional fulfillment in their family responsibilities. Parents in this category are also comfortable trying new techniques to deal with their children and adolescents. When they encounter problems, they may seek therapeutic support in order to maintain a healthy home environment. They understand the difficult period of adolescence and try to make the transition as easy as possible for their children. They foster independence, responsibility, and autonomy while providing a home that functions as a safety net.

Parental Personality Traits

Easygoing parents are usually emotionally stable and satisfied with their lives. They make a point of separating their personal difficulties or stresses from their parental reactions. Economic and other hardships can interfere with parents' ability to deal with their teen, and Easygoing parents make a conscious effort to be effective parents despite life's difficult circumstances.

Overall, they are happy, productive, and optimistic people: "Optimistic adults who become parents are more likely to display a more Authoritative parenting style" (Baldwin, McIntire, & Hardaway, 2007, p. 554). These adults adopt a parenting style that reflects their own emotional well-being. Their self-confidence often means that they are less likely to take their teen's behavior personally.

Parents' personality characteristics and approaches to dealing with life are congruent with their parenting behaviors:

> The results showed first, that parents who had a high level of self-esteem typically practiced an authoritative parenting style, characterized by positive attachment, the expression of affection, encouragement of the child's independence, rational guidance, and supervision of the child. (Aunola, Nurmi, Onatsu-Arvilommi, & Pulkkinen, 1999, p. 314)

In addition, these parents are more likely to have a healthy social life of their own. If married, their relationship is likely to be highly functional and happy. They usually have external support systems and are connected to members of their extended family. They understand that they need to be parents, not friends, but are also able to have a relaxed and enjoyable connection with their teen.

Adolescent Reactions

The Easygoing parenting style usually results in teen reactions that are age appropriate, reasonable, and emotionally stable. This parenting style does not preclude the teenager having the emotional ups and downs and moments of rebellion typical of adolescence. But such reactions are likely to be brief and do not result in unnecessary parent–teen conflict. Studies that have looked at teens' perceptions of their parents have found that most teens viewed their parents as "authoritative" and have also reported teens as having a healthy relationship with their parent (L. Steinberg, 2001).

Identity and Autonomy

Key tasks of adolescence are to develop an identity and self-concept and to separate from parents while maintaining a family connection. In the 1950s, a perspective referred to as family systems theory was developed (Bowen, 1978). It postulated that one of the tasks within the family system is the differentiation of self, which consists of finding a balance between individuality and fusion. *Fusion* refers to the degree of connection and dependency on the family. Healthy families discourage unhealthy dependency, encourage individuality, and strive for a comfortable and supportive familial relationship.

As individuality is accepted by Easygoing parents, their teens may be more willing to try on various styles of dress, music, interests, and behaviors. Only when these styles reach outrageous levels will Easygoing parents intervene. Because they are allowed to try various styles, these teens have more opportunities to find their own comfort level and are less likely to rigidly hold onto the more antisocial styles. Teens in healthy families are able to gradually transition from childhood to adulthood. They do not separate from their families suddenly or with anger, nor do they remain overly dependent.

Ryan, age 14, decided that he wanted to cut his hair short and add blue spikes, a style that was popular among his friends. Ryan's mother decided not to make an issue of this and agreed to allow him to decide on his own hairstyle. She took Ryan to her hairdresser, who bleached his dark brown hair blonde and then added blue tips. A subsequent trip to a water park with friends turned his hair an off green. Ryan opted to dye his hair back to brown and did not ask for further hair treatments.

Autonomy refers to an individual's ability to develop cognitive and emotional confidence and to be self-sufficient. Healthy individuals make decisions for themselves that reflect what is in their best interest and not that of peers or parents, a skill developed during adolescence. Teens in Easygoing families are usually given increased responsibilities within the family and in the outside world, and they are allowed increasing levels of freedom in which to test their own self-reliance. Like most teens, they may be impulsive and make mistakes, but they are offered the opportunity to learn from their mistakes. When the balance of responsibility and freedom is coupled with age-appropriate expectations, teens respond by developing self-reliance, confidence, a sense of competence, and good judgment.

Adolescent "Attitude"

The adolescent "attitude" is a well-known phenomenon. Beginning around age 12 or 13, children begin to adopt a different reaction to parental comments, suggestions, requests, and expectations. In addition, the worldview of a teenager takes on a more cynical overtone. Teens from the healthiest of families are not immune to this reaction. Somehow this teen attitude is a way of separating and individuating. Most of it is harmless.

Even teens from Easygoing families roll their eyes, sigh, make disdainful faces, and grumble at the prospect of taking out the trash or cleaning their rooms. But they do not let these brief encounters become hardened conflicts. Teens whose attitude provides a form of protection against the world are less likely to maintain a strongly disagreeable demeanor at home. So, although these teens may disagree with their parents and even engage in brief scuffles, their positive relationship provides for a quick recovery. Parents who allow teens the luxury of being disagreeable are far less likely to see them carry this attitude into their older adolescent years and adulthood. Angry feelings are an integral part of the adolescent experience and need to be appropriately channeled. Parents who acknowledge and support their teens can accept appropriate anger and help teens learn to deal with it in healthy ways.

Healthy Personality

Research has shown that adolescents from Easygoing families are far more likely to exhibit healthy personality characteristics (Aquilino & Supple, 2001; Lee et al., 2006; Rothrauff, Cooney, & An, 2009; L. Steinberg, 2001). Typically, teens from these families are friendly, cooperative, resilient, and optimistic. A study on optimism in college students found that

> one possible mechanism by which enhanced well-being occurs via the Authoritative parenting style may be that of optimism. There is an abundance of data which shows that optimists tend to be psychologically and physically better adjusted than their pessimistic counterparts.... Moreover, research shows that optimists tend to use more adaptive coping strategies compared with pessimistic individuals. (Baldwin et al., 2007, p. 554)

Easygoing parents are more likely to have teens who are realistic, logical, and less impulsive. When interacting with others, these teens are compassionate, empathetic, and caring. Teens from Easygoing families have been shown to have higher levels of life satisfaction and to be less likely to experience problems with depression and anxiety.

Academics

Adolescents with Easygoing parents are more likely to be academically successful. These teens usually do well socially and behaviorally as well. As their parents provide support and expectations of achievement, they are more likely to take responsibility for and ownership of their schoolwork. They work harder when the subject is difficult and are more likely to ask for help when they need it. In *Becoming Adult: How Teenagers Prepare for the World of Work,* Csikszentmihalyi and Schneider (2000) said,

> The most effective families appear to be those that give teenagers the sense that they are loved, together with the sense that much is expected from them. This combination is related to students' self-esteem, as well as to their feeling that their present actions contribute to the future. This combination appears to provide the best setting for teenagers' academic achievement and sense of security. The level of family support that students feel is strongly related to their optimism and sense of well-being at work. (pp. 138–139)

Students from Easygoing families are more likely to participate in after-school activities that reflect their own personal talents and interests. They effectively balance schoolwork with other activities. They are usually respectful of their teachers and are less likely to engage in disruptive behavior. This respect is not born out of fear of consequences but is a natural reaction to feeling respected at home. Hostility toward authority is rare, and many view their teachers as supportive. As these teens have been allowed to have their own opinions at home, they are also more likely to speak up in class, ask questions, and even disagree with the teacher. Unfortunately, some teachers are uncomfortable with being challenged by a student. Outspoken teens have to learn which teachers appreciate their speaking up and which are less likely to tolerate it.

Social Interactions

Adolescents who have been encouraged to express themselves, formulate their own opinions, and participate in decision making within the family are able to adapt these skills to their peer group. Studies have indicated that these adolescents are more socially capable than those raised with other parenting styles (McKinney, Donnell, &, Renk, 2008; S. J. Steinberg & Davila, 2008). These teens often enjoy peer group activities and experiment with various academic and recreational choices in order to clarify their interests. They are more self-confident and less likely to associate with unhealthy peer groups. Teens from Easygoing families are accepting of others and tend to have a variety of friends rather than being affiliated with one clique. Encouraged to develop social contacts, these teens are more likely to become involved in extracurricular activities, participate in church youth groups and other types of social groups, and even volunteer their time for various causes.

Because these teens have acceptance, support, and supervision in their family, they are more comfortable saying no to activities with which they are uncomfortable. It has been shown that "higher levels of parental monitoring [are] associated with lower levels of antisocial or delinquent behavior" (Jacobson & Crockett, 2000, p. 90). When confronted with an activity or behavior they are uneasy about, they can point to their parents' expectations or supervision as an excuse not to participate. For instance, a teen might tell a peer, "I'd better not drink, because my parents wait up for me to get home, and they would notice." These same teens would be willing to call their parents if they did drink and needed a ride home or if they needed help with an intoxicated friend. When there is a consistent balance between monitoring and warmth, adolescents are more likely to trust their parents and use them as a support system. Having this kind of relationship at home encourages peer group associations that are developmentally healthy.

Zima, 17, went to a homecoming party with a group of friends. Several of the other teens brought alcohol and encouraged Zima to drink with them. She decided to give it a try and drank several beers before the end of the evening. Realizing that she was slightly buzzed, she decided not to try driving home. She called her dad, who came for her. Dad did not make a big issue of the drinking that night, but made a point of thanking her for calling him. The next day, they had a family discussion on drinking. Dad did not condone the drinking but opted to stress the issues of safety and trust.

Romantic Relationships

During adolescence, emotional relationships change and develop. At three, a little girl is in love with her daddy, and at 13, it's the boy who sits next to her in history. The normal developmental process dictates a gradual shifting from having one's emotional needs met by parents to having more intimate relationships with peers. Teens from Easygoing families, like all adolescents, find themselves attracted to members of their peer group. Easygoing parents are not threatened by this process and will often be a resource for their teen's emotional relationships. Their teens are comfortable telling them about their interest in one of their classmates and asking them for guidance on handling the emotional and sexual issues that arise. Since adolescents from Easygoing families have a warm and respectful relationship with their parents, they do not enter the adolescent years with a strong need to become connected to others too quickly or to become sexually active at an early age.

Easygoing parents provide guidelines for healthy adolescent dating. Group activities usually precede individual dating. These teens are fairly comfortable allowing their parents to help establish guidelines (not controls) for their dating life. Even in Easygoing families, teens may find themselves involved in relationships that are too intense or conflicted for their age. In these situations, parents may need to intervene. When this does occur, the parents try to help the teen work through the problem and, if necessary, terminate the relationship.

This is a sticky issue for parents, as teens often resent any interference in their love relationships, even when the object of their affection is someone that the parent finds objectionable. Since teens can be very passionate about their love lives, Easygoing parents usually try not to insist that they sever a relationship unless absolutely necessary. Respect for the adolescent's romantic experiences is critical to the parent–teen relationship. Helping teens work through difficult dating situations allows them to learn how to handle future relationships and breakups. When the inevitable heartbreak does come, these teens will be able to turn to their parents as a source of comfort and understanding.

Short- and Long-Term Outcomes

Numerous studies have indicated that the Easygoing parenting style, which is similar to what others have called authoritative or balanced parenting, has the most positive long-term outcome for children and adolescents (Aquilino & Supple, 2001; Rothrauff et al., 2009). As a rule, adults who grew up in an Easygoing family have the easiest adolescent-to-adult transition and are less likely to carry unresolved issues from adolescence into their adult lives.

Personality Characteristics

The Easygoing parenting style results in the healthiest adult characteristics:

> Perhaps the most important conclusion to emerge from our work is that adolescents raised in authoritative homes continue to show the same advantages in psychosocial development and mental health over their non-authoritarian raised peers. . . . There is no question that authoritative parenting is associated with certain developmental outcomes . . . self-reliance, achievement motivation, pro-social behavior, self-control, cheerfulness, and social confidence. (L. Steinberg, 2001, pp. 8–13)

Adults raised in the Easygoing parenting style were guided and supported through the developmental journey that ends with individuation. As a rule, they have healthy self-concepts and are insightful and emotionally stable. They often have strong values and morals, and they rarely exhibit problematic behavior. They are usually responsible and self-reliant. Studies have indicated that they are the least likely to experience depression, anxiety, or substance abuse (Lamborn et al., 1991; Rothrauff et al., 2009; Weiss & Schwarz, 1996).

These individuals are more likely to handle life's difficulties in a productive and successful manner. Although no one is immune to stress or problems, these adults are probably better equipped to handle them. Overall life satisfaction is more common among these adults. As adults, they are also more likely to be responsible and are often financially secure.

Academics and Career

Adolescents from Easygoing families have been shown to do well in high school and college. E. A. Turner, Chandler, and Heffer (2009) studied the relationship between parenting styles and the academic performance of college students and found that what they called "authoritative parenting" (similar to what this book calls Easygoing parenting) "continues to influence the academic performance of college students, and both intrinsic motivation and self-efficacy predicted academic performance" (p. 337). A similar study concluded that

> an authoritative home world (one that consists of high levels of autonomy, demands, and emotional support) effectively imparts the elements of a mastery orientation toward schoolwork, which in turn prepares students for the world of American college, where self-regulation, persistence and autonomy are important for success. (Strage & Brandt, 1999, p. 154)

These studies clearly show that parenting style during adolescence has long-term implications for college and career success. This particular parenting style allows the development of behaviors and characteristics that are conducive to academic and career success.

Adolescents from this family style tend to be comfortable expressing themselves and their ideas, be more confident in their abilities, and show more persistence in attaining their goals. Teenagers who are allowed to develop their own interests are likely to have an easier time selecting a college major, and ultimately an occupation, that fits them. They are also more likely to choose a career that they find interesting and rewarding but not to believe that their worth is solely connected to their job. Work that is enjoyable and fulfills one's need to be productive results in a better work ethic, increased self-esteem, and life satisfaction.

As they become adults and enter the working world, they bring with them the healthy characteristics they developed with the support of their parents. Generally, these adults are responsible and creative and interact well with authority. As they have been taught to solve problems, they are more likely to find creative and realistic solutions to work problems. As they have been encouraged to succeed for their own sense of self-worth, their work product is likely to be of high quality. Relationships with colleagues are likely to follow similar patterns to those they experienced in their homes, where individuality and respect for others was practiced. Although these adults may be competitive, their competition is usually upfront and not underhanded. They prefer to be acknowledged for their own work and not at the expense of their coworkers.

Social Relationships

Easygoing families understand the need for peer relationships during adolescence; subsequently, these young adults are likely to have an easier time shifting their focus from family to peers. They are friendly, outgoing, and socially competent. They are likely to engage in various social and community activities as well as to be comfortable spending time alone.

Young adulthood marks the transition to mature intimate relationships. The basic skills involved in interpersonal relationships are learned in the context of both parent–teen and peer interactions. In addition, there is evidence that the parents' marital relationship affects a young adult's future relationships (for more on this subject, see chapter 8). Young adults may perceive their parents' relationship as a role model for their own, or they may internalize the interactional styles they observe. Easygoing parents often model healthy emotional relationships.

Easygoing parents' tendency to grant autonomy and individuality to their teens prepares the teens to move into adult relationships without feeling disloyalty to their parents. Parents who negotiate and problem solve various life difficulties with their children educate them on effective and healthy ways to deal with relationship issues. Healthy adults from Easygoing families are capable of sustaining long-term intimate relationships. Neal and Frick-Horbury (2001) analyzed the connection between attachment and parenting styles and found that "those students who were securely attached to their parents scored significantly higher on tests of personal intimacy and beliefs in [others'] abilities to be intimate" (p. 178). In essence, the authors found that although parenting style alone did not predict one's ability to be intimate, attachment to parents did allow individuals to have a more positive outlook on others' "accessibility, trustworthiness and responsiveness to one's needs" (Neal & Frick-Horbury, 2001, p. 181).

Parenting

Adults from Easygoing families are more likely to become Easygoing parents themselves. It is highly unlikely that adolescents raised with nurturance and appropriate supervision will become less than adequate parents themselves. The only limitation they may have is to be unprepared to handle difficulties in their own children that they themselves did not experience, such as significant behavioral problems or adverse life circumstances such as illness or divorce. On the other hand, the confidence and self-reliance that Easygoing parents instilled in their teens will translate into personal strength in times of adversity. Because family cohesion was an important part of their family life, as adults they will probably continue to be close to their own parents and siblings. These connections will serve as an ongoing support system and emotional stabilizer.

Lance and Jennifer had two teenagers, Frank, 16, and Mary, 14. Lance grew up in a family with a controlling, angry father, whereas Jennifer came from a balanced, highly functional family. The early years were relatively smooth, and Lance allowed Jennifer to take the lead in parenting decisions. As their children entered adolescence, Lance had more difficulty, especially handling the teenage "attitude." The more frustrated Lance felt, the more antagonistic Frank became. Lance quickly realized that some of his behaviors were reminiscent of his own father's actions, and he agreed to begin family therapy.

Within three months, the family had settled down into a more relaxed pattern of interaction. Jennifer's parenting style was more along the lines of the Easygoing parent, and she shared a more comfortable relationship with her children. Lance allowed Jennifer to help him be more aware of his tendency to be easily frustrated. He and Frank began regular Saturday outings to the golf driving range. Jennifer and Lance agreed to hold regular family meetings in which they listened to their teens' input on family decisions. The entire family acknowledged that the home environment became more harmonious once these changes were in place.

Summary

Easygoing parents have the healthiest parenting style. They raise their teens in a relaxed, warm environment that encourages individuality. Clear expectations are provided to keep the teens safe and allow the development of responsibility, compassion, and socially appropriate behavior. In these homes, parents and teens may disagree, but the connection between them remains. Teens from these families are able to differentiate without undue struggle. As L. Steinberg (2001) stated, "We can stop asking what type of parenting most positively affects adolescent development. We know the answer to this question" (p. 13). This style of parenting creates a legacy of emotional well-being and keeps families connected. It is the style of parenting that all parents should strive for.

PART THREE

PARENTAL LIFE ISSUES

CHAPTER EIGHT

Divorce and Remarriage

If teenagers live with broken promises, they learn to be disappointed.

—Dorothy Nolte and Rachel Harris,
Teenagers Learn What They Live

Case Example

Marla was a 14-year-old whose parents, Bob and Sue, had recently divorced. Marla lived with her father, and her mother lived about five hours away. Marla visited her mother sporadically.

Bob was 10 years older than Sue, and the couple had only dated for six months before Sue became pregnant. They had married shortly after finding out about the pregnancy. Marla was their only child. Both parents worked full-time, with Bob's income covering most of the family's living expenses. Marla considered her parents to have had a relatively normal relationship with only occasional disagreements, but admitted that these arguments often became very heated. A significant source of conflict for the couple was the difference in their parenting styles. Marla's father was permissive and indulgent, whereas her mother was more controlling. Marla often used this conflict to manipulate situations to her advantage.

Bob and Sue's divorce was particularly contentious and litigious. It was initiated by Sue, who said that she no longer wanted to be married and cited lack of attention from Bob, inequality in the household responsibilities, conflicts over Marla, and the age difference as the main reasons for her decision. Bob became extremely distraught, and initially focused on getting Sue to change her mind. Once it was clear that Sue was going through with the divorce, Bob became angry. Both adults shared their anger with Marla, and eventually engaged in a long, drawn-out custody battle.

Marla wanted to live with her father, as he was staying in the family home and her mother was moving several hours away to a small town. It was also evident that Marla's preference for her father was related to the fact that he was more permissive and financially able to give Marla what she wanted materially. Sue, not wanting to continue fighting with Bob, acquiesced and gave primary custody to him. Sue then moved away; her contacts with Marla became sporadic and often conflicted.

Initially, Bob was very dependent on Marla for companionship and would often confide in her his intense sadness and his hatred of her mother. Within six months of Sue's moving away, Bob started dating. Any time Bob had a date, Marla would become extremely agitated and accuse him of abandoning her like her mother had. Eventually Bob became seriously involved with a woman who had two teenage children, and the two started making plans to move in together. Marla was openly hostile to Bob's girlfriend and made it clear to her father that she did not want another woman in their home. The problems escalated when Bob's girlfriend perceived Marla to be spoiled and out of control and started encouraging Bob to be more of a disciplinarian with her. Eventually, the couple broke up because of their disagreements over Marla.

Overall, Marla had an extremely difficult time dealing with her parents' divorce. She had not perceived her parents' marriage as particularly conflicted and was surprised and confused when her mother announced that she was leaving. Marla struggled with being angry at both parents, alternating between who she perceived as being responsible for the divorce. With mom absent from the home, Marla found herself with a lot of unstructured and unsupervised time; she eventually became involved with an older peer group and started drinking and acting out sexually. Marla and her parents continued to struggle to restabilize their lives.

Divorce

One of the most significant events that can occur in adolescents' lives is their parents' divorce. Divorce is the legal, emotional, and physical dissolution of a marriage, and the end result is a significant alteration of the adolescent's family and life as they know it.

The decision to divorce can come at the end of a long series of problems or as a sudden surprise. Sometimes one spouse demands a divorce; in other situations, the decision is mutual. Divorce is often said to be an easy out, but most adults who have been through one would agree that divorce is an incredibly difficult decision and that the process is overwhelmingly stressful and painful.

Physical separation usually precedes divorce. One of the parents usually relocates, leaving behind most of his or her belongings and the children. This is the first experience of loss for the teenager. For some families, this separation is a relief from the constant tension; but it is always a significant life event for the teen. There is an abrupt restructuring of the family system. In most families, the mother becomes the primary caregiver and the father becomes a part-time visitor. As the process continues, a whole repertoire of emotions and situations arise for the parents and their teens. Whereas younger children are often sheltered from the experience by their parents, teenagers usually find themselves with a front-row seat to the drama, regardless of their parents' efforts to hide or disguise the conflict.

This change affects almost every area of the teenager's life. There are alterations in family finances, living arrangements, family structure, rules, and responsibilities. And almost always there are changes in parental behavior, an increase in the emotions expressed within the family, and an overall sense of loss. Divorce is particularly difficult for adolescents, as it has the potential to interfere with important developmental tasks that they are undertaking. Most teenagers are able to depend on their family to function as a safety net while they practice independence. Parental separation and divorce remove that safety net and make the work of adolescence more difficult.

Characteristics of Divorcing Parents

Adults embroiled in the divorce process develop what I often refer to in my practice as the "divorce crazies." For most adults, divorce is extremely difficult and results in personality and parenting style changes. Feelings about and reactions to the spouse can become intense. As the divorce unfolds, there is an increased level of conflict, and in some cases, outright hostility. For some, divorce is vicious and focused on revenge. Even in the most civil divorces, there are unavoidable areas of conflict. A colleague who is a family attorney has often said that once a couple reaches his office, the chance of reconciliation is significantly decreased—and that the presence of attorneys in the divorce process brings about a heightened level of conflict. In a sense, it legitimizes the anger between the couple.

The first advice that most adults get when contemplating a divorce is to take care of themselves and the second is to take care of their children. However, it is extremely difficult to take care of children when one's whole world is imploding. Another reality of divorce is that parents inevitably share too much information with their teenagers, drawing them into the process. Teenagers are generally aware of the issues that led to the divorce and are able to understand the complexities of the process. But this cognitive awareness does not necessarily protect them from the emotional repercussions of the experience. Teens can be drawn into the conflict between the parents and are often asked to decide who they want to live with, creating a loyalty dilemma.

Mindy was 16 when her parents divorced, and she was given the ongoing option to spend the night at either home. The divorce was amiable, and the parents did not want to draw their daughter into a custody fight, so they decided on an open custody arrangement, believing it to be in Mindy's best interest. Mindy's frustration with the process became evident when she said that she felt like she had to pick a side every single night: "I wish they would make it easier for me and just tell me where to go." Mindy's parents meant well but were unaware that their solution to the custody issue was not in her best interest. They had never thought to ask for Mindy's perspective. Protecting teens from the fallout of divorce is often an unattainable goal.

Emotional Reactions

Divorce is rarely a calm and mutual decision. Whereas marriage is the decision of two individuals coming together, divorce is usually the decision of one partner. A common scenario is that in which one partner finds him- or herself being left by the other. In *For Better or Worse: Divorce Reconsidered*, Hetherington and Kelly (2002) reported that in two out of three marriages, it is the woman who leaves. There are a number of possible reasons for divorce, including general unhappiness with the relationship, persistent conflict, adultery, or unwillingness to shoulder the responsibilities of the family. In some situations, one partner may have left symbolically, either by spending too much time at work or having an affair, and the other spouse eventually decides to end the empty marriage. I have worked with many adult clients who say that they had been telling their partner for years that they were unhappy, but the partner did not take the complaints seriously until the divorce papers were filed. Most individuals make the decision to leave a marriage only after considerable thought and anguish.

Common reactions to being left are denial, shock, and fear. Many persist in believing that their spouse is just upset and will change his or her mind. Some do not accept that divorce is a real possibility until their spouse moves out or formally files for divorce. Often, there is an overwhelming sense of betrayal and abandonment. When divorce comes as a surprise, the shocked parent may not filter the feelings he or she shares with teenage children.

For the individual who makes the decision to leave, there is also significant emotional upheaval. Guilt is often the primary feeling for parents who realize that they are breaking up the family because of their own unhappiness. They may also feel considerable anxiety at the thought of moving on with their lives without the security of marriage. The parent who has decided to leave has usually done so after considerable reflection and will usually take steps to protect the children from the fallout. But some such parents may share more information than necessary in order to justify their actions.

Some divorcing parents become depressed and withdrawn. They may become functionally unable to care for their children beyond the basics. Mothers, who often have primary custody, might become overwhelmed at the thought of having total responsibility for their children while dealing with the loss of their marriage. Many fathers have to move out of the family home and move in with friends or family members or into a small apartment. Many fathers with whom I have worked have talked about the incredible sadness and loneliness they feel during the first few weeks that they sit alone in an empty apartment.

During the divorce process, especially in the early stages, parents may experience a disruption in their normal functioning because of grief, stress, and feelings of abandonment. Insomnia, loss of appetite, headaches and stomach distress, inability to concentrate, and irritability are often the norm. Emotional suffering during this time is particularly acute, and many individuals take medication to help them deal with their anxiety and depression. During this initial stage of the divorce process, it is nearly impossible to protect teenagers from being acutely aware of the emotional upheaval that their parents are undergoing. Children, especially adolescents, experience a wide range of reactions to the news that their parents are separating.

Sarah, 48, had five children, three of whom were teenagers. Sarah's husband left her abruptly after she discovered that he had been seeing a woman in his office. Sarah would sit in her bedroom crying and screaming that she did not want to deal with taking care of five children by herself. She sometimes threatened suicide during these crying jags. The three older children made numerous attempts to comfort their mother, to no avail. They asked their father to come over and deal with her, but he refused.

Several weeks into the process, Sarah came into therapy at the insistence of her sister. It took several weeks of biweekly sessions to get Sarah's emotions under control so that she could even begin to consider the impact that her wailing would have on her children. The older children were so caught up in taking care of their mother and their younger siblings that they didn't have time to consider their own feelings about the situation.

Anger is another inevitable reaction to divorce. It can be subtle, passive–aggressive, or outright hostile. It is often primitive in nature, especially when a partner feels betrayed or abandoned. Women in particular handle their anger by becoming increasingly judgmental and critical about their ex-husbands. Some men may become intimidating and abusive. Some individuals obsess about the other person and may even stalk him or her. Many couples move past the anger and on with their lives, but some seem unable to do so. For some couples, the divorce emotions last longer than the marriage did.

Other possible reactions on the part of the divorcing parties are dependence and withdrawal. Some cannot deal with the loss and cling desperately to the hope that the marriage will survive. This is somewhat more common in women, especially those whose lives have been centered on the family. They may call repeatedly, beg for a second chance, seek out others to plead their case, and make efforts to block the divorce. Others simply walk away. They may move, refuse contact, at times abandoning their children in the process. This is particularly difficult for teenagers who remember their parent being a part of their "happy" childhood. As it is more common for the mother to have primary custody, it is often the father who chooses to walk away rather than deal with the emotions associated with the change in the family structure. I knew one father who asked if it would be okay if he stopped visiting his two daughters (ages 9 and 13) to avoid the constant conflict with his ex-wife.

The other possible reaction to divorce is a sense of relief and empowerment. For many adults who have been tied to a relationship in which they felt misunderstood, unhappy, disrespected, unappreciated, and in some cases even abused, the chance for freedom brings relief and hope. Some individuals take the opportunity to develop a more fulfilling life for themselves, perhaps to move into the workforce or advance in a career. A positive attitude makes even the most difficult adjustment easier.

Terri, a 44-year-old mother of three sons, 14 through 22 years of age, spent 23 years in an unhappy marriage. She reported a history of emotional abuse by her husband that had escalated in the last few years. They had made two attempts at marriage counseling, both of which he broke off, and a brief separation years ago. After her second child left for college, she started therapy and got up the strength to start divorce proceedings. Her husband's response was disbelief followed by intense anger and accusations of selfishness. She felt guilt and sadness, but also overwhelming relief and hope.

Terri told her sons the basic reasons she was leaving their father, but tried to keep them from feeling that they had to take sides. Her husband often called their sons to share his anger, loneliness, and bitterness. Terri encouraged her sons to spend more time with their father, although he had not been very involved in their lives. She acknowledged how difficult the divorce process was but felt that she made the right decision for herself.

Custodial and Noncustodial Parents

Parents who are the primary custodians have the greatest responsibility toward and impact on the adjustment of their children during and after divorce. In most cases, the mother has primary custody, whereas the father receives visitation rights. Although joint custody is becoming more the norm, there is usually one primary custodial parent. Most teenagers prefer to remain in the family home so that they can continue their peer relationships and school associations. Custodial parents who are able to provide a home environment similar to what their teenagers have known, maintain reasonable rules and expectations, and provide nurturance and support usually achieve the best outcomes. However, custodial parents typically have more day-to-day issues to deal with, struggle more financially, and have less personal time:

> Preoccupied by guilt, some custodial mothers put few limits on their children and allow them to run rampant; others, because of depression or self-involvement may neglect their children's needs and withdraw from them. But in the most common pattern, parental affection, positive involvement, and time spent with the child diminish, while parental irritability, punitiveness, and unpredictable, erratic discipline increase. . . . Where fathers fall short is in communication—in encouraging children to talk about their feelings and problems—and in adolescence, fathers often don't monitor their children's behavior well. They don't keep track of what their teenagers are doing, where they are, and who they are with. (Hetherington & Kelly, 2002, pp. 115, 117)

The behavior of noncustodial parents typically falls into one of three patterns. Some strive to remain active in their children's lives but are less involved in the discipline aspect and often choose to be the fun visitation parent. This may work well with younger children; however, it becomes somewhat trickier with adolescents, who prefer to be with their friends rather than their "other" parent. Other noncustodial parents step up and become more active participants in their adolescents' lives. Still others withdraw, visit irregularly, and in some cases even disappear. Despite research indicating that a large percentage of fathers abdicate their parental role following a divorce, many remain actively involved (Nielsen,1999; Wallerstein & Blakeslee, 2003).

In *We're Still Family*, Ahrons (2004) focused on how divorce affects different family members. The behavior and the adjustment of parents, during and after the divorce, has a direct impact on how their adolescents handle their own reactions. Ahrons (2004) reported the following:

> Parental separation ranges from, at best, a disruptive transition to, at worst, a traumatic event that has long-term consequences for families. . . . The good news is that about 40 percent of divorced couples had cooperative relationships, either from the start or within the first few years of divorce. The more distressing picture is that about 60 percent stayed mired in their conflicts or their anger actually increased over the first few years. (p. 171)

Parenting Style Changes

For a minority of parents, very little change occurs in parenting style during a divorce. But very few parents can go through such a fundamental change in their lives and not have it affect their parenting. During a divorce, parenting style is particularly dependent upon the inner issues and motivations of the parent.

My House, My Rules parents may find themselves unable to maintain as strict a position as they had previously held, especially with their adolescents. Mothers may have difficulty controlling their teenagers once the father is out of the home. Other authoritarian parents may become even more rigid because they have a strong need to control as much in their life as they can, and they think they can control their teenager. Others may become more demanding as a way of reassuring themselves that they are being responsible parents. Still others may attempt to control their teens because it is the one thing that they feel like they can do for them, especially when they have very little emotional connection to offer.

Parents' personal emotional upheaval makes it extremely difficult for them to maintain consistent control. Typically, control becomes erratic, rigid, and irrational. What is allowed one week is disallowed the next. Noncustodial parents may attempt to prove their position in the family by maintaining a tight rein on their children. This is a difficult position to maintain because of their irregular contact with their children. It is also particularly difficult with teenagers, who quickly realize that the noncustodial parent has very little power over their day-to-day lives. Noncustodial parents may try to intrude in the custodial parent's interactions with the teen. My House, My Rules parents quickly find out that, in a divorce, mutual respect and cooperation are more realistic goals with teenagers than control.

Jake, divorced for three years, continued to have regular contact with his two teenage children (14 and 16), who lived with their mother. Jake described his ex-wife as incompetent and weak as a mother and said that his kids liked living with her because they "get away with everything." Jake had a strong personality and struggled to assert some authority over his teens. When problems occurred, his two favorite forms of discipline were to cut off the cell phone or refuse to give them spending money. He was frustrated that his ex-wife did not support his actions and that they were not having any effect, especially on his 16-year-old son. Jake was encouraged to focus on his relationships with his teens rather than trying to control them from afar.

Many parents become more permissive during a divorce. They adopt the Cool parenting style for a number of reasons: "Mostly, our permissive parents were recent converts to the style, and their conversion was prompted by physical and emotional exhaustion, or by guilt" (Hetherington & Kelly, 2002, p. 130). Parents who were previously active and involved in their teenager's life find that they have very little emotional strength to deal with the teenage push for independence, so they acquiesce. Other parents befriend their teenagers because they need a friend and ally. Parents who start relying on their teenagers for companionship and comfort can easily cross the boundary between parenting and friendship. Some parents even regress to a pseudoadolescence. It is not unusual for these parents to start having teenage parties, complete with alcohol.

Some parents may have been controlling or enmeshed with their teen in response to the demands and expectations of the other parent. This is often the case in a household where an intimidating and authoritarian parent set the tone for family interactions. Once the controlling parent is out of the home, the response may be one of overcompensation, leading the custodial parent to become more permissive. Parents may also become permissive just to decrease the stress in the family. They don't want a power struggle with their teen; they want a peaceful environment after years of struggle.

Another common change in parenting style during a divorce is that parents become disengaged, some to the point of neglect. "Not now, I'm busy" takes on a whole new level of meaning in these families. Some mothers who have never worked before suddenly find themselves having to work to support their families. Other parents find themselves overwhelmed by the emotional toll of divorce and often have no strength left to deal with adolescents:

> Disengaged parenting is a form of emotional, psychological, and sometimes physical desertion. Essentially, the parent abandons children to cope with stresses of divorce on their own. Disengaged parents are focused on their own needs or survival. When a child interferes or makes demands, the parent responds with irritation or withdrawal. Some disengaged parents are just self-involved, narcissistic people.... Others neglect their children because of alcoholism or substance abuse or depression. Disengaged parenting is particularly common among defeated adults, who, overwhelmed by stress, have no time or energy left over for the children. (Hetherington & Kelly, 2002, p. 133)

This style of parenting occurs more frequently with adolescents for a number of reasons. Teenagers make it very difficult to maintain a strong stance on issues, and many stressed-out parents simply give in to teen demands.

Many parents also mistakenly believe that teenagers are mature enough to take care of themselves and often leave them alone for long periods of time. In homes where one parent is overwhelmed and disengaged and the other is absent, teens are left to fend for themselves. This can result in a very difficult adolescence for these young people. In these families, there is also the danger of adolescents becoming *parentified* or required to assume the role of primary caretaker. Many of these teens forsake their own developmental tasks and adopt a kind of pseudomaturity. They assume responsibility for the household, younger siblings, and even their parents' emotional well-being.

Noncustodial parents often slip into the Not Now, I'm Busy parenting style when they become overly focused on establishing a new life for themselves, particularly if they are dating. They may make plans with their teen and then cancel at the last minute because of another activity or work responsibility. Noncustodial parents who move out of the area tend to visit less often. Generally, any parent who lives more than a three- to four-hour drive away is less likely to visit on a regular basis.

Another primary reason for a parent to disengage from their teen is that finding activities to do with a teenager is not easy. Most teens have no interest in spending the weekend at their father's apartment, watching TV and eating pizza, while their friends are out socializing. Many noncustodial parents find themselves acting as chauffeurs for their teen's afternoon and weekend activities. Parents who are not receiving warmth and attention from their teens may withdraw. Conflict between the divorcing parents can also lead to a parent becoming disengaged.

Your Life Is My Life parents typically remain enmeshed with their children throughout the divorce process. The stress of divorce may intensify their need to live their lives through their teens' activities. Other parents may turn to their children for comfort and companionship—developing a stronger bond, but one that serves the parent's needs and is not in the best interest of the adolescent. Parents who do not move on with their lives may instead focus their lives on their children. In a few cases, an unhealthy relationship develops between a parent and a child of the opposite sex, creating a form of emotional incest. In these cases, the teenager becomes a substitute spouse. This can be extremely unhealthy for the adolescent and can seriously interfere with the development of his or her own relationships.

Adam was a 17-year-old only child whose parents divorced when he was 13. Shortly after the separation, his father moved out of state. Adam and his mother lived in a small, two-bedroom apartment, and his mother worked as a receptionist at the high school where Adam attended school. After the divorce, she focused all of her attention on her son. During the last year, she had started viewing Adam as her primary companion and pushed him to spend his evenings watching TV with her.

If Adam had activities planned with his friends, his mom asked him to invite his friends over to their house. When Adam protested, she talked about how sad and lonely she felt, making Adam feel guilty about leaving her home alone. Adam came into therapy after he started rebelling against this pressure. His mother's neediness and the absence of his father had resulted in an unhealthy situation for Adam, which affected his emotional development.

Easygoing parents might find it difficult during a divorce to maintain discipline and provide support, but some are able to continue doing so. Some become even better parents once they are free from an unhappy marital situation. Excessive marital conflict can drain parents' emotional resources; divorce may allow them to refocus on their teenagers. Parents who struggled with a spouse whose parenting style they did not agree with, but felt compelled to support, become able to parent in a way that they believe is healthier for their children. Overly controlling or permissive parents may adjust their parenting to a more balanced style after divorce. Divorce does not have to result in long-term negative effects. For some families, it becomes an opportunity to restructure themselves in a way that is more healthy and beneficial for all family members.

Special Situations in Divorcing Families

Special challenges to families undergoing divorce include interparental conflict, one parent's attempts to alienate a child from the other, remarriage, and stepfamilies.

Interparental Conflict

Conflict between parents during a divorce takes many forms, including arguments, passive–aggressive behavior, avoidant behavior, one spouse badmouthing the other, and continuous litigation. This conflict usually begins during the marriage, intensifies during the divorce, and continues for years after the divorce is finalized. Conflict between adults that continues after the divorce is called interparental conflict; Ahrons (2004) called such couples' conflict "habituated." Researchers agree that interparental conflict is probably the most damaging aspect of divorce for teenagers; the more extensive and long-lasting the conflict, the more harm is done to the teenagers (Buchanan, Maccoby, & Dornbusch, 1996; Forehand, Neighbors, Devine, & Armistead, 1994).

One type of interparental conflict involves overt and continual arguments between the parents—in person, over the phone, through e-mail and text messages, or in messages sent through the children. These arguments often become increasingly bitter and hostile and may take place as the teenager is being picked up or dropped off. Parents may use the teenager as a go-between, sending hateful messages to the other parent. They may seek retribution by disparaging the other parent to their children, for example by disclosing personal and negative information. Another way teens get caught in the conflict between parents is when parents quiz their teens as to events taking place in the other parent's home and then use what they learn as ammunition against that parent. It can be very frustrating for parents to see an ex-spouse having fun with their teenager, and consciously or unconsciously, they may try to interfere in that relationship.

Research has shown that interparental conflict and excessive and negative disclosures about the other parent negatively affect the adolescent's emotional well-being (Afifi & McManus, 2010; Kenyon & Koerner, 2008). A four-year study of adolescents reported that "a higher level of interparental conflict in divorced families was particularly detrimental for adolescents" and "conflict between divorced parents continues to be important in adolescent functioning up to three years after the marriage ends" (Forehand et al., 1994, p. 392). Another study reported that

> adolescent-reported parental arguing was associated with higher levels of depression and lower school effort among adolescents, particularly boys. Similarly every group . . . reported higher levels of overall deviance and a more severe "worst problem" in situations when parents argued frequently. (Buchanan et al., 1996, p. 89)

Parents need to be aware that their ongoing conflicts have significant implications for their adolescent's behavioral and emotional well-being. When anger is so ingrained, however, it is difficult to let it go, even when a child's emotional well-being is at stake.

Parental Alienation

Parental alienation refers to any effort, directly or indirectly, that has as its end result the alienation of a child from the other parent. In *Divorce Casualties*, Darnall (1998) identified three types of alienators: naive, active, and obsessed. Naive alienators make offhand negative comments about their ex-spouse but generally support their child's relationship with the other parent. Active alienators do not always control their negative comments about their ex; they may unconsciously benefit from sharing their negative feelings with the teen. Obsessed alienators purposely set out to damage the relationship between their teen and the other parent. They cannot separate their own anger from their teen's need to have a relationship with the other parent. They often actively deny that they are engaged in alienation.

Alienating behavior occurs more frequently with custodial parents. Children may so completely accept the negative view of the alienating parent that they are unable to differentiate their own thoughts and feelings from those of the parent. Even though teenagers are in the process of separating from both parents, they are still susceptible to alienation. Alienated teens often show intense anger, give unreasonable rationalizations for rejecting the other parent, and parrot the same stories and phrases as the alienating parent. When asked to look rationally and realistically at their opinions, they are unable to do so. They may become very defensive and intensify their rejection of the alienated parent.

John and Amy, ages 13 and 15, came into therapy because of a court order. The judge expressed concern that the divorcing parents were unable to reach agreement on visitation and noted that the teens expressed a great deal of anger toward their father.

The father had been hospitalized for several months for severe depression; upon his release from the hospital, his wife had refused to let him back into his home. During his hospitalization, he had lost his job and had been unable to provide financial support for the family. Shortly thereafter, the mother started divorce proceedings. In her view, depression was a weakness, and she felt abandoned by her husband.

During a separate individual session with the mother, she talked at length about her perceived injustices at the hands of her husband and admitted that she did not want her children to have a relationship with him. In follow-up sessions with the teenagers, they repeated many of the same stories, almost word for word. They insisted that they had nothing but disdain for their father and wanted nothing to do with him. No amount of rational discussion altered their feelings. Any questioning or comments about their mother brought intense defensiveness. They were seeing another therapist, who was reinforcing their right to their feelings. The teenagers were ordered to see their father under supervised conditions, but after a couple of years of extremely stressful and negative interactions, the father finally withdrew from his children's lives.

Parental alienation is a particular concern for adolescents, because it interferes with many adolescent developmental tasks. For teenagers, it may interfere with the development of their adult identity and it can also affect future intimate relationships. Using one's teenagers to get revenge is one of the most reprehensible emotional reactions to divorce.

Remarriage and Stepfamilies

Dealing with divorce becomes even more complicated for adolescents when one or both parents remarry. This represents a major life change for the adolescent. Most divorced parents remarry, often within five years, and fathers remarry sooner and more often than mothers (Crosbie-Burnett, 1991; Wallerstein, Lewis, & Blakeslee, 2000). Numerous studies have looked at the impact of remarriage on children and adolescents (Hetherington, 1999; Nicholson, Fergusson, & Horwood, 1999; Skaggs & Jodl, 1999; Wallerstein & Blakeslee, 2003). Some adolescents adjust very well and are able to develop a close and comfortable relationship with their stepparent. For other teens, the experience is more like the fairy tale stereotype of the wicked stepmother or evil stepfather.

Stepfamilies come in several varieties. When a parent with children remarries and brings the new spouse into the home where the children live, it is considered a basic stepfamily. A variation on this pattern occurs when the stepparent's biological children come for regular visits. In a more complex stepfamily, sometimes called a blended family, both spouses bring their children into the family. A newly married couple might have a child while also having full custody of the children of one or both parents from a previous marriage.

The impact of stepfamilies is complicated and depends on a number of factors. Studies have shown that many adolescents eventually adjust to the stepfamily situation. The success of the adjustment depends on a number of factors, including (but not limited to) continued connection with the biological parent, acceptance by the noncustodial parent of the custodial parent's remarriage, level of warmth and connection between stepparents and stepchildren, the presence of stepsiblings, the age and gender of the adolescent, and the adolescent's attitude toward the family situation (Henderson & Taylor, 1999; Skaggs & Jodl, 1999).

Remarriage and Parenting Styles

Just like divorce, remarriage affects parenting style. The most obvious changes result from the addition of another adult into the family system. Teens may resent having to share their home and their biological parent with another adult and possibly stepsiblings. It can be particularly difficult for teenagers with limited visitation to find that their noncustodial parent has suddenly become less available to them because of the presence of a new spouse. Teenagers can have difficulty dealing with a new adult in their lives and are more likely than younger children to resent the new parent's attempts to assert authority. At a time when teenagers are already battling parental authority, additional requests and demands are usually met with displeasure.

A recent study concluded that

> parent–adolescent relationships in recently remarried families face many stresses and are often characterized by less parental control, monitoring, and warmth and more negative behavior and parent–adolescent interactions than those found in non-divorced families. (Henderson & Taylor, 1999, p. 97)

Melinda was a 15-year-old whose parents had a joint custody arrangement in which each household had the teenagers for two week at a time. Melinda had an 18-year-old brother who was a senior in high school. Because of considerable problems between Melinda and her stepmother, her father sought therapy for his family six months after his remarriage. During the initial session with the parents, the stepmother reported that Melinda was difficult to deal with, was rude and sullen, and wanted her father all to herself. The stepmother said she felt Melinda was spoiled and manipulated her father into giving her whatever she wanted. It was clear that the stepmother had already developed some resentment toward Melinda.

When Melinda came into the session, she openly admitted being unhappy with her father's remarriage. Melinda reported that after coming into the home, the stepmother had immediately made a number of changes, including removing some family pictures that Melinda had carefully arranged on the front hall table and replacing them with pictures of her own family, without consulting the other family members. It was clear that Melinda was unhappy and that some of her unhappiness was related to the significant changes thrust upon her by the addition of this new woman to her family. It did appear that Melinda's feelings were often not sufficiently considered during the crucial adjustment period. The stepmother was also bewildered by the intensity of Melinda's rejection of her.

The presence of a new adult in the household can result in several possible parenting style changes. One such change occurs when a custodial parent marries a My House, My Rules spouse who, accustomed to being in charge in other areas, comes into the family expecting and demanding that the children obey him or her. The custodial parent, concerned with making the new marriage work, may unconsciously sacrifice the emotional well-being of the children in order to keep the peace. This parent may even have sought out a strong partner to help with the responsibility of parenting.

Adolescents used to a less controlling home environment are likely to struggle with this change in parenting style, especially if it occurs in the custodial parent's home. Teens may respond to parenting changes in the noncustodial home with less hostility but more withdrawal.

Research has shown that single parents often adopt more permissive or neglectful parenting styles (Demo & Acock, 1996; Nielsen, 1999). Single mothers have the most difficulty supervising their teenagers, particularly their teenage sons. For these parents, remarriage and the addition of another adult to help handle the family responsibilities can be quite beneficial. Single mothers tend to struggle financially, and a stepfather can bring financial security to the family. It is particularly beneficial for teenagers when they are able to appreciate and feel positive about the new stepparent. Research has shown that the mother's parenting style, economic status, psychological well-being, and self-reliance are the most important factors in the well-being of her children (Nielsen, 1999). The addition of a supportive stepfather, especially when he does not bring his own biological children into the family situation, may generate a significant improvement in the parenting style of these mothers.

Remarriage can provide a parent with support and stress release. Dealing with teenagers, especially during and after a divorce, is extremely difficult, and many parents feel overwhelmed by the task. A new partner may provide a needed sounding board for the parent and may result in a more relaxed parenting style. Healthy parenting takes place in an environment where all family members share open communication, warmth, respect, personal boundaries, fun, and clear rules and expectations. This is the Easygoing parenting style described in chapter 7. It has a better chance of developing when parents feel relaxed and supported and expect to have their needs met, not by their teenage children, but by a healthy adult companion.

Remarriage can also result in a parent becoming less involved in parenting, either by withdrawing or becoming too lax. When a marriage is in its early stages and the couple is focused on their relationship, teens may find themselves with even less supervision. The new parent may also, in an effort to befriend the teenagers, allow activities that were previously forbidden, like drinking or smoking, or give only lax supervision to teen relationships. If the teenage children are in late adolescence when the parent remarries, both the teens and the parents may push for the teens to mature more quickly and separate from the family, making way for the new marriage to take priority. Parenting style changes that do not provide structure, support, and nurturing can have negative consequences for the teen's emotional well-being.

Adolescent Reactions

Parents' divorce is a challenging experience for adolescents on many levels. It involves significant loss: of family identity, of a parent, and in some situations, of family income and the family home. Teens also grapple with issues of identity, trust, and increased awareness of their parents' imperfections. Teens may worry more about finances and their future. They have to adjust to two different residences, learn to interact with each parent separately, keep family secrets, and remember the different rules and expectations in each home. They often have to deal with two holiday celebrations and figure out how to share events, such as school and extracurricular activities, birthdays, and graduation, with two sets of parents.

Adolescents have an increased awareness of their parents' fallibility and often become critical of how adults are handling their own lives. Divorce during adolescence is particularly difficult and interferes with the developmental tasks that the adolescent needs to accomplish. The question is not whether teens will react, but how they choose to react. In general, teens do not respond well to divorce. Although most teens ultimately survive their parents' breakup, their path to adulthood is clearly affected by the life changes that accompany any divorce.

Denial

Many teenagers are aware of the problems and conflicts that exist in their parents' marital relationship, but few expect them to end in divorce. When the divorce is announced, they may not be completely surprised, but they still struggle to accept the news. In some cases, teens are unaware of their parents' problems, or the parental issues may have developed suddenly, for example through the discovery of one spouse's affair.

Either way, the first reaction of most teenagers is one of disbelief and denial. Even in the most contentious marital relationships, teenagers want an intact family. They want to believe that the family problems can be fixed and often implore their parents to reconcile. One teen told his mother that if she divorced his father it would ruin his high school years; the mother decided against divorce until he was in college. At that point, her son told her, "Do what is best for your life." Other teens simply withdraw from the family situation and engage more actively with peers, acting as if nothing is different at home. These teens often do not tell their friends what is happening at home. Very rarely do teens embrace the separation as a positive action. However, there are situations in which the home life is so stressful or abusive that the announcement of divorce is a welcome relief.

Reactions Based on Developmental Stage

Once teens have accepted that the divorce is proceeding, their response may vary on the basis of a number of factors: their age and developmental stage, the atmosphere in the family before the decision, the level of family conflict, and their ongoing relationship with their parents.

Early adolescents (ages 11 to 13) respond differently than teens in late adolescence. Divorce during the early adolescent period usually jump starts some of the more intense emotions and behaviors associated with this developmental stage. One fact that has been clearly established in the research is that divorce is particularly stressful during the early adolescent years—a time in which teenagers are beginning to venture out but still need the security and stability of home. Some researchers recommend against starting the divorce process or remarrying while a child is in the early adolescent period (Hetherington & Kelly, 2002; Wallerstein & Blakeslee, 2003). Divorce can affect the onset and duration of the adolescent developmental process. In *The Unexpected Legacy of Divorce,* Wallerstein et al. (2000) reported that "adolescence begins early in divorced homes. . . . Adolescence is more prolonged in divorced families and extends well into the years of early adulthood" (p. 299).

Teens at this age may feel more pressure to grow up too quickly. The negative attitude that begins in early adolescence is intensified. The normal disdain that young adolescents have toward their parents is magnified when teens feel that their parents, by divorcing, are taking away the security of their home. They may also be angry at one parent for making the other parent leave.

Another possible reaction during early adolescence is regression to an earlier emotional age. These teens become frightened of venturing out into the adolescent world and may become more clingy and emotional with their parents. They may unconsciously believe that if they act like children, their family will remain the same as it was when they were children. In a few cases, where there has been significant parental conflict, there is a sense of relief when the divorce process starts.

Teenagers in middle adolescence (ages 14 to 16) respond primarily with action. Normal developmental activities during this time center on identification with peers, experimentation with style, and moving away from parent-centered activities. Teens, angry and confused about the changes going on at home, often turn to their peer group for emotional support. This shift from family to peer group identification makes some adolescents vulnerable to peer pressure. Teens may also disengage prematurely from their families and develop pseudomaturity. Many teens at this age find a stable family model in the homes of their friends.

Teens in the midadolescent period engage in more active conflict with parents as they push to have their own way. Disillusioned with their parents' inability to handle their own lives, they may balk at accepting their parents' authority. Acting out can reach an extreme level in this age group. In *The Everything Parent's Guide to Children and Divorce,* Pickhardt (2006) wrote the following:

Two kinds of behavior often intensify when divorce coincides with a young person's mid adolescence: conflict and lying. . . . Conflict can be used to coerce or exhaust a parent into submission, particularly the one who hates, or is too tired to fight. Lying is used to cover up the truth of what was done or what is intended. (p. 113)

These behaviors also represent the emotions that the adolescent is feeling. Some of the behaviors may also be intended to make their parents pay more attention to what they are going through. Adolescents at this age are also developing their own sense of right and wrong and may find themselves morally outraged at the parent they deem responsible for the divorce, often selecting one parent as the bad guy and the other parent as the victim needing protection. Parentification and parental alienation often occur with teens in this age group.

Many parents believe that older adolescents (from age 17 to the early 20s) have matured sufficiently to weather the storm of divorce. This is only true for some teens—those who have sufficiently individuated and are less dependent on the family to meet their physical and emotional needs.

Teens in late adolescence are primarily focused on making life choices and developing intimate relationships. They may react to their parents' divorce by creating their own "families" through their emotional connections. Romantic relationships may be patterned after their parents' relationship, with conflict and struggles over trust. They may become more cynical and mistrustful of relationships, and they may also become afraid that their own relationships will fail.

The emotional upheaval in the family may affect teens' ability to make decisions that will take them away from the family, such as going to college or joining the military. They may also experience strong emotional reactions, such as depression and anxiety, which may forestall the development of autonomy and affect their move into adulthood.

College students are probably the most well-studied group in the United States. It is not surprising, therefore, that there have been a number of studies detailing the reaction of college students to their parent's divorce. Nielsen (1999) analyzed more than 210 books and articles and reported that most college students suffer few long-term consequences of parental divorce in terms of academic achievement, social development, emotional well-being, or relationships. Many of these young adults actually became more appreciative of others and more capable of understanding and respecting other people's opinions and perspectives. College students may use their parents' divorce as a springboard to their own independence.

Older teens do, however, experience some negative reactions. When the family was highly conflicted or the custodial parent was struggling emotionally, Nielsen found, many of these teenagers were concerned about abandoning their families to move out, go to college, or join the military. Older teens and young adults also expressed a mistrust of intimate relationships (Nielsen, 1999).

Gender Differences

Boys and girls appear to handle divorce differently (Nielsen, 1999; Skaggs & Jodl, 1999). Generally, boys act out more, whereas girls tend to internalize their reactions, becoming vulnerable to depression and anxiety. Boys may be vulnerable when parents divorce because of several factors: The absence of a father in the home, and a mother's negative opinion of her ex-husband, can affect an adolescent boy's sense of self. He may also feel a responsibility to take over the "man of the house" role. Girls tend to focus more on the loss and may align themselves more with their mother and perceive themselves as protecting her from their father, damaging the father–daughter relationship.

Anger

Anger is an inevitable reaction to divorce. Some adolescents take sides and become angry at the parent they feel is responsible for the breakup of the family, whereas others may express anger at both parents. Many adolescents are angry about the upheaval and uncertainty that divorce brings to their lives. Many struggle with accepting their parents' divorce but do not feel safe expressing their anger to their parents; instead, they become more aggressive with peers or act out at school. Teens who hide their anger from themselves and others often end up feeling depressed. Teens from families where there was continual and volatile conflict may become frightened of their own anger and suppress their emotions. Wallerstein and Blakeslee (2003) advised parents in *What About the Kids?*:

> While you should be prepared for an initial cool, almost detached response to announcement about the divorce, be aware that still waters run deep. Very soon you may be on the receiving end of a blast of anger from your teenager followed by crying spell or dramatic door slamming exit, depending on whether it's a girl or boy in your child's personal style. Your announcement evokes powerful fears and passions that lie very close to the surface. (p. 100)

Anger is not only felt during the initial stages of divorce; it can continue in different forms for many years. After all, divorce changes many circumstances in the adolescent's life.

Withdrawal and Loneliness

Although teens are able to understand the process of divorce, many still want to deny that it is happening to their family. In order to maintain this denial, many teens withdraw from the situation by refusing to discuss the particulars of the divorce, spending more time with friends, isolating themselves in their room, or creating other ways to emotionally numb themselves from the family chaos going on around them. Maintaining emotional distance from the changes going on in the family requires a degree of vigilance. This vigilance can result in anxiety and loneliness. The loneliness felt by many teens stems from their awareness that their parents are less available to them. Teens may also minimize interactions with their parents, so as to avoid taking sides. Many teens also find themselves with more time alone following the divorce, as one parent may have moved away and the other parent works.

Aaron was 14 when his parents announced that they were divorcing after 20 years of marriage. Aaron had two older sisters who were away at college. Both parents worked very hard to make the transition as easy as possible. Aaron listened quietly to his parents' explanation and then, with little comment, went up to his room.

During the next few weeks, Aaron appeared to be handling the divorce very well. The only change was that he seemed to withdraw from family activities and was somewhat more negative toward his mother. Several weeks after the announcement, Aaron's school counselor called to say that he was in her office after fighting with another boy on campus. During a discussion with the school counselor, he acknowledged being very angry with his mother for leaving his father and disrupting his family life. Being the only child left at home, he felt alone and abandoned.

Maturity and Responsibility

Divorce can bring about changes in a teen's responsibilities. Many teens find themselves responsible for younger siblings or care of the house when the custodial parent returns to work. At times, this caretaker role extends to taking care of one or both parents, who the teen may view as emotionally weak. When the role of caretaker becomes the primary responsibility of the teenager, the result is parentification, a role reversal in which the teenager becomes the parent and the parent becomes the child. Parentifed teens often sacrifice their own developmental needs in order to take care of the family.

As parents focus on the complexities of their own lives, their children may feel pushed to become more autonomous. Younger teens may become pseudomature and assume the behaviors and responsibilities of older teens:

> The teenager may accelerate her separation from family in response to the parent separating the marriage. . . . Some teenagers may feel driven to act more grown-up because, deserted by the unified family they could once count on, they now feel more impelled to grow up quickly and operate on their own. (Pickhardt, 2006, p. 115)

As teens push to appear more mature, they may skip important steps in the developmental process; the result can be a superficial identity that lacks important core characteristics.

Older teens have a better chance of developing healthy ways of coping with their parents' divorce. They may accept more responsibility for their own self-care, decisions, and activities, ending up with a feeling of control over the changes going on in their family. Teens who are able to master the responsibilities of young adulthood without feeling thrust out of the family usually go on to succeed in their own lives.

Manipulation

Teens are not above manipulating situations to meet their needs, and divorce can provide an opportunity for them to manipulate their parents to their advantage. Most teens do this in small ways, such as asking to stay overnight at the home of the parent who is more likely to give permission for a certain activity, or trying to get more privileges by pitting one parent against the other. Some parents may encourage their teen to manipulate the other parent, for example by asking the noncustodial parent for more money to pay for items that the custodial parent would normally be expected to take care of. This manipulation takes on a more negative connotation when teens use the threat of moving in with the noncustodial parent to get their way.

Acting Out

For most teenagers, emotions become behavior. Emotions that divorce can evoke in teenagers include anger, sadness, fear, confusion, mistrust, and grief. Many teens experience these feelings in reaction to their parents' conflict even before a divorce is announced, but divorce forces them to accept the true extent of the problems in the family. During a divorce, teens are also more susceptible to peer influence, which can result in various types of acting out. These behavioral reactions can range from emotional outbursts at home to behavioral problems or even instances of criminal mischief outside of the home. Studies have shown that teens whose parents are involved in a highly conflicted divorce exhibit more academic problems, substance abuse, sexual acting out, truancy, and delinquency:

> One in four of the children in the study started using drugs and alcohol before their fourteenth birthdays. By the time they were seventeen-year-olds, over half of the teenagers were drinking or taking drugs. . . . Of those who used drugs, four in five admitted that their school work suffered badly as a result. . . . Early sex was very common among girls in the divorced families . . . in our study, one in five had had her first sexual experience before the age of fourteen. Over half were sexually active with multiple partners during their high school years. (Wallerstein et al., 2000, p. 188)

Multiple studies (Amato, 2001; Amato & Keith, 1991; Buehler, Benson, & Gerard, 2006; Fauber, Forehand, Thomas, & Wierson, 1990; Peris & Emery, 2004) have shown that teens with the poorest outcomes come from families with high levels of conflict that subsequently went on to divorce; however, teens in high-conflict intact families exhibit the same behavioral problems. Clearly, parental conflict and family disruption can provoke acting out in adolescents.

Bella, age 23, was sober for two years when she came into therapy to work on her family issues. Bella's parents divorced when she was 13, after her father left her mother for another woman. Bella reported that her mother had a very difficult time adjusting to the divorce and basically abdicated her parenting responsibilities for about a year and a half.

Bella acknowledged that she dealt with the divorce by seeking out older peers, drinking, and acting out sexually. She started skipping school, and her grades dropped. When Bella's mother finally tried to establish some authority in the home, Bella actively resisted her efforts. Bella continued to drink heavily throughout her adolescence. She eventually went to Alcoholics Anonymous and became sober. She was trying to reestablish a relationship with her mother and came into therapy to help her work through the trauma of her parents' divorce.

For many, the impact of divorce extends into adulthood. Parental divorce is a common topic in many adult therapy sessions.

Depression, Anxiety, and Other Emotional Reactions

Divorce is an extremely distressing experience for everyone involved. Many people focus on the emotional well-being of the adults and miss teens' emotional cues that show that they are struggling with the loss of their family as they know it. This loss can invoke grief, anxiety, or depression. The depression can be a reaction to loss of an intact family, loss of a parent, loss of friends and neighborhood due to relocation, and lack of attention from preoccupied parents. Depression and anxiety do not always have the usual outward signs in teens. Many teens express depression through increased irritability, deteriorating grades, withdrawal from friends, isolation, and an overly intense focus on the family situation. Anxiety can develop when adolescents feel confused and insecure about the changes taking place and when they find themselves caught between their warring parents. Adolescents can also find the divorce process confusing and frightening, especially if they are dragged into a custody battle.

Conduct and eating disorders have also been linked to divorce. Oppositional defiant disorder and conduct disorder are two behaviorally based psychiatric disorders seen in adolescence. Reactions to parents' divorce can include unhealthy and persistent acting out. Eating disorders, which can be complex and dangerous, are often an attempt to exert some kind of control over one's life by controlling food intake. They can involve eating too little in an attempt at physical perfection or overeating and using food as comfort. Behavioral and emotional disorders developed in adolescence may continue into adulthood, especially if unattended to during adolescence.

Changes in Parent–Teen Relationships

Divorce often results in changes in the way parents and teens relate. These changes, whether initiated by the parent or the teen, are often detrimental to the teen's development. As discussed earlier, parentification may result from a teen's reaction to perceived parental stress or weakness or when a parent encourages the teen to take over adult responsibilities in the household. Even though teens may appear to accept the additional responsibilities, they often resent them. But when parents reassure them that, despite some additional responsibilities around the house, they are still being taken care of by their parents, the disruption to their development is likely to be minimal.

Divorce can lead parents to treat their teen like a confidant. Parents may share too much information and confide their hurt and anger. This occurs more frequently in same-sex parent–child relationships. Teens make convenient companions, available whenever a parent needs to talk or complain or cry or spout hateful comments about his or her ex. Teens placed in this position often find themselves having less time to spend with their own peer group, yet often do not neglect the needy parent. Guilt can develop when a teen is unable to meet the parent's perceived needs.

Sometimes a parent designates his or her teenager as a replacement companion. This is particularly harmful when it occurs in opposite-sex parent–teen relationships. Children respond with attention when a parent expresses acute sadness or loneliness, and over time, an unhealthy dependency can develop that interferes with the adolescents' development of their own personal relationships and their separation from the parent. Adolescents who get locked into unhealthy codependent relationships with parents can suffer long-term negative consequences.

Reactions to a Parent's Remarriage

Most divorced adults remarry within a few years (Crosbie-Burnett, 1991; Wallerstein et al., 2000). Teens usually do not respond favorably to this addition of a new adult into their world. They do not want to get close to another adult, especially when they are still dealing with the changes within their own family. Adolescence is about separating from parents, not developing a complex relationship with a new parent. Initially, teens may seem unconcerned or even friendly when a parent introduces a new love interest. However, once that person marries into the family, teens usually react with displeasure. In all of my years of working with adolescents, I have never encountered a teenager who welcomed, without reservation, a new adult into the family.

Remarriage changes a teen's relationship with both biological parents, sometimes upsetting whatever delicate postdivorce balance had been achieved. Remarriage can also result in the custodial parent relocating, separating teens from their friends and exposing them to a new school and neighborhood, or the noncustodial parent moving further away. Many adolescents experience the addition of the new family member as a threat to their relationship with the biological parent. Others experience a conflict of loyalties as the remarriage removes any hope of reconciliation between their parents. The situation is intensified when the new marriage partner was involved in an affair with the parent prior to the divorce. Teens' acceptance of a new stepparent can be influenced by how the other biological parent responds to the remarriage.

Adolescents' reactions to a new stepparent can include anger, anxiety, jealousy, resentment, ambivalence, and in some cases, cautious hope. Most teenagers engage in power struggles with a new stepparent. "Few teenagers accept the parent's new partner as a parent. It's normal for them to challenge your authority at every opportunity. The harder that you try to act like a parent, the more likely are they are to resist" (Ahrons, 2004, p. 148). At a time when adolescents are questioning the validity of a parent's rules and expectations, a new adult coming into the household and attempting to establish him- or herself in an authoritarian position will be met with resistance.

Generally, boys have more difficulty accepting the authority of a new stepfather, whereas girls struggle more with stepmothers. In addition, younger adolescents engage in more conflicted relationships with stepparents than do older adolescents. This is probably related to the fact that younger teens engage in more parental rebellion and that older adolescents have already successfully individuated and have less overall need for parenting. The most successful stepparents are those who come into the family with the goal of developing a connection with the teen and providing a supportive relationship rather than focusing on establishing their authority.

One recent study (Crosbie-Burnett & Giles-Sims, 1994) established that adolescents react negatively to stepparents who attempt to exert authority without having previously established a close connection. The study also found that a disengaged parenting style was related to the poorest outcomes for adolescents and concluded that a supportive stepparenting style resulted in the most positive adolescent–stepparent relationship. "These results suggest that stepparent support is more important than control in promoting adolescent adjustment and/or that relatively well-adjusted adolescent will accept some controlling behavior from the stepparent, if support is also present" (Crosbie-Burnett & Giles-Sims, 1994, p. 398).

For some families, remarriage provides a more stable home environment. When the custodial parent has experienced significant financial and emotional struggles, the addition of a new supportive adult can be a welcome and stabilizing influence. Chances for successful inclusion in the family increase when there is adequate time for the adolescent to establish a comfortable and supportive relationship prior to the marriage. Some teenagers appreciate the opportunity to observe and experience a healthy relationship between two adults. Many also respond favorably when they can see that the new stepparent brings their parent happiness. Other teens feel positive about the new stepparent when he or she relieves them of some of their household responsibilities. Teenagers are usually able to quickly assess whether the new addition to the family is going to be beneficial for them or create new conflict.

Complex stepfamilies, which include children from both families, can experience a more complicated adjustment process. The addition of stepsiblings to the family unit opens up additional issues for both parents and teenagers. Comparing simple and complex stepfamilies, researchers found better adjustment in the simplest stepfamily situations (parent, children, stepparent). As the number of individuals and the complexity of the interrelatedness grew, more difficulties in adjustment and poorer long-term outcomes were found:

> In complex stepfamilies, the challenge of dealing with the diverse biological relationships between parents and children, shared and nonshared family histories, and varied alliances in complex stepfamilies may contribute to more problems in adolescent development. (Skaggs & Jodl, 1999, p. 146)

In all kinds of stepfamilies, researchers have found significant differences between the ways that parents responded to their biological children and to their stepchildren. Parents were more likely to provide warmth, support, and behavioral monitoring to their biological children than to their stepchildren, especially in complex stepfamilies. Overall, mothers and stepmothers provided more warmth and monitoring of teens than did fathers and stepfathers. And adolescents were more positive and affectionate with their biological parents than with stepparents; this finding held for both mothers and fathers (Crosbie-Burnett, 1991; Henderson & Taylor, 1999; Hetherington, 1999; Nielsen 1999).

Teens often focus on the issue of fairness, and complete equality and fairness are rarely possible in a stepfamily. When a noncustodial parent remarries and takes on the parenting role with stepchildren, teens can feel even more isolated and angry, creating hostility between the teen and the new spouse and stepsiblings. These feelings can be particularly acute when teens feel that the noncustodial parent, who has been unavailable to them, is now sharing affection, attention, and resources with another family. Stepparents can benefit from guidance to help adjust to their new role, especially if they do not have children of their own.

In positive stepparent–teen relationships, teens respond with acceptance, respect, openness, and warmth. But they may also react to stepparents with hostility, coldness, aloofness, disrespect, and wariness. In extreme cases, they actively work to come between the stepparent and the biological parent. Conflicts with stepchildren can create tremendous marital stress and even cause the marriage to fail. A healthy stepparent–teen relationship is the primary responsibility of the adult, but the teen's role is also very important. The success of the new family depends on the relationship established between the stepparent and the teen, and not on any arbitrary position being assumed by one or the other.

Long-Term Consequences of Divorce

Parents' divorce can affect teens' academic accomplishments, vocational choices, relationships, emotional well-being, social adjustment, and financial management skills. But most teens emerge from divorce with few problems that can be directly linked to it. As Marquardt (2005) said in *Between Two Worlds*,

> We don't look much different from anyone else. We might seem a bit more guarded, a bit slower to make new friends, a bit more anxious about life in general. But we do manage to make friends, fall in love, accomplish goals, succeed at work: some of us do quite well. (p. 189)

Divorce by itself does not necessarily produce long-term consequences for the adolescent. However, studies have shown that the difficulties experienced by adolescents in divorced single-parent families and stepfamilies are related to the amount of interparental conflict and that similar effects exist in families that stay intact but have high levels of dysfunction (Forehand et al., 1994; Ruschena, Prior, Sanson, & Smart, 2005; Zill, Morrison, & Coiro, 1993). Studies have also found that there can be positive long-term outcomes when high-conflict families divorce and that the new family systems function in more healthy and supportive ways (Buchanan et al., 1996; Hetherington & Kelly, 2002). Divorce does not necessarily result in a negative outcome for adolescents; rather, the behavior of the parents and the teenager's reactions are the crucial components that determine that outcome.

Love and Commitment

Adolescence is the time when sexual and romantic interests develop. Divorce, and the ongoing relationship between the divorced parents, can have a powerful impact on an individual's ability to establish successful intimate relationships. "It's in adulthood that children of divorce suffer the most. The impact of divorce hits them most cruelly as they go in search of love, sexual intimacy and commitment" (Wallerstein et al., 2000, p. 299). Teens experiencing the breakdown of their parents' marriage inevitably question what they have come to believe about love and marriage. It is inconceivable that, after that experience, they could face their own intimate relationships with naiveté and trust. In *The Love They Lost*, Staal (2001) discussed the emotional impact of divorce:

> I have built up walls, rarely letting anyone in. I have trouble living in the moment, and often find myself wondering how things will end, even as they start. I feel like the rug could be pulled out from underneath me at any time. I constantly set up tests, forcing people to prove their love to me. I have a hard time trusting. I am so scared of being abandoned. (p. 6)

Teens with divorced parents frequently struggle to trust that someone loves them. They enter relationships half expecting them to fail. Statistically, children of divorce have a greater chance of getting divorced someday themselves (Wallerstein et al., 2000). Some teens experience more than one divorce in their family; they may come to view marriage as an institution that one enters and departs, depending on one's level of personal satisfaction.

Divorce often brings out intense anger, and some teenagers end up equating love and anger. This perception is not too far off. These teens may witness heated parental arguments that include claims of continued love for the other parent. Many adults, though divorced, continue to maintain a connection with their ex-spouse through anger. Their adolescents often develop relationships that show patterns similar to the conflict that they saw expressed between their parents. If infidelity was an issue in their family, teens may view it as a particularly critical relationship issue or as an expected part of a relationship.

Stella was 37 years old and married; she came into therapy with her husband of nine years. The couple had two school-age children. Stella had an erratic temper, and at times overreacted to small disagreements with her husband. Stella was extremely suspicious of her husband and had often accused him of being interested in other women. Her husband denied any interest outside of his marriage and expressed dismay at being unable to convince his wife of his love and fidelity.

Outside of the issues of trust and Stella's difficulty in dealing with basic marital disagreements, both reported a happy and fulfilling relationship. Stella's parents had had a contentious relationship and had divorced when she was 14, following the discovery of her father's affair. Her father immediately married the other woman, and after that, Stella saw very little of him. Stella's mother remained bitter about the divorce and even refused to attend her wedding if Stella's father was invited.

Once they understood the connections between Stella's family history and their current marital problems, the couple was able to work toward stabilizing their own relationship.

Personality Traits

The emotional problems of adults with divorced parents may be due to the divorce's interruption of their adolescent developmental tasks. During adolescence, important adult characteristics are developed, stabilized, and ingrained in the adult personality. Adolescents develop these characteristics by observing the behavior of the adults around them and by their own coping strategies. Positive characteristics that may develop include resilience, self-reliance, self-esteem, empathy, determination, tolerance, and forgiveness. More negative characteristics include self-centeredness, manipulation, entitlement, vindictiveness, and distrust.

During particularly difficult divorces, teens often become center-stage observers of their parents' negative behaviors. When a parent uses less than ethical actions to achieve the best divorce outcome for him- or herself, teens learns to deal with others in self-centered, manipulative, and unethical ways. In homes with continual interparental conflict, teens learn to treat others with disdain, disrespect, and—at times—outright cruelty. This lesson is intensified when parents use the teenager to send negative messages back and forth. I once worked with two divorced parents, both remarried, who had not spoken to each other in 10 years except through messages, often negative, sent through their two adolescent children. When the families finally came together, at my request, to discuss their teens' extensive problems, they were unable to articulate why the hostility had continued for so long.

In many custody battles, parents say, "At least my children will know that I fought for them." Unfortunately, what the adolescents actually learn is that they are being fought about, not for, with their custody as the ultimate prize. Many parents are not above using unethical tactics to win a custody battle. Teens observe not only their parents' behavior, but that of the attorneys involved, and in most cases, the lessons they learn are not about truth and justice. Parents who choose to handle custody issues with fairness, consideration, and empathy teach their adolescents these important values. Adolescents are able to observe, think for themselves, and use the divorce experience to learn which types of characteristics they want to emulate and which to reject.

Social Relationships

The move from parent-centered relationships to peer-centered relationships, which takes place during adolescence, is important because it allows individuals to function independently in the world, make friends, establish relationships, interact appropriately with coworkers, and make decisions for themselves. During the divorce, teens may find themselves more tied to their families, supported in their quest for independence, or pushed out to fend for themselves.

Divorce can encourage adolescents either to develop appropriate peer relationships or to establish superficial peer relationships in order to escape the family chaos. These choices can affect the establishment of adult characteristics such as self-reliance, identity, social skills, resilience, empathy, and fairness. Peer relationships can also be influential in the development of boundaries, with individuals needing to learn when to respond to others' needs and when to take care of themselves. Generally, adult children of divorce do not know how to set appropriate boundaries. Many teenagers who experienced divorce become lifelong caretakers; others set up walls to keep people at a distance.

Future Family Relationships

Changes occur in the parent–child relationship when an adolescent becomes an adult. Although divorce can result in closer parent–child ties, most families experience a distancing of relationships. Custodial parents probably remain more closely connected to their adult children, whereas noncustodial parents, especially those who remarry, are more likely to disengage from the children of their first marriage. For adolescents, there is less time after a divorce for parents to reestablish a stable family identity; therefore, many young adults focus on establishing their own family rather than on maintaining closeness to their family of origin.

"Although relationships between biological parents and adolescents in stepfamilies improved over time . . . those between stepparents and stepchildren tend to remain more problematic and disengaged" (Henderson & Taylor, 1999, p. 97). Relationships with stepparents may improve when an adolescent moves into adulthood and the issue of parental control and authority is taken out of the equation. Many adults are able to establish a healthy and comfortable relationship with their stepparent. However, most adults with whom I have worked over the years differentiate between a biological parent and a stepparent, and most refer to a stepparent as their biological parent's spouse rather than as their parent, even when the relationship is close. There is also an increased likelihood that, when conflict occurs between adult children and their families of origin, they will blame the conflict on the stepparent. On the other hand, relationships with stepparents can be instrumental in helping an adult develop the ability to make new and close connections, accept change and diversity, and in many cases, see that healthy and happy marriages do exist.

Another long-term consequence of divorce is the change it creates in sibling relationships. This can be particularly difficult when siblings end up living with different families or when stepsiblings are brought into the situation.

Martha was 51 years old and divorced; her parents divorced when she was 12. Martha was the middle child of five. Initially, she lived with her mother; her father moved out of state and married within one year of the divorce. As Martha entered adolescence and began to experience normal conflict with her mother, she was sent to live with her father and his new wife. In discussing her adult relationships with her mother and her siblings, she reported often feeling left out and described herself as feeling like a misfit. Despite Martha's effort to maintain a connection with her mother and siblings, she felt that she had never been able to be fully integrated into that side of the family. The sadness that Martha felt about the situation was clearly evident as she talked about it. Martha also struggled with feeling that she did not quite fit in at work and in many social environments.

Academics and Career

Another area of impact is academic achievement and career management. Numerous studies have shown that adolescents struggling with their parents' divorce often suffer academically (Buchanan et al., 1996; L. Steinberg, 2002). The degree to which teenagers' grades or interest in school is affected is directly related to the amount of ongoing conflict in the family, parents' ability to pay for college, and the degree to which the custodial parent promotes higher education. During the divorce process, many parents get sidetracked from providing supervision and support for schoolwork. There is also evidence that the high school dropout rate is higher for teens from divorced families than for those from intact families (Nicholson et al., 1999; Zill et al., 1993). Some of this effect can be related to stress from family conflict, the changing economic status of the custodial parent, and a greater pressure to move out of the family and become independent.

The good news is that most of these adolescents eventually refocus on their studies, and many establish successful careers. Although the academic and vocational aspects of one's life are connected to the quality of early life experiences, divorce, in and of itself, does not reduce teenagers' chances of becoming productive and successful in their adult lives. In a many cases, the experience provides teenagers with the life skills to persevere in their goals and become successful. These life skills include resilience, flexibility, adaptability, problem solving, self-reliance, and determination.

Financial Skills

Divorce reduces many teens' economic standing. Many learn that they don't need the latest fashion or the newest electronic device. As adults, they are realistic about their expenses and purchases. They learned from the divorce how to manage money, save for the future, and differentiate between needs and wants. Other teens, including those whose parents used money and presents to assuage their guilt (this can be a greater temptation for noncustodial parents), may develop an unrealistic sense of entitlement. "Disneyland dads" may leave their kids with the impression that they should be able to have a vacation or other special treat whenever they want. One father I worked with offered his 15-year-old daughter a $500 a month allowance above and beyond the child support he was paying to her mother.

Positive Long-Term Outcomes

Despite the number of negative outcomes that divorce can create, some adolescents experience healthy outcomes. Teenagers may learn to evaluate relationships in a more mature and realistic manner, so that their choice of partners is healthier and more stable than that of their parents. Many delay getting married until after they have established themselves as responsible adults. Some teens' parents handle their divorce with dignity and grace and later move on to establish a healthy independent life for themselves and their children. These teens learn the value of self-care and how to handle difficult situations while maintaining one's self-respect. Another possible positive outcome is that these teenagers are more likely to view divorce as an acceptable solution to an unhappy situation.

Some positive emotional characteristics can be linked to teens' experiences of their parents' divorce—such as the ability to take care of themselves, assume responsibility, handle transitions, make the best of difficult situations, and find strength and happiness in the midst of turmoil.

Summary

Adolescents whose parents divorce experience life-altering events while they are becoming adults. Adolescence is the time to clarify and stabilize an identity, perfect social skills, acquire relationship skills, and make career choices. Because of this, it is hard to imagine that many adolescents experience the divorce of their parents neutrally. Research has produced conflicting results but has established some basic realities about the impact of divorce on adolescents. Divorce, in and of itself, does not appear to have a significant long-term impact, but it does have some notable short-term effects. Studies have found specific factors in the divorce process that affect adolescents, including interparental conflict, remarriage of one or both parents, economic changes, and the continued involvement of the noncustodial parent (Chase-Lansdale, Cherlin, & Kiernan, 1995; Peris & Emery, 2004; Ruschena, Prior, Sanson, & Smart, 2005). A teenager's temperament, personal strengths and weaknesses, intellectual capacity, and life opportunities play a large role in how divorce affects him or her.

Parents influence this outcome by their behavior during the divorce process. Ongoing interparental conflict, parental reactions, and changes in parenting style have the most effect on adolescents during these critical developmental years. A four-year study with over 500 adolescents found that how parents handle their parental responsibilities affects how the teen will handle the divorce:

> Our data suggest that, after divorce, when parents' rules and expectations for the child are inconsistent, this can generate conflict between the residential parent and child as well as loyalty conflicts. Parent–child conflict and loyalty conflicts are particularly likely, in turn, to be associated with depression in the adolescent. . . . Furthermore, inconsistent parenting . . . is linked to higher levels of antisocial deviant behavior on the part of the adolescent. . . . It appears that adolescents do have difficulty—particularly emotional difficulty—when parents do not establish consistent routines and styles of control in the two postdivorce homes. (Buchanan et al., 1996, p. 272)

The adolescent journey is a difficult one and disruption in the family exacerbates the issues that can arise between parent and child. For adults, divorce and remarriage can take the focus away from the teen's needs and create additional stress for everyone. Parents who stay attuned to their teens' feelings and reactions will ultimately make the transition easier for themselves and their children.

CHAPTER NINE

Physical Illness, Psychiatric Disorders, and Substance Abuse

If teenagers live with healthy habits, they learn to be kind to their bodies.

—Dorothy Nolte and Rachel Harris,
Teenagers Learn What They Live

Case Example

Kristin was 38 years old and married. She came into treatment to deal with issues related to her family of origin. She had been married for seven years and had no children. She worked as a marketing specialist, and her husband was in software development. The couple's families lived out of state, limiting their family contact. Kristin had a history of depression and alcoholism. She was in Alcoholics Anonymous and had been sober for over 10 years. She was on medication for depression.

Kristen's parents divorced when she was 12. She had one sister, two years younger, and a brother, three years older. Reportedly, her parents had a very contentious relationship, and her father departed abruptly after a particularly heated argument. Kristen's father remarried six months after the divorce to a woman from his office. After his remarriage, he saw his children only sporadically. That marriage ended four years later. After her parents' divorce, Kristin reported, her father became intensely religious, and in his later years he spent a lot of time quoting the Bible and preaching. Kristen did not realize at the time that her father was suffering from undiagnosed schizophrenia. Eventually, she had to limit her contact with her father because of his religious obsession.

Kristen's mother was extremely bitter about the divorce; during Kristen's adolescence, her mother started drinking regularly. By the time Kristen was 15, her mother was an active alcoholic and often unavailable for Kristen and her siblings. Kristen's mother was prone to rages while intoxicated, and her anger was often directed at Kristen.

Kristen admitted that she did not handle her parent's divorce and her mother's alcoholism very well. At 15, she started drinking alcohol and smoking marijuana. Seeking the attention and comfort of others, she became sexually active at an early age. In retrospect, Kristen realized that she was also suffering from depression during those years. As a young adult, Kristen continued to struggle with alcoholism and was involved in a series of unfulfilling and unhealthy intimate relationships. In her late 20s, she sought help, joined Alcoholics Anonymous (AA), and became sober. She met her current husband in AA. Both she and her husband had difficulty with issues of trust and insecurity, but with insight and therapy, including couples therapy, they forged a good relationship.

At times, Kristen still struggled with depression, but she sought therapy as needed. She was still actively involved in AA. Her mother continued to drink, and Kristen pulled back from that relationship after she realized that her mother was not likely to get sober. Her father died recently after a brief illness. Kristen was aware that many of her difficulties came from the fact that her adolescent years were spent dealing with her parents' issues and that many of her reactions only exacerbated her own emotional problems. She was working on being able to let many of these family issues go and build a healthy life with her husband.

Situations arise during the course of one's life that will have a significant effect on the family. The previous chapter discussed the effect of divorce on family functioning and adolescent development. This chapter explores how physical illness, psychiatric disorders, and substance abuse affect parenting behaviors, teen reactions, and long-term development. Physical illnesses include cancer, HIV/AIDS, and chronic pain. Psychiatric disorders include bipolar disorder, depression, personality disorders, and schizophrenia. Substance abuse includes alcoholism, drug abuse, and misuse of prescription medications.

Physical Illness

A number of physical illnesses can significantly affect the family. Cancer is a particularly devastating diagnosis for families. Many cancers are treatable, but the diagnosis and the effects of the treatment are felt by all members of the family. Cancer can be a long and difficult illness and, in some cases, terminal. HIV/AIDS can also result in a protracted and debilitating illness and premature death. The diagnosis of HIV can create fear within the family. Heart disease, Parkinson's disease, and multiple sclerosis can also result in changes within the family. An illness that results in a parent being unavailable or creates the possibility of loss can produce considerable anxiety in the family system. Other medical conditions that involve chronic or recurring pain or discomfort—such as arthritis, migraines, and chronic fatigue—can also alter parenting style and affect the tasks of adolescence.

Cancer

When cancer is diagnosed, the first reaction of most family members is fear. The diagnosis of cancer usually requires a number of doctor's appointments and invasive tests to establish the diagnosis, severity, prognosis, and treatment plan. From the moment a family knows that cancer is suspected, family members redirect their focus to the affected individual. When it is the mother or primary caretaker who is diagnosed, there is a major shift in the family functioning. The ill parent may turn his or her attention away from parenting responsibilities and become more self-aware and focused on self-preservation. Many parents struggle to maintain as normal a family life as possible, but treating cancer takes time and energy.

HIV/AIDS

HIV/AIDS is a devastating diagnosis for parents and their children. Besides the fear that the diagnosis evokes, there is also the issue of the method of transmission. AIDS can be transmitted through intravenous drug use, sexual contact, or other forms of blood contamination. Parents who have used intravenous drugs or had unprotected sex are likely to feel shame or guilt and remorse that their choices are now affecting their family. Parents who were infected through contaminated blood or other accidental methods deal with a great deal of fear and anger. AIDS is never an easy diagnosis to deal with; it often brings with it a sense of secrecy and shame for the parent and the adolescent.

Chronic Pain

A number of chronic pain conditions can affect parenting style, including migraines, fibromyalgia, rheumatoid arthritis, and back and neck problems. Most of these conditions develop slowly, but when they are in their acute state, they can be debilitating. Chronic pain is physically and emotionally taxing and brings with it the issue of pain control, which for many means the use of strong painkillers. Persistent and debilitating pain can result in a parent's inability to fulfill parenting responsibilities. Increased irritability can exacerbate conflict between parent and adolescent. Many chronic pain conditions are not life-threatening, nor are they easy to see, which makes them less likely to evoke fear or sympathy on the part of the sufferer's spouse or children. As the condition worsens, family functioning deteriorates further.

Effect on Parenting Style

When a parent is diagnosed with a serious medical condition, the normal functioning of the family is usually altered. Household routines, responsibilities, and priorities may change. There may be new financial problems. Most importantly, the parent may become less available, physically and emotionally. In most families, the impact is more dramatic when it is the mother who has been diagnosed, as mothers are often the primary caretakers and responsible for coordinating family schedules. Cancer's effect on parenting has probably been studied the most, but other studies have addressed changes in parenting style brought about by HIV/AIDS and chronic migraines (Azizi, 2009; Fagan, 2003; Osborn, 2007; Visser et al., 2007). Research has shown that the levels of stress in the family increase during parental illness.

When a parent becomes ill, it is not unusual for adolescents to be expected to help more with housework and care of younger siblings or even to help care for the parent. Cancer patients spend a lot of time at doctor's appointments and in treatment, and their resultant fatigue and physical discomfort often necessitates these changes. Many may find their parenting style shifting to "Not Now, I'm Busy"—or more accurately, "Not Now, I'm Sick." Adolescents can experience a form of parentification, in which they assume the primary caretaking role for the parent and household, either out of necessity or because they want to help.

A parent who is ill may also become focused on his or her own life, having the sense that there is not much time left to fulfill cherished goals. In this situation, the spouse may choose to participate in activities with the ill parent or assume a larger role in the parenting department. When there is an older adolescent in the home, many of these parents will assume that the adolescent has the necessary abilities to take on more of their own self-care.

Time-consuming and physically draining treatments for cancer and other serious illnesses can lead to increased irritability. Teenagers, experiencing their own stress, can become more prickly and demanding at the same time. Some parents may find raising an adolescent too much of a drain on them and disengage. This disengagement can be related to the physical demands of the illness or to the difficulties associated with parenting a teenager.

Marilyn was a 48-year-old married mother of two teenage children who had recently been diagnosed with ovarian cancer. The prognosis was poor, and the expectation was that Marilyn had less than two years to live. Initially, the family focused on caring for Marilyn as she underwent chemotherapy. Six weeks after chemotherapy ended, tests showed that the cancer had returned. In reaction to the news, Marilyn and her husband decided to take an extended European cruise, leaving the two teenagers in the care of their paternal grandparents. Both teenagers felt abandoned by their parents, and their behavior and schoolwork reflected their emotional turmoil. Their mother's departure also made it very difficult for the teenagers to deal with their grief over her anticipated death.

Other parents who become seriously ill begin to focus less on the responsibilities of parenting and more on having a connection with and enjoying their teen. Parents may have a hard time saying no to their teen and may begin to allow behaviors they previously disapproved. For these parents, becoming "cool" feels like an easier and more enjoyable way to relate to their teen. "Life is short, let's have fun" becomes their philosophy.

Despite the strain of chronic and serious illnesses, many parents strive to maintain as normal a life as possible for their teenagers:

In spite of the difficulties, they were striving to be good parents. Positive aspects of illness reported were a shift of priorities and change of values that often brought family members closer together. The parents would face the challenges of illness by making the best of it, putting the needs of the children in focus and trying to maintain normal family life. The overall aim of parenting would be to protect the children and make the illness situation as secure and normal as possible for them. (Helseth & Ulfsæt, 2005, p. 38)

Adolescent Reactions and Long-Term Effects

Teenagers struggle emotionally when a parent is diagnosed with a chronic and debilitating illness. When the diagnosis is life-threatening, the first reaction of most teenagers is fear and uncertainty. Teenagers are old enough to know and understand their parent's illness, and most want to be given sufficient information about the illness to allow them to participate in the experience. Teenagers live in a world of instant information, and many immediately seek out information about the diagnosis. However, information available on the Internet is often incomplete, confusing, and frightening. The most complete and realistic information about the parent's situation comes from the parent's treatment team. Teenagers may want to be present during the parent's medical appointments. Whatever decision is made about how to share medical information with teenagers, it is important that they be given enough information to allow them to be aware of what is happening with their parent. Secrets make teenagers increasingly anxious, and they may make false assumptions about possible outcomes of illness. Even conditions such as chronic migraines can be frightening for a teenager, especially a younger teenager, who does not completely understand the parent's symptoms.

Research has shown that most difficulties experienced by adolescents with a parent who is seriously ill are less a function of the actual diagnosis and more a function of the family environment; poor communication; and the parent's own anxiety, depression, and coping style (Azizi, 2009; Hall & Webster, 2007; Osborn, 2007). Support and open communication with a healthy parent have been found to be positively related to adolescent well-being.

REACTIONS AT DIFFERENT AGES. Younger adolescents may have a harder time dealing with a parent's serious medical condition because they still depend a great deal on family for validation and security. Younger teens also need more active involvement from parents, even if it consists only of transportation to various activities. These teens may regress and become more immature and needy. Other teens' fear and confusion about the diagnosis may create a need to push away from the family. Increased rebellion may be disguised fear and anger about the parent's illness.

Older teenagers (ages 16 to 19) may be able to handle the diagnosis in a more mature and realistic manner. These teens have established a strong enough sense of identity and resilience to cope with the changes in the family. This is not to imply that they won't be devastated by the diagnosis, but their method of handling it may be more mature. Most older teens want and expect to actively participate in decision making and treatment. They are also the most likely to assume adult responsibilities around the house and a caretaking role for the ill parent.

DENIAL. Denial is possible when a teen is unable to accept the severity of a parent's illness. When the relationship between parent and adolescent was stressful to begin with, the teen's reaction to the diagnosis may be more intense and problematic. Denial, followed by avoidance of the family and refusal to participate in the parent's treatment, may appear uncaring. In reality, some teens simply do not have the emotional strength to deal with such a devastating possibility as the death of their parent.

Sasha was an 18-year-old who recently graduated from high school and lived at home with her parents. She came into treatment at the insistence of her mother, who had been diagnosed with lung cancer six months earlier. Sasha and her mother's relationship had been quite conflicted. Sasha was working part-time and attending a local community college. She stayed out late and had become heavily involved in alcohol and drug use.

Sasha refused to discuss her mother's illness and had not participated in any of her mother's medical appointments. When pushed to discuss her mother's illness, she insisted that her mother would be okay and that she didn't need to worry about her. Sasha's mother had made efforts to connect with her daughter but reported that Sasha avoided her. The mother was terrified that she would die without having resolved the issues between herself and her daughter.

Sasha worked in therapy on issues related to interpersonal relationships and future plans but steadfastly refused to discuss her mother. After three months, she stopped therapy. Nine months later, her mother died. Sasha called to let the therapist know of her mother's passing but denied needing to talk about it. Two months later, she called for an appointment.

ASSUMING RESPONSIBILITIES. Parentification (assuming adult caretaking responsibilities) is a common occurrence in many homes in which a parent is physically or emotionally unable to perform household tasks and parenting. Teens who are given new responsibilities may have mixed feelings, including resentment. A study on the impact of parentification on children whose parents had HIV/AIDS found that parentifcation led to increased emotional distress, behavioral problems and substance use (Stein, Riedel, & Rotheram-Borus, 1999). Resentment and other negative responses are more likely when the parent's condition is chronic but not life-threatening or when the teen believes that the parent is capable of doing more but is using the illness as an excuse to avoid responsibility. Other teens may find comfort in having something they can contribute to the household. These responsibilities can result in teenagers growing up faster and developing a sense of confidence and self-worth when they are able to contribute so significantly to their family.

The researchers followed up with the same adolescents six years later and found no observable negative long-term outcome of the parentification. Instead, many of these young adults exhibited better coping skills, more resilience, and less drug and alcohol abuse than their peers (Stein, Rotheram-Borus, & Lester, 2007).

EMOTIONAL RESPONSES. It is inconceivable that a teenage will not experience many emotional reactions to a parent's serious medical illness. The responses will vary depending on the type of diagnosis, the teenager's temperament, and the quality of the parent–teen relationship. Several studies have explored the psychological impact of parental cancer on adolescents. Osborn (2007) reviewed a number of these studies and concluded that adolescents, especially daughters, are at a slightly increased risk for stress reactions, anxiety, and depression but that there was no strong evidence linking behavioral problems in adolescence to a parent's illness. There was also no evidence that social competence was negatively affected by a parent's diagnosis; in some instances, these adolescents had better levels of social competence. It may be that teenagers with a seriously ill parent develop an increased awareness of others' needs and are less likely to be caught up in the more petty issues of the teen world. No matter how well the adolescent handles the situation, there is a need for teens to have a strong support system during a parent's illness. Many may benefit from counseling.

REACTION TO A PARENT'S CHRONIC PAIN SYNDROME. Chronic pain or other non–life-threatening illnesses can also cause changes or difficulties in a family's functioning:

> Studies suggest that migraine may be related to family disharmony, instability and conflict. . . . [Children of] parents with chronic physical pain received higher scores on a measure of delinquency, exhibited poor general adjustment, and had poorer social skills than children of parents with no pain. . . . Results showed that adolescents of parents with depression or arthritis reported lower self-esteem and fewer school activities than adolescents of parents who were not ill. (Fagan, 2003, p. 1044)

Chronic pain may result in more problematic adolescent emotional reactions and behaviors in that the parent is physically and emotionally available only part of the time. Illnesses that are not life-threatening, especially if they do not have obvious physical symptoms, are less likely to generate concern and sympathy from the teenager. Teens may find themselves angry that their parent is unable to carry out many normal parenting tasks. Parental abdication of some of the household and caretaker responsibilities is common in these homes.

Not all teenagers react in the same way to a parent's chronic physical pain. Many react with concern and compassion and willingly step in to help when the parent is not feeling well. In healthy, functioning families, there is open communication about a parent's physical problems and the parent strives to limit the problems' impact on the adolescent.

Julie was 15. Her mother had been diagnosed with fibromyalgia and was overweight. The mother brought Julie in for therapy, saying that she was uncooperative and disrespectful. Julie complained that her mother sat in her recliner, screaming orders at her to take care of household chores. Mother was also often unable or unwilling to drive Julie to peer social functions.

Julie believed that her mother used her diagnosis to avoid her household responsibilities and was resentful that her mother expected her to take over these tasks. Julie's father agreed that his wife tended to scream too much but didn't want to fight with her over these issues. In therapy, Julie learned how to better deal with her mother and not to take her mother's negative statements personally.

REACTION TO A PARENT'S DEATH. Loss of a parent following a terminal illness can be devastating. I have worked with many adults who still struggled with the loss of a parent during their teen years. Research with adolescents whose parents died from cancer found that these teens "exhibited symptoms of depression and associated psychological problems including anxiety, behavior problems, decreased social competence, and lower self-esteem" (Pfeffer, Karus, Siegal, & Jiang, 2000, p. 1). However, this study found that most children did not report depression levels greater than those found in the general population. The authors surmised that their study may have not been able to adequately account for some of the important factors related to grief over the loss of a parent. They acknowledged that the impact of this loss may have been more covert and subtle than the emotions and behaviors assessed by their study.

Loss of a parent to cancer or other illness can have devastating long-term effects, but what my experience has shown is that the outcome is highly dependent on a number of different factors. The way adolescents faced with a parent's terminal illness react often depends on their particular family environment. Teenagers who, prior to the illness, had a stable, high-functioning, and close-knit family may exhibit more problematic reactions, as the illness is such a monumental change. Teens who have more experience adjusting to chaotic family environments may be better able to cope with the changes, whereas dysfunctional families may result in more unhealthy responses. All families must find a way to address the issues that the illness and subsequent death brings about.

Psychiatric Disorders

Adolescence is an emotionally challenging period for teens and parents. Parenting style is associated with a parent's emotional and intellectual functioning. Parenting well is an emotional and intellectual challenge. Psychiatric disorder, by its nature, has a significant impact on an individual's emotional state. Many psychiatric disorders can interfere with a parent's ability to assess a teen's behavior and react appropriately.

Families that experience brief and situational emotional difficulties, such as grief over a lost family member, usually process this experience in a healthy way and restabilize within a short time. A greater long-term challenge is faced by families in which one or both parents have a chronic psychiatric disorder. According to the Substance Abuse and Mental Health Services Administration, in 2009 an estimated 11 million adults had a serious mental illness, and the majority of them were women. Of these, 65 percent of the women and 52 percent of the men are parents (National Survey on Drug Use and Health, 2009). Further, children of parents with psychiatric disorders are at risk for the development of emotional and behavioral problems. The extent of the unhealthy or harmful responses to a parent's diagnosis depends on a number of factors including the parent's severity of illness, the impact on parenting style, and the teen's internal resources.

Depression and Bipolar Disorder

The majority of psychiatric disorders in the United States today are affective disorders, meaning that the major area of impact is on the emotional functioning of the individual. One of the most common and well-known psychiatric disorders in the United States is major depressive disorder. Although it is possible for an individual to experience a single depressive period, most people who suffer from depression experience recurrent episodes. It is often difficult to predict or prevent depressive episodes, despite recent advances in mental health treatment. The same is true of bipolar disorder, which is characterized by both depressive and manic episodes. Although much is now known about these illnesses and their symptoms, and medication to treat them has become much more effective, they often go undiagnosed. This means that many families experience their impact without a clear understanding of the underlying forces, and many parents don't receive the treatment that could help them.

Depression is probably the most well-studied psychiatric disorder in terms of its effect on parents and subsequently on their children. Parents suffering from depression have a difficult time maintaining consistent parenting practices. They may be either too controlling or too uninvolved. They often lack the emotional and physical energy to deal with the needs and expectations of adolescents.

Prior to the development of SSRIs (selective serotonin reuptake inhibitors), many children grew up with memories of depressed parents isolating themselves in their rooms for days on end. Even today, depression can go untreated, and most depressed parents tend to be lax in monitoring, disciplining, and supporting their teens. Few have the energy to engage in an argument with a determined teenager, so they simply give in to requests and demands. They are also often emotionally unavailable as most of their personal resources are focused on dealing with their own issues. They are less likely to be willing to listen to the small details and drama of the adolescent's life or deal with complicated homework assignments. Thus, depressed parents may adopt the Not Now, I'm Busy style—not by choice, but by lack of physical and emotional capacity.

Depression often causes impatience and irritability. Many depressed parents end up functioning in an "I can't deal with this right now" parenting style. They have difficulty with compromise and often lack the ability to problem solve with their teens. They may adopt a My House, My Rules style, even if they enforce the rules inconsistently, because it gives them some sense of control over their lives. These parents can also easily become "screamers"—with little patience and few resources, they erupt over minor incidents or issues and respond to their teens with yelling and even verbal abuse. They may take difficult adolescent behavior personally. Negative thinking and feelings of hopelessness and helplessness are characteristic of depression.

Parents with depression also often have marital difficulties, and many parents with depression are divorced—an additional challenge to their ability to function in a consistent and healthy manner.

A recent review of the literature related to parental mental health issues found that parents with depression are less likely to be emotionally available and affectionate and are often less sensitive and competent as parents. Researchers found that mothers with depression were often disorganized, anxious, unhappy, and inconsistent (Mayberry & Reupert, 2009). Although most studies have focused on the effect of depression on mothers' parenting abilities, research also indicates that fathers' depression has similar effects on adolescent behavior and outcome.

Jerome was a 15-year-old who lived with his mother. He was referred by his school counselor for truancy and poor school performance. His parents were divorced, and he had little contact with his father, who lived out of state. Jerome's mother had been diagnosed with bipolar disorder, with depression predominant. She worked evenings as a waitress and made little effort to monitor Jerome's activities. When he was called in for a truancy hearing, she failed to accompany him. Despite his mother's inconsistent parenting, Jerome was quick to defend her and blamed her inadequacies on her job and emotional problems.

Personality Disorders

Personality disorders are a category of psychological disturbance featuring enduring and personality-specific characteristics that usually include significant distortion in interpersonal relationships, perception, self-awareness, and personal motivation. They include borderline personality disorder, narcissistic personality disorder, and antisocial personality disorder, all of which can significantly affect parenting. Personality disorders probably create the most distorted types of parenting, as parents with these problems find it hard to focus on or relate to the needs and well-being of their children. Parents with personality disorders are often inconsistent in their parenting and may be overly involved and enmeshed or withdrawn and neglectful.

Parenting practices often have more to do with the parent's current emotional state than with the teen's behavior. Johnson, Cohen, Kasen, and Brook (2006) found that mothers with personality disorders often engage in a number of significant and problematic childrearing behaviors, including inconsistent rule enforcement, poor supervision, low educational aspirations, possessiveness, excessive use of guilt, poor communication skills, verbal abuse, and harsh punishment.

Parents with a personality disorder are more likely to struggle with a teen's quest for independence. In *Stop Walking on Eggshells*, Mason and Kreger (1998) asserted that parents with borderline personality

> may feel threatened by children's normal behavior. As children grow and become more independent, the BP [borderline personality parent] may feel abandoned and become depressed and may rage at the children. The BP may also unconsciously try to increase their children's dependence on them. Children thus may have a hard time separating from the parent or feel competent at handling their own life. When children become angry themselves, the BP may take it personally and rage back, escalating the situation. (p. 181)

Parentification (saddling a child with adult responsibilities) and parental alienation (turning the child against the other parent) are often associated with parents who have a personality disorder. These parents have a strong need for control of and acceptance by the child. They interact with their children in ways that meet their own needs rather than their children's. During divorce, this need, coupled with anger toward and rejection of the spouse, can lead to parental alienation. These parents need their adolescents to play a consistent role in their life script, and efforts by adolescents to become more independent are often met with anger. They see any effort by the child to maintain a close relationship with the other parent as a betrayal, and they send the message "if you're not with me, you're against me."

Schizophrenia

Schizophrenia is a serious psychiatric disorder in which the individual experiences distortions of reality, including hallucinations, delusions, and dissociation. Although it can often be controlled by medication and therapy, it is never cured, and patients are prone to relapse. The primary concern for these parents is to be able to effectively separate their schizophrenic symptoms from their interactions with and perceptions of their child. Schizophrenic parents are often withdrawn, passive, and unsure of themselves. During a delusional phase, they may include their teen in their delusions or hallucinations.

Schizophrenic parents are often emotionally unavailable and have difficulty engaging in everyday parenting activities. They may be unable to provide consistent and clear emotional messages; they may also misinterpret their teen's emotional cues. Schizophrenic parents are rarely able to provide consistent structure, supervision, and emotional support. They often care deeply for their children and desire to be good parents, but the unpredictability and severity of their illness often makes this difficult for them.

Adolescent Reactions

Adolescents exhibit a wide range of emotional and behavioral reactions to a parent's psychiatric condition. Teens are often aware that their parent is struggling and seek out information to help them with their understanding. Other teens, unaware that a parent has a psychiatric disturbance, may be frightened or confused by the parent's behavior. They are often unable to distinguish when the parent's response is simple parenting and when it is influenced by the parent's illness. Home may feel like an emotional minefield; teens' reactions can be as erratic as their parents' behavior. A teen's reactions can depend on the parent's psychiatric illness, the parent's behavior, the teen's emotional state, and the issue at hand.

KEEPING FAMILY SECRETS. Depression and other disorders do not carry the same stigma that they once did. Information available on the Internet, media coverage, commercials for antidepressants and other medications, and other sources of information give adolescents substantial information about psychiatric disorders. Although teenagers are cognitively and emotionally able to understand mental health issues this does not necessarily protect them from feeling confused and ashamed of their parent's behavior, especially when it is particularly erratic.

Most teenagers are likely to keep information about a parent's emotional problems within the family, sharing very little with friends. This need to maintain the family's privacy often prevents teens from inviting their friends to their homes. Teens may also be concerned that they might inherit their parent's emotional condition or that their friends will begin to see them as similar to their parents. The need for secrecy can prevent the teen from reaching out to friends and other adults who could provide a support system for them. This may also limit teens' ability to develop appropriate strategies for coping with their parent's illness.

COGNITIVE DISTORTIONS. Achieving separation, individuation, and autonomy are key tasks of adolescence. Despite their increasing dependence on peers, adolescents are still very aware of and influenced by their parents. Of particular importance is the impact that the parent's thinking style has on the teen's own developing perceptions and thought processes. Psychiatric disorders cause distortions in thinking, perception, and attitudes. Schizophrenic parents may have difficulty with reality; depressed parents are often negative and pessimistic; anxious parents are worriers and fatalists. Even if teens appear not to be listening, they are absorbing their parents' view of life. Parent's negative thoughts may make it more likely that teens will be negative about the present and have a harder time feeling hopeful and positive about the future. It is also difficult for teens not to incorporate their parent's distorted perceptions of them into their sense of their own identity. This is particularly true for teenagers of personality disordered parents whose perception of their child is influenced by their own psychological issues rather than the reality of who their teen is.

TAKING ON RESPONSIBILITIES. Added responsibility for younger siblings, the household, and even the parent is common among teens with a mentally ill parent. These responsibilities may be adopted by the teenager out of a belief that it is necessary for the functioning of the family. Some teenagers may become overly invested in taking care of their parent at the expense of their own developmental tasks. Other teenagers may not be given a choice; the additional responsibilities are simply required of them. Some teens may become angry and resentful about these additional responsibilities, especially when they do not fully comprehend the need. Others may use the opportunity to develop more positive characteristics, such as resilience, maturity, and a sense of purpose.

WITHDRAWAL. Some teens have a difficult time understanding and coping when a parent has a psychiatric disorder. They may be confused or frightened by the parent's behavior, especially if the parent threatens or attempts suicide. The parent may require hospitalization and thus be unavailable for periods of time. When teens are overwhelmed by the situation at home, one option for coping that they may choose is withdrawal. This can take many forms; some teens isolate themselves in their rooms, avoiding contact with family members and friends; some avoid the house as much as they can, preferring to spend time with friends. Other teens may simply shut down emotionally, numbing their feelings about what is going on with their parent. However, these reactions do not help them to develop appropriate coping skills.

Leanne was a 48-year-old single mother with one daughter, Misty, 18. Leanne had a history of schizoaffective disorder. Leanne divorced Misty's father when Misty was three; after that, he had only infrequent contact with Misty. Over the years, Leanne had been hospitalized several times for her psychiatric problems. However, she had become more stable in the last few years and had not required hospitalization since Misty was a freshman in high school.

For many years, Misty had been very close to and protective of Leanne. However, beginning in Misty's senior year, their mother–daughter relationship became increasingly contentious. Misty became angry and hateful, avoiding her mother by staying in her room or staying away from the house with friends. Leanne struggled to maintain a connection with Misty and hold onto the parent role.

Misty also showed signs of depression but refused to see a therapist. It was clear that the normal adolescent separation experience was particularly difficult for both of them. Misty had been her mother's companion and protector for many years, and neither of them was prepared for the changes that high school graduation would entail.

ANGER AND RESENTMENT. Anger, frustration, and resentment are possible reactions to living with a parent with a psychiatric disorder. Although most teenagers understand that their parent is not suffering from a psychiatric disorder by choice, they may view their parent's condition as a personal weakness. Teens are aware that treatments are available for emotional problems, and they may feel resentment when they believe that the parent is not trying hard enough to get better. A parent's failure to take prescribed medication or follow through on therapy appointments can create frustration for the teen. Parent behaviors that interfere with the everyday functioning of the adolescent, such as allowing their participation in school and peer activities or driving them to a social event, can also cause anger and resentment. These teens still also experience the normal angry reactions to parental decisions and actions that come with adolescence.

BEHAVIORAL REACTIONS. Even though teenagers have a growing capacity for cognitive awareness and emotional insight, they often act out their feelings. Behavioral reactions to a parent's emotional condition include becoming more oppositional, increased conflict with parents, academic problems, increased aggression, and drug and alcohol use. Experimentation with alcohol and drugs may be an attempt on the part of the adolescent to find some relief from the stress at home. The home environment may not be conducive to academic accomplishment. Worry about their parent may make it difficult to focus on school.

Parenting behavior that is distorted by a psychiatric disorder can provoke parent–teen conflict and extreme acting out. In some cases, the teen's rebellious behavior is an effort to provoke the parent into paying attention to them and reassuming important parental functions. Teens may also act out as a way of separating themselves from their parents. When a parent is overly dependent on a teen or struggling with allowing the teen to individuate, that teen may react by separating in a more intense and oppositional manner.

EMOTIONAL REACTIONS. Adolescents with a parent with a chronic emotional disturbance are more likely to develop emotional disorders themselves. "Young people growing up with parents dealing with emotional problems are at a greater risk of having behavioral/emotional problems themselves due to genetic factors and harmful psychosocial experiences" (Sherman, 2007, p. 27). Sherman identified a number of studies showing that these youths are at risk for depression, anxiety, developmental delays, and behavioral problems.

Many studies have found that teenagers, girls in particular, are likely to react to the family situation by internalizing the stress, which can result in anxiety, depression, insecurity, and poor self-esteem (Rutter, 1990; Timko et al., 2008; Weissman, Warner, Wickramaratne, Moreau, & Olfson, 1997).

Some teens develop an eating disorder, which is an attempt to maintain some control over themselves and their environment. Adolescent daughters of mothers with an eating disorder often develop distorted perceptions of eating, weight, and body image (Park, Senior, & Stein, 2003). A study of suicidal risk in young adults found that individuals whose mothers had major depressive disorder or bipolar disorder were more likely to "report suicidal thoughts and behaviors by adolescence ... [and] were at a higher risk for the more severe forms into a suicidal content" (Klimes-Dougan, Lee, Ronsaville, & Martinez, 2008, p. 538).

Anxiety is another possible response, particularly when the parent's behaviors are confusing, frightening, or unpredictable. Younger adolescents are more likely to struggle with their internal reactions to distressing parental behaviors, whereas older adolescents have more coping skills with which to deal with and understand the parent's disorder.

HEALTHY REACTIONS. Dealing with a parent with a psychiatric disorder may provide adolescents with a unique opportunity to develop some positive and healthy traits. In the face of family need, many adolescents respond with concern and maturity. The situation challenges them to develop coping mechanisms that allow them to remain involved with their family and at the same time to continue the process of individuation. They develop empathy and learn to consider others' needs as well as their own. In *When a Parent Is Depressed*, Beardslee (2002) discussed the characteristics of resilient children in families with depression. He reported that they are realistic about the situation, develop strategies to offset the effects of their parent's illness, and believe that they can make a difference.

Teens, with their cognitive abilities and awareness of the power of emotions, are often able to separate themselves from their parent's illness. In studying children's reactions to living with a mentally ill parent, Mordoch and Hall (2008) found that teens are capable of taking care of themselves while staying connected to their parents. In describing the activities undertaken by these teens, the authors reported that healthy responses "included conserving energy, gaining respite from the illness, providing self affirmation, developing identities, increasing connections with others, finding solutions to problems and space, exerting control, [and] seeking opportunities for developing and managing emotions" (Mordoch & Hall, 2008, p. 1136). High-functioning teens are able to focus on their schoolwork, interact with peers, have fun, and move forward with their lives while maintaining closeness to their families.

Short- and Long-Term Outcomes

Research has indicated that adolescents who live with a mentally ill parent experience more emotional and behavioral difficulties and that these problems extend into adulthood (Goodman & Gotlib,1999; Jaser et al., 2005; Mowbray & Mowbray, 2006). The severity of the issues carried into adulthood depend on a number of factors, including the severity of the parental illness, the presence of a healthy parent in the home, the coping skills used by the adolescent, and the social support system available to the family and the adolescent. In reporting on a number of outcome studies, Mowbray and Mowbray (2006) stated that research on adult children of parents with mental illness shows increased mental disturbances, lower self-esteem, less social support, more alcohol consumption, less social adjustment, more social avoidance, and more anxiety, somatization, and depression symptoms. . . . Studies have also examined non-mental health outcomes and found negative effects. . . . Offspring of depressed parents had lower scores on social adjustment (for work, family, marital, and overall functioning), fewer children and are less likely to seek mental health treatment, even when they felt they needed it. (p. 131)

The degree to which individuals experience these difficulties depends on the factors previously discussed, including individual abilities and family environment. Adults whose parents were the most severely disturbed, and those whose parents continually involved their teenager in their emotional problems, are more likely to have a difficult long-term adjustment.

Substance Abuse

Data from the federal Substance Abuse and Mental Health Services Administration for 2002 to 2007 indicated that more than 8.3 million children (age 18 or younger) lived with at least one parent who was alcoholic or engaged in some form of substance abuse. Almost 7.3 million had an alcoholic parent, and 2.1 million had a parent who was dependent on illicit drugs. There is a slightly higher rate of substance abuse among fathers than among mothers (National Survey on Drug Use and Health, 2009).

Alcoholism is a widespread problem that significantly affects family functioning. Alcoholics may drink beer, wine, or hard liquor. They may drink daily, only at night, only on weekends, or in binges. Alcoholism creates emotional and behavioral changes. Since the early 1960s, attention has been given to the long-term impact of alcoholism on a person's development. The challenges facing adult children of alcoholics have been researched and discussed in professional journals, books, newspapers, and family magazines.

Substance abuse—including regular use of marijuana, narcotics, or prescription pills—will have a significant impact on the family's functioning. The abuse of prescription pills has become increasingly common. Prescription medication addicts often deny that their use is excessive and may also feign or create pain in order to get additional prescriptions. Although there is considerably more information on the effects of alcoholism, the impact of drug abuse is similar and may even be more severe in certain situations. The illegal nature of drug abuse adds to the level of secrecy and places families in jeopardy of becoming involved in the legal system. There is also a greater chance of misuse and even overdose with drug abuse.

Although more information is available on the impact of alcoholism, the effects of alcohol and drug abuse on parenting are similar; the terms "alcoholism" and "substance abuse" are used interchangeably in this chapter. The impact that parental substance abuse has on teenagers and their subsequent development varies depending on the parent, the behavior of the nonusing parent, the severity of the use, the presence of other illnesses, and the effect of the problem on parenting skills. This section examines the impact of substance abuse on parenting style and the adolescent's emotions, behaviors, and long-term consequences.

Effect on Parenting Style

Parenting and substance abuse do not make a good combination. Parenting, especially of adolescents, requires patience, awareness, communication and negotiation skills, and mutual trust and respect. Substance abuse requires secrets and denial. Alcoholics are often focused on having access to alcohol without being judged by family members. A parent may, for example, drink while the children are at school and then hide the bottle or conceal the alcohol in a coffee cup or glass of soda.

Some substance abusers are so addicted that they do not care whether family members are aware of it. Parents may drink openly and keep excessive amounts of alcohol available, whether it's beer in the refrigerator or bottles of scotch on the counter. If questioned by their teens, they are likely to become angry and defensive, claiming that they're just having a drink to relax after a hard day.

Other parents may only drink outside of the home and believe that their drinking will not be noticed by the family—for example, stopping off at the local bar on the way home and then claiming to have worked late. Here's the reality: Alcoholism is rarely a secret. Although younger children may not be fully aware of a parent's alcohol use, teenagers are acutely aware of it. In many households, it is a well-known but unspoken fact.

Healthy parenting and substance abuse do not mix. A study on the parenting practices of narcotics addicts found that

> relationships with their children were characterized by high levels of conflict and by numerous interpersonal issues. . . . Drug abusing parents are not generally willful in their dysfunctional parenting but are overwhelmed by the serious problems related to their addiction and often cannot function responsibly in the parental role. (Nurco, Blatchley, Hanlon, O'Grady, & McCarren, 1998, p. 55)

Addicts and alcoholics are often emotionally immature, have impaired cognitive functioning, struggle to maintain effective control in their home, have low frustration tolerance and low self-esteem, and are often socially isolated. Substance abuse usually results in emotional and cognitive numbing, rendering the parent unavailable, especially while intoxicated or during the hangover phase. Substance abusers are often ineffective parents and poor role models.

Substance abuse is often associated with other psychiatric disorders, including depression, anxiety, and personality disorders. It is also often associated with marital conflict. The sober parent is often focused on protecting and controlling the alcoholic, leaving little time to focus on other family members. Stress and loneliness may make single mothers particularly susceptible to alcoholism.

NEGLECTFUL PARENTING STYLES. Substance abuse is often associated with the more neglectful styles of parenting. Teenagers may find their parents at home but unavailable, and in some cases unconscious. These parents are heavily involved in their addiction and may even resent the time and effort that it takes to parent. They may deny a teen's request simply because it requires too much energy. Lack of confidence in their parenting abilities may lead them to avoid interactions that would reveal their inadequacies. They may be aware of their substance abuse and therefore not trust their own judgment.

CONTROLLING PARENTING STYLES. The My House, My Rules parenting style may also be associated with the abuse of alcohol or drugs. Alcoholic parents have very little patience or time to spend on problem solving or negotiating with teens. For these parents, it is easier to come up with a nonnegotiable rule. Also, teenagers are likely to argue, and substance-abusing parents are often not open-minded or tolerant. Coupled with a decrease in emotional control, this often results in higher levels of conflict between parents and teens and in anger and stronger efforts at control on the part of the parents. A parent may suddenly decide that the teen has crossed an unspoken line and respond harshly, even with physical violence. Often these parents are insecure and overwhelmed by their parental role. In these families, there is little respect between parent and teen.

PERMISSIVE PARENTING STYLES. The Cool parenting style is also often associated with substance abuse. These parents deal with their alcohol or drug dependency by attempting to incorporate it into their relationship with their teenager. They convince themselves that alcohol, marijuana, or other drugs are not that harmful; providing these to their teenagers proves that their use is simply recreational.

Such parents focus less on providing structure, supervision, and boundaries and more on having a superficially close relationship with their teen. This works especially well when the parent wants someone to talk to late at night or needs someone to share their good times. In addition, these parents may use the adolescent as a sounding board for their complaints about their spouse, their job, or other problems. They insist that they have a close relationship with their teen, when they are actually using their teen for their own social and emotional needs.

Alcoholic parents may claim that they are better parents when they are more relaxed after a few drinks. They may go so far as to provide alcohol for their teens' parties, arguing that they are teaching their teens to drink responsibly by allowing them to drink in the home. In reality, they are just reassuring themselves that their own drinking is not inappropriate. In addition, Cool parents may allow their teens to use drugs because confronting them could bring their own use into question. When alcohol or pills are missing, the parent may look the other way.

Deena was a 17-year-old who recently moved in with her father and stepmother after running away from her mother and stepfather. Since she turned 15, Deena had been using a variety of illegal substances, mostly marijuana and alcohol, and this caused numerous conflicts between her and her stepfather, precipitating her move to her father's home. Deena said that her stepfather drank beer daily and that their fights were worse when he was drinking. She said that her father also smoked pot and drank on occasion; since she moved in with her father, her drug and alcohol use had continued but had not escalated. Her father made some effort to curtail her use, but acknowledged that his own use made it hard for him to set too many limits. Deena's schoolwork showed some improvement after she moved in with her father, because there were fewer family arguments. Deena agreed to come to therapy to help her cut back on her drug use, but her attendance was irregular.

Substance Abuse and Other Disorders

Two issues often associated with substance abuse that affect parenting style are the presence of additional psychiatric and medical disorders and the effect of a parent's substance abuse on the nonusing parent and the marital relationship.

Substance abuse often coexists with other illnesses such as depression, anxiety, and personality disorders. It may even be an attempt at self-medicating for the other illness. Medical conditions, especially those involving chronic pain, may also bring about increased substance abuse, which may turn into a bigger problem than the pain. In many cases, the pain syndrome becomes secondary to the drug abuse, and it is not unusual for an individual to feign or even create a pain syndrome to obtain additional medications.

When substance abuse is coupled with a psychiatric disorder, the impact on the family, particularly on parenting ability, is intensified. A recent study of the effect of depression and alcohol dependence on mothers found that the alcohol-dependent and depressed group included mothers "whose attachment was poorer, who were less involved with their children, provided fewer boundaries or guidance, and were more hostile and critical of their children. This environment, therefore, provided less concern and warmth, and greater criticism" (Woodcock & Sheppard, 2002, p. 238). The same authors noted that when mothers are depressed and alcohol dependent, the situation is "particularly pernicious and debilitating." Mothers who suffer with chronic pain and abuse pain medications are more likely to have significant deficits in their parenting ability.

Partner Reaction to Substance Abuse

Substance abuse has a major impact on the relationship between spouses and even ex-spouses. The sober partner may take on one of several roles. The role of enabler is well defined and frequently discussed in the field of alcoholism and substance abuse. Enablers help make it possible for an addict to continue using. They can be spouses, parents, or even the adolescents themselves. They pick up the pieces, smooth out the edges, cover up, and support addicts' denial. Enablers may buy them beer, drive them home, put them to bed, call in sick for them at work when they're actually drunk or hung over, and create cover stories for the children and neighbors. They protect alcoholics and drug abusers from having to face the consequences of their behavior. Being the enabler may be due to codependency or may provide the enabler with some form of secondary gain (an outcome that is desired but not obvious). For example, a spouse may tolerate drinking if it prevents the spouse from requesting sex.

Other spouses may see themselves as victims of their partners' addiction and take on the role of martyr. They are often angry and depressed but feel trapped in the situation. Stay-at-home mothers who are financially dependent on their alcoholic husbands often do not have the resources to leave. Parents who do have the resources to leave may not be willing to give up the lifestyle with which the marriage provides them. Others may come to enjoy the role of martyr and the attention they get because of their difficult situation, and they may not take advantage of opportunities to escape or improve it. But the message they send to their teenagers is that they have to put up with being unhappy and find a way to get a secondary gain from the situation.

Other spouses of substance-abusing parents become angry, resentful, or passive–aggressive, allowing the marriage to become a power struggle in which their awareness of the substance abuse is the ultimate trump card. They may provoke arguments and constantly belittle the substance-abusing parent. They may share their disgust with their extended family, their neighbors, and—in a form of parental alienation—their children. Substance abuse by one parent—and anger, screaming, insults, hostility, shaming, and rejection by the other—can become a vicious circle. Both partners become locked in this dysfunctional relationship, with the children being unwilling players in the game.

Adolescent Reactions

Substance abuse by one or both parents elicits more intense emotional and behavioral responses from adolescents than any other family problem. Teenagers are cognitively and emotionally capable of recognizing and understanding the presence and impact of substance abuse in a parent. The manner in which the teen reacts depends upon the family environment, the behavior of the substance-abusing parent, and the individual personality and temperament of the teen.

PHYSICAL DISORDERS. Adolescents who have a difficult time finding an outlet for the emotional stress they experience in the family may show this distress in physical ways. Physical reactions can include stomachaches, intestinal distress, headaches, or even impairment of the immune system.

KEEPING SECRETS. One of the key features of families with a substance abuse problem is the importance of maintaining the family secret. This prevents teenagers from being able to talk about their situation with friends or other adults. Teens may be embarrassed by their parent's substance abuse, ashamed to bring friends home, and afraid that the parent will behave inappropriately. Keeping family secrets increases teens' isolation. The shame and secrecy can create problems well into adulthood. Many of my adult clients who grew up in alcoholic families eventually find that they need to deal with the anger, shame, and secrecy.

ANGER AND RESENTMENT. Anger and resentment are common and natural reactions to a parent's substance abuse. Adolescents are aware of the damage that drugs and alcohol do to an individual and a family. They have been taught in school that they have a choice about using alcohol and drugs, and they resent the fact that their parents have made the choice to use. Although many adolescents realize that alcoholism is a serious problem, they still believe that their parents should be making the effort to overcome it. Adolescents often are particularly angered when a parent breaks a promise to stop using or lies about his or her use. They also may be angry at the nonaddicted parent for not doing more to change the situation or protect them.

This anger may be expressed in oppositional behavior, disrespect, refusal to cooperate, physical aggression, or verbal aggression such as sarcasm. Teenagers may resort to passive–aggressive actions such as pouring out the alcohol, not passing on important messages or information, doing chores in a half-hearted manner, and withholding affection.

TAKING RESPONSIBILITY. In homes with substance-abusing parents, many adult responsibilities fall on the shoulders of the adolescents—often not because parents demand it but because teens see the need and assume responsibility. They may make dinner, wash the dishes, clean the house, and help with younger siblings. Parents may start a chore but not finish it. Dinner preparation, after several glasses of wine, may suddenly become the responsibility of the teenager.

COGNITIVE DISTORTIONS. The home environment plays a large role in the thought processes and perceptions of different family members. In a home where secrets and denial are common, teenagers may develop a distorted way of thinking. They may fantasize about what their parents would be like sober. They may find reasons to believe that their parents will quit as promised and then develop justifications when they do not. They may make excuses for the parent or adopt the parent's rationalizations, such as "my mom needs the pills, her back hurts" or "my dad needs a drink, he has a stressful job." This thinking may pave the way for the adolescent's own drug or alcohol abuse. Dysfunctional families are not good at problem solving, which can make it difficult for the teen to learn this skill.

Children are rarely aware that activities going on in their family go against the norm until they've had enough experiences outside of the family to make this assessment. Teens have the opportunity to see different family systems but may need to hold onto the belief that their family is normal, even when the family dysfunction is severe. Some of the most distorted thinking comes when the teenager needs to justify the parent's abusive or out-of-control behavior. Teens may blame themselves for the problems or believe it's up to them to help make the parent's life easier. They may also adopt some of the pessimistic and cynical "life is unfair" thinking that substance abusers use to justify their drug or alcohol use. When teenagers begin to think in negative and distorted ways about life, they are more likely to experience unhappiness, dissatisfaction with life, and depression.

EMOTIONAL EXPRESSION AND REACTIONS. The ability to accept and express one's emotions is developed in the family. Families with substance abuse problems may have difficulty acknowledging and expressing feelings. Emotions such as anger, love, affection, fear, frustration, and sadness may be muted or exaggerated, creating discomfort for the teenager. Adolescence is a time when intense emotions about self and others surface, and when the family environment does not provide comfortable, secure, and effective examples of how to handle these emotions, teens have a difficult time dealing with them. They often show

> emotional instability, inability to control emotions, confusion about sexual role, and viewing oneself as being different from others in terms of psycho-pathology and increased depression. The latter is not manifested as a disorder of mood, but as a tendency toward withdrawal and defeatism, as a derogatory attitude to oneself and other people, as well as increased uncertainty and apathy. (Tomori, 1994, p. 951)

Teens in particularly stressful and dysfunctional families suffer from feelings of insecurity and low self-esteem. Because they cannot trust their parents, they often do not trust their own emotions or reactions. They may withdraw from others because they feel different and not good enough. It is particularly difficult for them to attend events when other parents are present and sober and their parent is not. Some teens' family environments are a struggle from which they find no acceptable way out, and so they internalize their feelings in the form of depression or anxiety. Anxiety and depression may also stem from concerns and fears about the parent.

SOCIAL SKILLS. Like the skill of effectively handling feelings, social skills are also first developed within the family. In adolescence, there is an increased desire and need for social interaction with peers, which allows teens to practice and refine their social skills. Studies have shown that teens in substance-abusing families may be uncomfortable in social situations, avoid socialization, or align themselves with peers from other dysfunctional families (Jacob & Johnson, 1997; Leonard et al., 2007; L. Steinberg, 2002). They may gravitate toward peer groups that engage in inappropriate and even illegal behaviors such as truancy, shoplifting, gang involvement, and drug use.

Other teens may gravitate toward a high-functioning group such as a church youth group, high school band, or sports team. They may do well in school and escape their family problems through achievements in other areas. They may also seek out the families of friends in order to spend time with a healthy family. In fact, they may spend an inordinate amount of time at friends' homes but rarely invite their friends to their own home. Other members of the extended family, such as grandparents, may provide a safe alternative. This form of disengagement from the alcoholic environment is a healthy response to a difficult and unhealthy situation.

BEHAVIORAL REACTIONS. Teens are reactive. When parents say, "I need a drink, I've had a hard day," they teach their teens that covering up emotions is preferable to dealing with them. Teenage children of alcoholics are often diagnosed with conduct disorders and are at risk for delinquency. When teens live with parents who have difficulty controlling their own anger, they may respond by acting out outside of the home. The anger they feel at a parent may be directed at peers in the form of bullying or gang involvement. They may become hostile, uncooperative, disrespectful, and belligerent with a parent whose authority they do not accept or respect. Though many parents believe that authority is their inalienable right, it is actually derived from the mutual respect between parent and child. Teens with substance-abusing parents learn that selfish actions and reactions are more appropriate to life situations than problem solving, coping, or empathy.

Academic problems including poor grades, truancy, behavior problems at school, and failure to finish high school are possible reactions to a family environment of substance abuse. Teens whose parents are engaged in loud and drunken arguments may find it difficult to do their homework. They may also be unwilling to share with their teachers what is happening at home.

Some teens react to substance abuse problems in the family by becoming overly responsible and achievement-oriented. They push themselves to be successful and to appear happy. They are often perfectionists who can never quite believe that anything they've done is good enough. They may fill their time with extracurricular activities, including after-school clubs and part-time jobs, staying active to keep their emotional turmoil at bay. But at some point, they have to go home and deal with what is happening there.

Preston, 16, appeared to have it all together; he was a good student and a basketball star. He worked part-time at the local movie theater. But the reality was that Preston hated to go home. His father drank heavily, and his parents fought constantly. They paid him little attention except for occasional pats on the back for "my son, the basketball star." Preston was determined to leave home as soon as he graduated.

ALCOHOLISM AND DRUG ABUSE. Teens living with alcoholics or drug addicts have a higher than average chance of becoming alcoholics or drug addicts themselves (Guo, Hawkins, Hill, & Abbott, 2001; Sher, 1997). According to Sher (1997),

There is probably no more robust finding in the area of alcohol research than the finding that COAs [children of alcoholics] are somewhere between 2 and 10 times more likely to develop alcoholism than non-COAs. . . . Additionally, parental alcoholism appears to be associated with other substance use disorders in their offspring, such as drug abuse, drug dependence, and tobacco dependence. (pp. 249–250)

Drinking and smoking pot may seem like a way to connect with their parent or to prove that they are grown up. This is not true of all teenagers from substance-abusing families. "Although COAs generally are at increased risk of becoming alcoholic themselves, more than one-half of COAs exhibit no alcohol problems. . . . Many COAs show great resilience in these difficult environments" (Jacob & Johnson, 1997, p. 208). Some avoid all drug and alcohol use; they may become active in activities directed at preventing teen alcohol abuse. Teens whose parents are the most severe and chronic abusers may be more likely to avoid alcohol and drugs as their experiences at home will have increased their desire to avoid these substances.

STRENGTH AND RESILIENCE. Many teens are intelligent, resourceful, creative, independent, and resilient. They take difficult situations and make the best of them. They find ways to get their needs met and accomplish the developmental tasks that lead to adulthood. The National Institute on Alcohol Abuse and Alcoholism (n.d.) has asserted that although there are negative consequences to parental alcoholism, many of the adolescents from these homes do not develop serious problems:

These resilient children shared several characteristics that contributed to their success, including the ability to obtain positive attention from other people, adequate communication skills, average intelligence, a caring attitude, a desire to achieve, and a belief in self help.

In addition to the above characteristics, teens who function successfully in alcoholic homes are insightful, realistic, knowledgeable, and able to use humor effectively. They often maintain a close connection with their parents, making allowances for their shortcomings and feeling empathy for their struggles. These teenagers have an internal drive to take care of themselves.

Short- and Long-Term Consequences

Adolescents must accomplish important developmental tasks in order to emerge as independent, responsible, and emotionally healthy adults. These tasks are always affected by the family environment. Parental misuse of alcohol or drugs interferes with a number of important tasks. Healthy separation from the family does not imply detachment or rejection but is a process by which young adults become able to stand as separate and complete individuals while maintaining an emotional connection with the family. Adolescents need opportunities to develop autonomy and to become comfortable developing and maintaining relationships with others. They must also learn to appropriately handle and express their emotions. Many of these tasks become problematic for teenagers who are struggling to deal with the stress created by a substance-abusing parent.

A variety of studies have looked at the long-term impact of parents' alcohol and drug abuse on their children. The results have been complex and difficult to generalize owing to the many factors involved in the development of the adult personality. Some studies have suffered from poor methodology or choice of sample populations. Sher (1997) examined a number of studies conducted in the 1980s and 1990s and noted discrepancies in their findings but found certain patterns. According to Sher (1997), the evidence indicates that "as a group, COAs are at a higher risk than non-COAs for a number of psychological disorders in both childhood and adulthood and that they seem to be more impulsive and possibly more neurotic than people without alcoholic parents" (p. 253).

FAMILY ROLES. Children and teenagers in alcoholic families often take on certain roles within the family. These roles, identified in the 1980s, are the hero, the scapegoat, the lost child, and the mascot (Wegscheider, 1981). The hero, usually the oldest child, takes care of the parent and the household. These teenagers are often the family's shining star: the football player, cheerleader, or valedictorian. The scapegoat is the rebellious one. This teen is often angry and acts out the family's anger. He or she often exhibits problematic behavior and bears the brunt of the parent's disappointment and rage. The lost child withdraws, often suffering depression that doesn't get noticed or treated, feeling helpless to change the situation. The mascot is the family clown, trying to lighten the mood in the family with humor or other efforts to cover up the tension.

In some situations, teens may assume one role for a time and then change when they find that the role does not help them deal with the situation. The family mascot, for example, may get discouraged and become withdrawn and disconnected. Although children in substance-abusing families don't always take on these exact roles, they are likely to assume roles that allow them to function within their troubled family rather than develop their own unique personality. These roles usually don't serve them well when they move into the adult world. And they can hinder the development of a complete and self-sufficient individual.

ADULT CHILDREN OF ALCOHOLICS. The concept of adult children of alcoholics was developed by Woititz in the early 1980s. Many adult children of alcoholics have issues, behaviors, and personality characteristics in common as a consequence of growing up in an alcoholic family—or a family with another form of substance abuse. According to Woititz (1990), adult children of alcoholics often have the following traits:

- They guess at what normal behavior is.
- They have difficulty with interpersonal relationships.
- They overreact to changes over which they have no control.
- They constantly seek affirmation and approval from others.
- They are overly responsible or highly irresponsible.
- They are impulsive.

These are often the consequences of growing up in a home with unrelenting stress, secrets, and conflict, in which the teen's developmental needs are secondary to the parent's addiction.

ACADEMICS AND CAREERS. Adolescents and young adults from substance-abusing families often have difficulty with academic achievement (National Association for Children of Alcoholics, 1998). Even in homes that encourage school attendance and homework, the home environment, especially in the evenings, is often not conducive to studying. Research indicates that these adolescents have a higher than average dropout rate (Parsons, 2003).

During junior year of high school, students must decide whether to apply for college. This is a difficult and complicated task that requires parental input. Although some guidance is available through the schools, most students who apply for college are actively encouraged and supported by their families. This may be more problematic in substance-abusing homes. In addition, adolescents in dysfunctional families are less likely to be comfortable with the concept of moving away from the family. Parentified teens are particularly reluctant to leave the family.

Decisions about career choice also begin in late adolescence. Skorupa and Agresti (1998) investigated the differences in how adult children of alcoholics and other adults approach their career decisions. They found greater anxiety, indecision, and irrational thinking among the adult children of alcoholics, which made decision making more difficult.

Many adolescents with substance-abusing parents find themselves taking care of their parent or siblings. Many develop a strong sense of responsibility and concern for others and enter professions that involve taking care of others such as nursing, physical and occupational therapy, and social work.

RELATIONSHIP ISSUES. Adolescence is the time in which individuals begin developing intimate romantic relationships. Teenagers from dysfunctional families often have a more difficult time developing healthy relationships. Some emulate their parents' poor relationship styles. Others are too busy taking care of the family, or guarding the family secret, to develop their own relationships. They may experience problems with trust and jealousy. Homes in which one or both parents are drinking or using drugs do not give adolescents the opportunity to observe a healthy, high-functioning relationship. They are more likely to see a codependent relationship, in which one partner takes care of the other at the expense of his or her own feelings, ideas, and needs.

Adult children of alcoholics also have a greater tendency to marry an alcoholic, even when they try to avoid this. They may discover after they are married that their spouse is alcoholic, even when there was no indication of this during the early part of their relationship. Teenagers who grow up with substance-abusing parents often learn to associate love with familiar behaviors and emotions that are actually dysfunctional and associated with alcoholism.

Those who grow up in a substance-abusing home often find it a struggle to be trusting and open and to understand what a healthy relationship entails. Even when they become involved in a healthy relationship, issues related to their past may surface.

PERSONALITY CHARACTERISTICS. Adults who grew up in substance-abusing households often continue to show emotional difficulties well into adulthood, such as impulsivity, low self-esteem, emotional constriction, poorly defined identity, inadequate social skills, and perfectionism. Sher (1997) found evidence that these individuals "appeared to have lower self-esteem than non-COAs in childhood, adolescence and young adulthood. . . . COAs may be characterized by higher levels of negative emotionality" (p. 251). Similar outcomes are found in families with other types of dysfunction, but alcoholism and drug abuse are clearly significant determinants of future emotional and personal problems.

Adolescents in alcoholic families may have difficulty performing in their adult roles, as they are accustomed to functioning in a disorganized and unhealthy system. "Children of alcoholics bring from their family of origin ways of coping that may interfere with their ability to form a mature identity and capacity for intimacy, and make commitments to adult roles and responsibilities" (Crespi & Sabatelli, 1997). The behaviors that worked for them while they were growing up are often not transferable to adult environments. In addition, these adults may have difficulty with financial management as many alcoholic homes spend a large portion of their income on alcohol or drugs, and financial problems are often the source of conflict between the spouses.

EMOTIONAL PROBLEMS. Depression, anxiety, and other emotional problems are often the result of living with tremendous stress, mistrust, and conflict. Teenagers in these homes often neglect their own emotional well-being as they struggle to simply survive each new crisis. Research has also indicated that adult children of alcoholics continue to be affected by their parents' unremitting substance abuse.

POSITIVE OUTCOMES. Adolescents raised in substance-abusing homes can become healthy, independent adults. Although addiction is a common response to growing up with addicted parents, teenagers are aware that substance abuse can have a damaging impact on the family, and they often choose not to follow in their parents' footsteps. They also often reject other negative coping styles (such as lying and denial) used by their parents. They may find alternative role models, either within their own extended family or elsewhere. Adolescents who assume responsibility for their siblings and household are often able to take on their own life responsibilities once they are legally adults.

One of the most important characteristics of these healthy young adults is their ability to let go of anger and resentment. They individuate and develop a strong sense of self despite the chaos in their families. Many stay focused on academics and are able to go to college. As young adults, they may choose to detach from their families, or at least maintain a safe distance. Many are able to learn from their parents' mistakes.

Summary

Parenting style is influenced by life situations, including medical and psychiatric disorders and substance abuse, and these disorders have a significant impact on the well-being of adolescents. Medical problems may come on suddenly or develop over time but, when they are in their chronic state, can alter the family's routine. Psychiatric disorders may develop slowly but are often unrecognized or untreated until they have resulted in a noticeable change in the parent's functioning. Substance abuse can be particularly damaging to an individual's ability to parent in a healthy manner. Many families pull together to meet the challenges, especially in cases of serious medical illness. Psychiatric disorders and drug abuse often limit the parent's ability to supervise their teen and decreases their sensitivity to the teen's emotional issues. The changes and behaviors that come from these issues become risk factors for the teen's successful transition to adulthood. Teenagers recognize and respond to changes in a parent's health and this may create negative and unhealthy reactions, including anxiety, depression, low self-esteem, and poor school performance. Alcohol and drug use has been found to be more common in teens with substance-abusing parents. Adolescents are often quite resilient, and many teens will respond to these family problems with strength and compassion. Knowledge that aids in the teen's understanding of the illness and a good support system is helpful in the teen's development of adequate coping skills and may reduce the long-term effects. The challenges of physical illness, psychiatric disorders, and substance abuse involve a tremendous number of changes, and these life events can either disrupt teens' development or bring out their inner strengths.

PART FOUR

ASSESSMENT AND CHANGE

CHAPTER TEN

Parenting Style—Become the Parent You Want to Be

Your children are not your children.
They are the sons and daughters of Life's longing for itself.
They come through you but not from you,
And though they are with you yet they belong not to you.
You may give them your love but not your thoughts,
For they have their own thoughts.
You may house their bodies but not their souls,
For their souls dwell in the house of tomorrow,
which you cannot visit, not even in your dreams.
You may strive to be like them,
but seek not to make them like you.
For life goes not backward nor tarries with yesterday.

—Kahlil Gibran,
"On Children"

The Parent Effect: An Allegory

A group of adolescents go to play a game of soccer accompanied by their parents.

The My House, My Rules parents immediately step in to take charge, establish the rules, and clarify who's playing which position. They reserve the right to change or add a rule as they see fit.

The My Life Is Your Life parents choose their favorite position, demand that their teen be allowed to play it, and then pressure their teen to score. They may also play alongside their teen, offering constant praise and blocking any player who interferes with their teen's actions.

The Cool parents show up a little late, bringing snacks. Casually dressed, they give high fives to the other teenagers and cheer enthusiastically for all the players. They allow their child, and any of the other teenagers, to go in and out of the game and change positions at will. When the teens come off the field, they may offer them soda or beer, because after all, the kids are thirsty.

The Not Now, I'm Busy parents come sometime after the second quarter and slip into the stands. During the game, they look up periodically from their smartphones to offer a congratulatory cheer. Just before it's time to leave they get another important phone call, so they ask another parent to take their teenager home.

The Easygoing parents accompany their adolescents to the game and immediately take their position on the sidelines. They offer support and praise as needed and do not interfere or give advice unless they see their teens step out of bounds. If their teens behave inappropriately, they temporarily remove them from the game. Afterward, they will congratulate their teens on their soccer skills and sense of fair play.

As the game gets under way, the coach intervenes and offers some helpful suggestions to the teens and their parents. To the My House, My Rules parents, the coach suggests that they allow their teens to have input in deciding the rules for the game and give them the opportunity to try out the various positions to see what they feel most comfortable with. To the Your Life Is My Life parents, the coach suggests that they find a comfortable seat in the bleachers and try cheering from afar. The coach also suggests that they pay more attention to their teen's choice of position rather than trying to choose for him or her.

The Cool parents are informed that they need to establish more clear boundaries between themselves and the teenagers and that bringing beer for minors is inappropriate and illegal. The coach also suggests that they might benefit from paying more attention to their own teen instead of the group as a whole. When the Not Now, I'm Busy parents finally arrive, the coach points out to them that, by being late to the game, they missed some important plays in which their teen was involved and suggests that they turn their smartphones off and focus on their teen's impressive talent and team spirit. The coach congratulates the Easygoing parents on their support of their teens and stresses the importance of their role modeling appropriate sporting behavior.

At the end of the game, the parents, teenagers, and coach leave the field feeling a little more connected to the game and to each other. Sometimes changing the rules of the game can make a difference in the long-term outcome.

Parenting Teens

Parenting teenagers is one of the most challenging life experiences that any adult will ever undergo. Teens can be contrary, sullen, dismissive, and stubborn; they can also be fun, endearing, thought-provoking, and lovable. The eight or so years between childhood and adulthood can be a roller coaster of feelings, activities, and changes. The overwhelming majority of parents strive to provide their adolescents with the life lessons they believe are necessary for their development. However, many factors and issues affect parenting style, and it is not unusual for parents to be unaware of the impact their actions have on their teen's development. Being able to realistically evaluate one's parenting strengths and weaknesses can help parents to make important changes and positively affect the adult that their teen will become.

Parenting teens requires patience, flexibility, humor, consistency, and knowledge. Teens are impulsive, and it is the parent's job to provide structure and limits. Teens are sexually inquisitive, and parents must teach them responsibility and morals. Teens are risk takers, and parents need to encourage them to make good decisions. Teens seek freedom, and parents need to help guide the way. Parenting is a challenging but satisfying experience with long-term benefits for parent and child.

The goal of this book is to provide parents with information about the impact of different parenting styles and empower them to make changes that will provide their adolescents with the best possible chance for a healthy, productive, and happy life. This is not a message of blame but of responsibility and possibilities. All parents have circumstances and experiences that consciously or unconsciously affect their parenting style, but awareness makes change possible.

In all the years that I have worked with families, I have rarely met a family unwilling to make changes to improve their family environment. Most parents have been happy and surprised to see the changes that take place in their parent–teen relationships after making some adjustments to the way they deal with their teen. When families seek help, all too often the focus remains on the teen's problems and fails to adequately address the parents' role. This chapter offers suggestions for parents who want to make changes in their parenting style. Professionals who work with adolescents will also find it helpful.

Characteristics of Healthy Families

Healthy families have certain characteristics in common. These characteristics have little to do with socioeconomic status, parental age, or educational level.

- Healthy families show unconditional love and acceptance.
- Healthy families have clear boundaries.
- Healthy families are accepting of individuality.
- Healthy families allow feelings to be expressed.
- Healthy families have appropriate levels of give and take.
- Healthy families have open communication, and their messages are clear and free of hidden agendas.
- Healthy families have a basic set of norms to guide them.
- Healthy families allow for independence.
- Healthy parents are flexible and can adapt their response to the situation and the individual child.

- Healthy parents are comfortable with parental authority and set limits that are reasonable and age appropriate.
- Healthy parents provide adequate supervision.
- Healthy parents take the time to listen.

Healthy Adolescents

Just as families have characteristics that reflect their level of emotional well-being, teenagers who show certain personality traits tend to be emotionally and behaviorally healthier than their counterparts. In most families, these traits are encouraged. Teenagers are a work in progress, and many of these characteristics develop gradually during adolescence.

- Healthy adolescents feel good about themselves.
- Healthy adolescents are able to deal effectively with their feelings.
- Healthy adolescents feel capable of handling life's issues.
- Healthy adolescents are able to show concern for others and have the ability to be empathetic.
- Healthy adolescents can control their impulses and are able to make good choices for themselves.
- Healthy adolescents are able to delay gratification.
- Healthy adolescents are able to spend time by themselves and have the ability to self-comfort.
- Healthy adolescents feel productive.
- Healthy adolescents are capable of making and maintaining emotional attachments.
- Healthy adolescents can think for themselves and are able to consider alternative ways of seeing things.
- Healthy adolescents are able to see their parents as humans and allow their parents to make mistakes.
- Healthy adolescents learn from their mistakes.
- Healthy adolescents tend to be optimistic about life.
- Healthy adolescents follow through on their promises.
- Healthy adolescents are able to establish goals for themselves and persevere in attaining these goals.
- Healthy adolescents can have fun.

What Teens Need

Chapter 1 outlined the important developmental challenges that all adolescents undergo on their way to adulthood. The hope is that a teen living in a functional family and successfully accomplishing the tasks of adolescence will grow into an emotionally healthy adult. Adolescence is about creating a stable identity that will allow the teen, and the adult he or she develops into, to interact successfully and productively with the world. This identity needs to provide a strong sense of self-worth and be socially appropriate. Adolescents must acquire a set of values and morals that guide their actions. They must eventually establish a life separate from their family of origin, define their sexual and social roles, and develop social and intimate relationships. As adults, they need to find purpose and meaning in their actions and life choices, including a satisfying and life-sustaining career. Healthy adults are able to think abstractly and deal effectively with the problems and issues they encounter.

To develop the strengths they will draw on as adults, teens need a number of things.

- Teens need attention and acknowledgment from parents, teachers, and peers.
- Teens need to be listened to and have the opportunity to express their opinions.
- Teens need supervision that keeps them safe while allowing them to develop independence and responsibility.
- Teens need opportunities and encouragement to develop their own interests, talents, and strengths, and to set goals.
- Teens need to be respected and allowed to have some degree of privacy and personal space.
- Teens need to feel appreciated for what they contribute and to be valued for who they are.
- Teens need to feel secure, loved, and cared for.
- Teens need to develop their thinking skills and learn problem-solving skills.
- Teens need to have some sense of power over their life, including the ability to have their way some of the time.
- Teens need to be able to trust the adults in their life and have parents that are honest and keep their promises.
- Teens need a home without excessive conflict.
- Teens need role models and heroes.
- Teens need to be given responsibility so that they can learn to be responsible.
- Teens need the opportunity to have fun and to interact socially with peers.
- Teens need to be able to establish and follow through on their own goals and to have purpose in their life.
- Teens need to see adults love, respect, and show affection to each other.
- Teens need exposure to spiritual or religious concepts.

When teens have these basics in their lives, they are able to develop a healthy adult identity, become involved in a committed relationship, be productive, and develop financial responsibility.

Parenting Styles and Their Challenges

The environment in which children are raised has a major impact on their long-term well-being. This book has explored five parenting styles and has endeavored to help parents become more aware of the critical role they play in their teens' lives. The following brief review highlights the main characteristics and likely outcomes of each parenting style and identifies challenges for change.

My House, My Rules

These parents have a strong need to deal with their adolescents in a rule-driven and structured manner. They find obedience to their rules and adherence to their values to be the most important aspect of the parent–teen relationship. Often rigid in their thinking, they may become angry when their authority is questioned.

Teens dealing with authoritarian parents often rebel, and this parenting style can lead to highly conflicted parent–teen relationships. Other teens become overly compliant and have difficulty developing their own ideas and goals. Despite parental pressure, these teens do not do as well in school as teens from families with more flexible parenting styles. Many of these teens use drugs or alcohol, which they go to great lengths to hide from their parents.

Challenge: The challenge for My House, My Rule parents is to relax their expectations and demands and allow their teens to take a more active role in decision making. These parents need to stop seeing conflicts with their teens as power struggles and accept that a certain amount of teen "attitude" is normal and even healthy.

Your Life Is My Life

These types of parents exemplify a method of dealing with their teens that is based on their own specific motives and unmet needs. The characteristics vary with the type of need that they are seeking to meet. Some parents try to fulfill their unmet dreams through their children, others to enhance their stature in the community through their teen's accomplishments. Yet others are so enamored of their offspring that they indulge their every desire and strive to protect them from all of life's heartaches.

Teen reactions to this type of parenting are as varied as the parent's motivations. Some do their best to meet parental expectations, whereas others fight to establish themselves as separate from their parents. Some grow into extremely driven, Type A adults, whereas others end up lacking focus and a strong sense of self.

Challenge: These parents often have the most difficult time changing because their whole lives revolve around their teens. Their challenge is to recognize that their teens are separate individuals making their own choices about interests and activities and not to pressure their teens to meet their expectations. They often also need to find more adult social activities that they can enjoy on their own.

Cool

Some of these parents provide their teenagers and their friends with alcohol. They maintain that they are doing it to provide a safe environment for their teens to drink. However, what the majority of these parents are really striving for is to be considered "cool" by their teens and their friends. They are less concerned with the responsibilities of parenting and more concerned with being their teen's friend. Other parents in this category are afraid to anger their teens and therefore find it easier to simply allow them to make their own decisions.

Although it might seem that most teens would enjoy this type of parenting, in reality most want responsive and responsible parents. Many teen children of Cool parents act out in an attempt to push their parents to provide structure and set limits for them. In teens with this type of parents, there is a higher likelihood of alcohol and drug use and indiscriminate sexual activity. Other teens may take over their own parenting and develop a kind of pseudomaturity.

Challenge: The primary challenge for Cool parents is to grow up and assume the parental role. If they are afraid to assert authority over their teens or worried about being inadequate, they need to get help addressing these concerns. They also need to engage in more appropriate adult social interactions and supervise their teens' activities rather than participating in them.

Not Now, I'm Busy

Parents in this category abdicate a lot of their parenting responsibilities because they are too busy or do not have the energy to parent an adolescent. Other parents in this category are frightened by the challenges of the teenage years and back away rather than chance making a mistake. Not Now, I'm Busy parents do not maintain an active presence in their teen's life. Many are not necessarily neglectful, simply unavailable.

Although teenagers often say they want more space, they continue to need and want parental supervision. A teenager who is not being noticed will often up the ante by behaving in ways that require parental attention. Other teens enjoy functioning under the radar, but may be less driven and slower to learn responsibility. Like the children of Cool parents, these teens are more likely to be involved in inappropriate and impulsive behavior. They often end up in peer groups (such as gangs) that use alcohol or drugs or commit crimes.

Challenge: The challenge for these parents is to get off their cell phones and laptops, leave work a little earlier, and pay attention to their teens. They need to become less preoccupied and more involved, which means coming up with creative solutions to their time management problems. They also need to be willing to exert the energy that it takes to parent a teenager.

Easygoing

The Easygoing parenting style is the healthiest parenting style discussed in this book. These parents strive to be present in their teens' lives without being too rigid and controlling or too indulgent. They find time to enjoy their teens, support their accomplishments, and give them the freedom to develop their own sense of identity. They are the most likely to use available information on adolescent development. They generally come from healthy families themselves, or have made a concerted effort not to let their personal issues interfere with their parenting decisions.

In general, the teenagers in these families are the best adjusted and have the healthiest parent–teen relationships. Although this parenting style does not guarantee that teens won't have difficult periods or sometimes behave inappropriately, these teens usually grow into well-balanced and healthy adults.

Challenge: The challenge for Easygoing parents is not to get too confident and comfortable. Teens can change with each year, school semester, and new friend made. Easygoing parents need to be open to adjusting their approach as their teens change, constantly keeping a balance between providing structure and encouraging independence. They also need to be aware of how their personal issues and stress may affect their reactions.

Assessing Your Parenting Style

The questionnaire in chapter 2 allowed you to determine which parenting style is closest to your own. After reading about the various parenting styles, you may want to reassess some of your parental practices and philosophies. Perhaps you became aware of certain aspects of your parenting style that negatively affect your adolescent. It is important to be gentle with yourself as you think about any behaviors you may need to change.

Parenting is never simple; it is a complex equation made up of past experiences, emotional needs, life stresses, and a few unknowns. Evaluating your parenting style with an open mind is the first step in being able to make changes. Some of these changes may be minor, whereas others may be more difficult and require determination. The following sections present a number of exercises that can help you make adjustments to your parenting style. Answer questions in any format that works for you—short statements, detailed paragraphs, or even poetry. You may want to record your answers in a journal, to which you can add or refer back as needed.

Origins and Motivations

Think about how you were influenced by your family of origin. Answer the following questions in any manner that feels sufficient for you to have a good sense of your family of origin legacies.

1. What parenting style did your parents use?
2. What parental messages do you remember hearing? (These may include "You never do anything right!" or "This is my house!")
3. What do you know about your parents' family life?
4. How often do you find yourself echoing comments you heard from your parents?
5. How easy or difficult were your own adolescent years?
6. In retrospect, which aspects of your parents' style do you find positive, and which ones do you find negative?

The following questions are designed to help you assess your personal motivations with respect to your parenting style.

1. What needs of yours are met through your interactions with your teen? (Did anything you read in the sections on motivations and origins of the various parenting styles strike a chord with you?)
2. Sometimes an interaction can have a secondary gain. For example, teens who fight with their parents might be punished but at the same time get some attention; the attention is the secondary gain. Do you derive any secondary gains from your interactions with your teens?
3. What are your long-term goals in raising your teenagers? (Examples could include your teen being able to attend college or become an NFL football star.)
4. What is your understanding of the developmental tasks of adolescence? How do your parenting actions encourage the successful accomplishment of these tasks?
5. Which aspects of parenting adolescents do you enjoy? Which do you dislike?
6. What concerns do you have about your adolescent's development?
7. Do you have any concerns about your life after your teenager leaves home?
8. How would you characterize your personal life aside from your parenting role?

Make a note of any areas that you feel are problematic or would benefit from some adjustments. Remember, change takes knowledge and courage.

Face Your Past

Parenting style is often passed down from generation to generation. Even the most knowledgeable and determined parents sometimes find themselves parenting in ways that remind them of their parents. It is important to take the time to deal with your own past, particularly in terms of how it affects your parenting. It can be hard to escape the influence of one's family history. I recall a 62-year-old woman who asked, sobbing, if it was normal to be her age and still struggle with feelings about her mother. Most books on adult emotional difficulties stress the influence of parent–child interactions on adult problems. Facing one's past is not an easy task and requires honest reflection and emotional strength.

The following exercises can be helpful for understanding and reducing the impact of childhood legacies. Try at least three of these techniques to give you a better idea of the impact that your family of origin has on your current parenting style.

1. Create a timeline of significant events that took place in your life before your 21st birthday. Draw a line lengthwise across the center of a piece of paper. Place ages or dates along the center line. Because you will probably have more memories of the later years, you may want to place the earlier dates closer together to leave more space on the page for the later years. Note your most important life events, using the upper half of the page to note positive experiences and the bottom half to note unhappy experiences.

Next, chart events by placing them in the upper half or lower half of the page. Record an event higher or lower in relationship to the center line to indicate degree of importance or intensity. Remember, situations or experiences above the line are positive in nature, whereas those below the line indicate difficult or painful memories.

If you wish, you can connect the dots to see the pattern that emerges; for example, you may notice a definitive drop in happier events during your early adolescent years but an increase in positive events later in your adolescence. Example:

```
Trip to Hawaii                          Got puppy
   11————————12 ————— 13 ————— 14————————15
                       Parents' divorce        Dad remarried
```

2. Another commonly used technique for dealing with childhood and adolescent family issues is to write a letter to your parent expressing your thoughts and feelings about your childhood. You do not need to send the letter; the purpose is to become aware of unresolved feelings and issues you may have. It is often helpful to keep a journal and add to it periodically rather than trying to express all your thoughts and feelings at one time. It is not unusual for individuals to find out that they have a lot more issues and feelings connected to their childhood than they realized. We often avoid remembering painful situations.

3. Talking with family members may be helpful in getting a clearer and less biased view of the family in which you grew up. Siblings often have different recollections of similar events. It is also not uncommon for siblings to have different relationships with a parent. Aunts, uncles, cousins, and grandparents may also be a good source of family information. You may try bringing up a specific incident that carries emotional weight for you and asking your family members for their recollections of this event. If you find that siblings have very divergent views on their upbringing, it may indicate a need to explore the family dynamics in more detail. In highly dysfunctional families, memories of events may be altered in order to allow individuals different ways of coping with stressful situations.

4. If your family environment was particularly stressful or dysfunctional, you may want to seek therapy to help you work through the resulting issues. Therapy can provide a safe environment in which to explore past issues, understand their impact, and bring about some closure. As the saying goes, those who do not remember the past are destined to repeat it. Not facing your past allows it to continue to have a powerful hold that may be reflected in your parenting.

5. Another activity that can help you identify the positive and negative parental influences that you bring with you is to list the techniques that your parents used that you found helpful and those that you swore you would never engage in. Perhaps your parents made a point of telling you that they loved you as you were walking out the door to spend an evening with friends, and this was their way of reminding you to behave in a way that allowed them to trust you. You can also make a list of your parent's rules that you recall and then specify whether you thought

each rule was fair or ridiculous. Remember, not all rules are clearly stated; some may be communicated through parental reactions. For example, if your parents glared at you every time you laughed during dinner, you quickly realized that laughing at the dinner table was unacceptable.

6. It can also be helpful to visit with your parents, either in person or over the phone. If you feel comfortable, you can discuss some aspects of your childhood. It is a good idea to interact with your parents on several separate occasions. Often adults lament how going back home makes them feel like a child all over again. During these visits, be aware of the various emotions that your parents evoke in you, and see if you can link those emotions to specific parental behaviors. Is your mother still critical of your weight? Does your father still make you feel like you're not good enough? Then ask yourself whether you are creating any of the same feelings in your own teenager.

Assess Your Current Life Stressors

The next step in making changes to your parenting style is to assess the issues, problems, and stressors in your current life. Many people are familiar with the Life Stress Assessment Scale, which lists a number of life stressors (for example, divorce, job loss, relocation) ranked by degree of intensity (Holmes & Rahe, 1967). Every family has life stressors that affect its functioning. Identifying your stressors can help you identify actions you can take to reduce the stress.

1. List your stressors. List as many stressors as you can think of, especially those you encounter regularly. Next, prioritize your stressors by intensity. Some will be more intense and significant, whereas others will be relatively small or fleeting. Minor stressors could include rush hour traffic or helping your teen with homework. Major stressors could include a recent job loss or marital conflict. Finally, highlight any stressors that you feel are affecting your parenting.

The following are some common stressors encountered by parents with adolescents:

- Marital discord
- Job loss
- Heavy homework load
- Aging parents
- Taking out the trash
- Depression
- Conflicts over clothing style
- Teenage driving lessons
- Teenage drug use
- Money problems

2. Another method of identifying your stressors is to take a few minutes at the end of each day to list the stressors you encountered that day. Think about how you handled each stressor at the time it occurred. Saving up all of your stress from work, with the belief that you can alleviate it once you get home, often results in parent–teen conflict over insignificant issues. Once again, highlight those areas that you think may affect your parenting.

3. Stress is a reality of today's life and even more of a reality when living with teenagers. Methods for reducing stress are common subjects for magazine articles

and books. Failing to deal with stress can create an incredibly unhealthy situation within the family. Now that you have identified your stressors, you can begin to consider ways to deal with them. What stress-relief techniques have you already tried? Which have been helpful, and which have not?

Some methods of reducing stress are described briefly here.

Breathing exercises: Stress often results in more shallow breathing, which decreases blood and oxygen flow to the different parts of the body, including the brain. Slowing down and taking deeper, more even breaths can help reduce tension. One method is to breathe in through your nostrils until you feel your abdomen expand and then exhale slowly through your mouth, counting to four as you exhale. Repeat this several times until your breathing becomes more rhythmic. Do not breathe too deeply or rapidly, as this could cause lightheadedness. Another simple technique is to simply focus momentarily on a specific object and then allow your breathing to slow down.

Relaxation exercises: Numerous relaxation exercises are available online and in books that you can find in your library or bookstore. A technique I commonly teach my clients is to relax their muscles by tensing and relaxing each of the major muscle groups, starting at the top of the head and working down to the toes. The exercise consists of tensing a specific muscle as you inhale and then exhaling and releasing the muscle tension. For example, in order to tense and relax the muscles in your forehead, simply arch your eyebrows, hold them tightly in that position, and then exhale and let your forehead relax. When you get to your toes, simply curl them inside your shoes and then relax and let them go. Another approach is to simply focus on each body part and imagine that part relaxing.

Some people relax by taking a few minutes to listen to music or read a few pages of their favorite novel. Any activity that takes you away from the stress and allows you to immerse yourself in a relaxed and enjoyable activity, even if only for five minutes, is beneficial.

Take your music player and go for a stroll. It's not only good exercise, but it's incredibly relaxing. Take your dog with you.

Laughter is always a good way to relieve stress. Allowing yourself to use humor, especially during some of the tense moments with your teenager, goes a long way toward reducing the stress of parenting.

Be creative and find your own method of relaxation. Whatever method you choose, do it three to four times a day, not only at the end of the day. Avoid letting stress build up.

Identify Your Parent–Teen Issues

Identifying your stressors is just one step in the process of clarifying the issues that you need to work on in order to be the parent you want to be. The next exercise highlights the problems that you are currently experiencing with your teenager.

Begin by identifying some of the behavioral and emotional issues that your teen is experiencing and areas of conflict between you and your teen. This is an important step, as it identifies problems that you may be able to address by changing your parenting style.

Examples of issues include difficulty with trust, hassles over homework, or not getting chores done. Major issues may include such difficult situations as suspected drug use, friends you fear are a bad influence, or failing grades. If you are having difficulty identifying areas of concern, you can do the following . . .

1. Make a list of all the issues and conflicts that you and your teenager have engaged in during the last two weeks, including minor irritations as well as major eruptions, and then rank them in terms of difficulty. Among other things, if you find that many of the conflicts are over inconsequential issues, you may be able to let those go and focus more on the important issues.

2. Another exercise that can be helpful in increasing awareness of your parent–teen interactions is to review a recent conflict from the standpoint of an outsider. Pretend that you are your neighbor looking in the window at the argument between you and your teenager. Be as honest as you can about the behavior you see. Ask yourself the following questions:

- Was I raising my voice unnecessarily?
- Did I say unkind things or belittle my teen?
- Did I threaten consequences as a way of controlling the discussion?
- Did I allow my teen to present his or her position on the issue?
- Did I allow myself to take the time to fairly consider his or her request?

It's surprising how often we would act differently if we knew a neighbor was watching. Maybe it's important to remember that our adolescents are watching our actions and judging themselves on the basis of these interactions.

3. It may be helpful to sit down and have a conversation with your teens as to what they perceive to be issues or problems within the household. It is important to reassure them that nothing said in the discussion will be held against them or subject to punitive actions. The following are some questions that you might ask your teen:

- If you could change something about how our family functions, what would you change?
- What do you think are the primary topics that we disagree about?
- Is there an area that you think that we, as parents, are being unfair about?
- What do you think we don't notice about you that you wish we would notice?
- What areas in your life do you feel we focus on or appreciate?

These are just a few examples of questions you might ask your teen to generate a conversation. Remember, the goal is to adjust your parenting style so that it promotes the type of characteristics that you hope your adolescent will acquire. Open communication is an excellent goal for families and will be of value to your adolescents for the rest of their lives.

Identify Your Goals for Your Teen

Now that you have identified some of the difficulties that are occurring in your home and between you and your teenager, you may want to establish more specific goals for your teenager and for yourself. It is tempting to simply deal with the day-to-day problems without stopping to think of the overall picture. In many workplaces, employees are asked to establish a set of goals for themselves and list the projects they wish to accomplish in the next year. Often these goals are used to assess the individual's work performance. Even though there is no one to actually evaluate your parenting performance, except perhaps the adult your teen will become, the same exercise can be useful. The following steps can help you develop a usable set of parenting goals.

1. Identify the long-term goals that you have for your adolescent. What do you hope your adolescent will become or accomplish? These goals may be tangible or abstract—such as the following:

- I want my teenager to become a doctor.
- I want my teenager to grow up being concerned about the environment.
- I want my teenager to have a strong religious faith.
- I want my teenager to be self-sufficient.
- I want my teenager to be fiscally responsible.
- I want my teenager to have a good marriage.

These goals are more often hopes, wishes, dreams, and expectations and cannot be guaranteed. But if you identify the aspirations that you have for your teen, you will be in a better position to encourage and support the behaviors that are likely to result in your teen being able to meet his or her own dreams and goals. This exercise will also allow you to be more cognizant of any goals for your teenager that are really more about your dreams than theirs.

2. Next, make a list of the goals that you want to accomplish with your teen in the next year. These will vary from year to year and depend on the adolescent's age and maturity level. When establishing these shorter term goals, keep in mind the long-range goals that you established earlier.

At this juncture, it is best to establish goals and expectations that focus on behavior, because this allows both teen and parent to gauge when goals are being accomplished. You may also have a few expectations that are more abstract in nature, but whenever possible, couch them in behavioral terms for clarity. If the goal is for the adolescent to be able to do his or her own laundry, think through all the steps it will take to accomplish this goal. You may need to show the teen how to do laundry several times, and to allow for some mistakes and possibly even ruined clothes. Keep in mind that setting up goals for your adolescent must include appropriate action and reaction on your part so as to allow him or her to feel successful. Some sample short-term goals:

- Do their own laundry
- Complete chores without being reminded
- Complete homework on their own
- Budget their allowance
- Spend an evening with the family without any conflict
- Solve problems on their own
- Ask parents for advice when they need it

Establishing Parenting Goals

The next important step in changing your parenting style is to develop a realistic set of goals for yourself. In this section, you will develop a contract with yourself as to how you want to parent and what you want your parenting behaviors to elicit in your teen. Developing parenting behaviors that produce the outcomes that you are looking for requires that you are realistic as to the impact of the parenting approaches you use now. For example, if your parenting style discourages negotiation and one of your goals for your teen is to resist peer pressure, stressing compliance without discussion is not going to achieve this outcome. The following exercises can help you set parenting goals.

1. First, identify at least five parenting behaviors that you normally exhibit. This is not an easy task, as it requires you to be reflective and critical of your own actions. Describe the philosophical beliefs that guide your parenting methods. Did any of the beliefs described in the discussions of the five parenting styles strike a chord with you? How about the challenges listed in the parenting style summaries at the start of this chapter?

Here are some examples of parenting behaviors that you might list:

- Frequently commenting on teen's choice of clothes
- Snooping through teen's room
- Allowing parties at the house with little supervision
- Refusing to allow discussion of parental decisions
- Pressuring teen to spend more social time with parent

2. Next, beside each parenting behavior, list the ways your teen reacts when you do this and the long-term outcome that this parenting behavior may elicit. Individual teens may respond differently, so be as realistic as possible when making note of your teen's reactions. This may not be easy, as some teen reactions are hard to connect with parental behaviors, or the connection may be painful to acknowledge. Different teen reactions and long-term outcomes are described in the chapters on specific parenting styles. For example, refusal to allow discussion of your decisions

may evoke anger and rebellion in one teenager, whereas another teen may withdraw and shut down. Neither reaction is healthy.

Identifying the primary parenting behaviors and teen reactions in your family can be the foundation for developing a more realistic set of goals for yourself and making changes in your parenting style.

3. The third part of this exercise is to list problematic or recurrent behaviors exhibited by your teen on a regular basis and then to identify the parenting behaviors that may be responsible, in part, for the behaviors you have identified. This usually requires some backtracking, as you notice a teen reaction and then try to identify any parenting behaviors that may have elicited it. Sometimes the relationship is fairly obvious. For example, criticizing your teenager's friends may produce an angry or disrespectful response. At other times, it may take a little more thought. For example, if your teen is becoming increasingly rude and sullen in the evening when you come home from work, perhaps your late hours are beginning to make him or her feel neglected. Of course, not every behavior has a clear-cut antecedent, but if you look at the overall patterns, you will uncover important connections.

4. Another important technique for improving parenting style is to establish a new set of guidelines and behaviors for yourself. Begin by making a list of changes that you want to make or new behaviors that you want to try. Be brutally honest with yourself. Your goals should be clearly stated and describe specific behaviors, so that later on, you can easily evaluate what you accomplished. Here are some sample goals:

- Stop controlling my teen's choice of clothing styles
- Allow my teen to spend more free time with peers
- Call my teen daily from work and spend a few minutes chatting
- Develop my own social activity
- Don't badmouth their father

Once you've made the list, begin by changing just one or two items at a time. Give yourself at least two weeks to become comfortable with the changes and see some results. After you've accomplished the first set of goals, go on to the next. It may be helpful to group changes so that you can focus on one or two areas at a time. For example, you could begin by adjusting the way you handle schoolwork. You may want to start with the changes you think will be easiest to accomplish or that are particularly important for you.

Making these changes and having them stick requires that you to find a way to accomplish and reinforce them. This may be as simple as a daily reminder to yourself of your new goal. To accomplish that, you could make small signs listing your goals and post them in appropriate places, such as your bathroom mirror or the dashboard of your car. Or you could make a pop-up reminder on your schedule that shows up just before you get home. Another technique might be to quickly check your reflection in the mirror when you find yourself upset with your teen. You will also benefit from periodic reviews that allow you to be more aware of your parenting behavior.

You are more likely to accomplish your goals if, when you establish them, you also come up with mechanisms for ensuring their success. Examples of goals for each parenting type, and methods for accomplishing them, are listed below.

"My House, My Rules" Parents

Goal: Allow more teen input on decisions.

Method: (1) Set up family meetings to make decisions about major teen requests. Listen to your teen's requests and reasons, and write them down. Consider the validity of the reasons. Ask for any additional information you need. Make a decision on the basis of information. (2) When you feel like saying no, ask yourself, "Why not?"

Reminders: Make a note at the top of the family meeting agenda to listen. Remind yourself not to react to teen "attitude."

"Your Life Is My Life" Parents

Goal: Stop asking for details on your teen's text conversations.

Method: (1) Leave the room when your teen is texting. (2) If your teen is texting while riding in the car with you, listen to the radio.

Reminder: Put a post-it on your bathroom mirror with the words "texts are private."

"Cool" Parents

Goal: Stop allowing alcohol at parties.

Method: (1) Consider saying no to parties at the house. (2) Research teen alcoholism. (3) Tell teen about new "no alcohol" rule.

Reminder: Post a copy of the state laws on serving alcohol to minors on the refrigerator.

"Not Now, I'm Busy" Parents

Goal: Spend more time with teen in the evenings.

Method: (1) Plan a simple family meal three times a week. Ask all family members to attend. (2) Set up a 15-minute "check in" chat every evening. Limit conversation to light topics. Think of topics to share in advance.

Reminders: (1) Put your scheduled family time on your work calendar. (2) Post it on the family bulletin board.

"Easygoing" Parents

Goal: Teach teens to do their own laundry.

Method: (1) Set up an appointment to familiarize your teens with the laundry room. (2) Show teens how to use the washer and dryer. (3) Write out instructions and post them on the washer. (4) Give teens a deadline date for taking over their own laundry. (5) Ignore piles of dirty clothes in their rooms. (6) Enjoy your free time.

Reminders: Smile to yourself when your teens start wearing the same shirt four days in a row because they ran out of clean clothes.

5. An important part of parenting is to take care of yourself. Just like you put on your own oxygen mask first in an airplane emergency, you need to have sufficient outlets and coping skills to parent an adolescent. Healthy parents take time for themselves. This could include having an evening out with your spouse, taking a hot bath, doing a puzzle, playing games, spending time away from the house with friends, or any other activity that helps you relax. Having a good support system, whether it consists of family members or friends, helps make parenting easier.

Schedule Family Meetings

Another important technique for improving parenting style is to hold a family meeting once a week or every other week. Weekly gatherings cut down on some of the off-the-cuff parental reactions. All family members sit down and discuss how the family is functioning. It is important that each family member has an opportunity to speak and be heard and that there are no negative repercussions for what people say during the meeting.

This is a time for parents and teens to talk over problems, make changes in family rules, and plan family outings and other events. It should not be a complaint fest but a discussion that improves parent–teen functioning. Rules should be established that reflect the democratic orientation of these meetings. All household members should attend, and decisions should incorporate input from all. If the meeting is only an opportunity for parents to assert their authority, it will soon dissolve into anarchy. Meetings can help unengaged families find time for quality interaction. Try posting an open agenda on the refrigerator several days before the meeting and inviting all family members to add ideas.

Negotiate Family Contracts

Family contracts can help families begin to function on a healthier basis. Contracts can help sidestep parenting style problems as they outline ways to deal with teens' behaviors that don't require emotional reactions. The contract should outline the behaviors expected of the teenager and list any consequences for failing to follow the guidelines. It can specify privileges or rewards that the teen can earn for behaving appropriately or meeting certain goals. Expectations that the parents intend to meet for themselves or specific teen requests may also be included.

Contracts should be negotiated between the parent and teenager and allow for teen input. Negotiation is important in order to assure the teen's cooperation. Sample contracts are shown at the end of this chapter. They can be changed as much as necessary to address the specific issues of each family.

More Thoughts on Effective Parenting

Now that you have had the opportunity to assess your parenting style and are on the road to improved parent–teen relationships, a few additional tips may come in handy. The following suggestions can help you become more effective and comfortable during the difficult but exciting adolescent years.

Parent–Teen Interactions

The good news is that parenting can be a cooperative effort. Parenting teenagers involves interaction between the parent or parents and the teenagers in the family. The little-known secret about teenagers is that they tend to be more cooperative and enjoyable with parents who make them feel valued and respected. Once children become adolescents, you really can't make them do much of anything. Gone are the days when you could physically carry them to their rooms or take a toy and put it on top of the refrigerator. Parenting requires agreement and respect on the part of the teenager. Any environment that functions well does so because everyone involved feels like they have value and are contributing. Families should be democracies with caring leaders (parents) rather than dictatorships.

Another important component of successful parenting of adolescents is the amount of warmth and affection between family members, which is evident in the way that individuals acknowledge and treat each other. Love should feel unconditional, and discipline should focus on the behavior, not the person. Teens in particular need attention and validation. Parents and teens need to experience interactions that are pleasant and enjoyable.

A recent study (Parker-Pope, 2010) reported that marital satisfaction is more likely in relationships in which five or more positive interactions occur for every negative one. In my work, I often encourage parents to be aware of the number of positive, neutral, and negative interactions between themselves and their teen. Positive interactions include asking about their day or commenting on what a nice job they did with the dishes. Walking in the door in the evening and immediately assessing everything that the teen did not do or needs to get done is not a positive interaction. Teens often tell me that within 10 minutes of coming home, their parents have already made them feel worthless. An important step in the process of changing parenting style is to change the small everyday interactions.

Listening and Communication

"My teen doesn't listen to me" is one of the most common statements I hear from parents. This is probably true; teenagers tend to talk more and listen less as they go through adolescence. Teens also report that their parents don't listen to them. If parents want their teens to hear them, they need to learn how to listen. There may be times when teenagers appear to be listening, but they don't really hear, understand, or care what their parent is saying. Lectures are often tuned out. Communication is a two-way experience. One of the most important aspects of communication is listening, and listening to teenagers is indeed an art. Teens say a lot between the lines, and only parents who listen are able to hear what their teen is trying to tell them. Open and clear communication is an important goal for all families.

Communication with teens occurs at three different levels. The first level is the one that allows individuals to function within the same family. This includes basic requests and the sharing of everyday information—for example, "What do we need at the store?" and "I have basketball practice after school today."

The second level is social. It includes conversations between teens and parents about everyday topics of interest, such as movies, news events, and weekend plans. During the adolescent period, this type of communication often decreases as schedules become hectic and peer group activities become more important. But it is critical because it allows family members to have a relaxed, open, and enjoyable relationship. It also shows interest and respect for the individuals in the family. Without it, the other two levels of communication become more strained.

The third level of communication occurs when parents and teens discuss important or emotional issues. This can include such difficult topics as financial problems or problems in the teen's personal and social life. This is the most difficult level of communication, but essential to healthy family relationships. Ongoing communication on the first two levels make the teen and parent feel more comfortable engaging in topics with higher stakes. Parents often tell me that their teenager can tell them anything, whereas those same teenagers tell me that they wouldn't talk to their parents about many of the issues that they discuss in therapy and with friends. Too often, adolescents believe that their parents wouldn't understand their concerns. Often this discrepancy in family communication is a matter of perception and can be rectified by increasing the amount of quality interaction and communication.

When you want to have a conversation or make a request of your teens, the first step is to make sure that you have their attention. This may be as simple as calling out their names and taking a moment to notice whether they have focused on you. If they don't respond, try again. All humans can tune out the world around them when they're focused on something that's of interest to them. When you have gotten your teens' attention, make your request as pleasantly and as clearly as possible. Just because they're family doesn't mean it's okay to be short or rude in your request. "Billy, please take out the trash, it's overflowing" is nicer than "Billy, can't you see that the trash is overflowing?!"

When you want to have a discussion related to a specific concern—such as what's going on with your teen who just came in the door looking unhappy—you need to make sure that you use a type of listening that invites conversation instead of shutting it down. This is often referred to as reflective listening or active listening. The goal is to encourage continued communication and to reflect to your teen that you are interested in what he or she has to say. This can be accomplished in several ways:

- Make eye contact and show interest.
- Reflect back what you hear your teen saying.
- Ask open-ended questions.
- Offer suggestions, not advice.

- Share some relevant information about yourself.
- Thank your teen for talking to you about the issue.

The bottom line is that if you want your teens to talk to you, you need to listen to them. If you want your teens to respond to your requests, ask in a way that encourages cooperation. When you take the time to listen to your teens and interact with them about everyday life events, you might find that parenting adolescents is not quite so stressful.

Setting Boundaries

All parents struggle with setting appropriate boundaries for their teens. Despite their grumbling, teens need and want structure and discipline. Adolescents from controlling and disengaged families exhibit the most behavioral problems. Teens from controlling families rebel, whereas those from disengaged families act out to get noticed. What are some of the optimal ways to avoid those two extremes and establish healthy boundaries and rules for teenagers?

Setting rules for teens needs to take into account the teen's age, maturity level, and temperament. Teens do better with rules that they find realistic and fair. It is also better to have a small number of rules that cover the important issues rather than a lot of small, nitpicky rules that the teen is likely to spend a lot of time finding a way around. Sometimes, it helps to differentiate for the teen the difference between rules, expectations, and maturity privileges: *Rules* are specific statements about what behaviors are acceptable or unacceptable; *expectations* are guidelines as to what the family considers reasonable or normal behavior for a particular individual or within the family; *maturity privileges* are privileges that the teen earns or is afforded on the basis of age and maturity and level of responsibility. Two examples follow:

- *Rule:* Alcohol use is unacceptable. *Expectation:* Attend school and do your best. *Maturity privilege:* You may drive the car to school.
- *Rule:* No boys are allowed in the house when we're not home. *Expectation:* Show respect for authority. *Maturity privilege:* One-on-one evening dating

There should be a few significant rules, a reasonable number of expectations, and an escalating number of maturity privileges. Each rule should have clear boundaries and a brief explanation. Rules should be enforced with appropriate consequences for infractions. Expectations are often the result of family conversations, family norms, and role modeling. They should be encouraged and supported, with periodic reviews in the form of family discussions. These conversations should be supportive and encourage teen input. Sometimes an expectation may become an issue for your teen and you may need to be a little more direct in expressing your expectations. Sometimes expectations may need to become rules for a period of time.

Remember, expectations are not meant to fulfill your dreams but the teen's. Doing well in school is an expectation. Being the cheerleader captain may be your dream.

Maturity privileges should reflect increasing responsibility and freedom. As the goal of adolescence is to allow teens to differentiate and assume increasing accountability for themselves, the years from 12 to 18 should function as a training ground for these life skills. Allow teens to try out new activities and responsibilities and give them increasing opportunities to make decisions for themselves. Misuse of a maturity privilege should result in loss of that privilege for a short time. Always give teens another opportunity to earn maturity privileges.

Discipline

Discipline is one of the most difficult issues for parents during the adolescent years. It is a primary topic in books on dealing with teenagers. Discipline is the method by which parents direct, control, and protect their teenagers. The five parenting styles described in this book use a wide variety of consequences. My House, My Rules parents often depend too much on punishment, whereas Cool parents don't offer enough feedback on misbehavior.

The word discipline comes from a Latin word meaning "to learn." Discipline is not about punishment—which is the imposition of pain, directed at controlling behavior. Many parents mistakenly believe that punishment must include a form of physical or emotional discomfort in order for their children to learn the lesson. This is simply not true. Discipline is about teaching socially appropriate behavior and encouraging the acquisition of healthy life skills and should encourage self-control and confidence. Discipline can involve loss of privileges that are being misused, logical consequences, additional chores, or learning activities such as writing an essay about the infraction.

The components to discipline are limit setting, monitoring, and consequences. Consequences should be logical and reasonable and allow teens to make the connection between their behavior and the outcome. Examples of logical consequences include the following:

- Missing the bus means that they need a ride to school; therefore, they are going to clean your car this weekend.
- Failure to complete chores on time means that they need to stay home on Saturday morning until the chores are done, plus have an additional chore assigned.
- Coming home 15 minutes after curfew means that they will have to come home 30 minutes before curfew the next night. A second infraction could mean that they lose the privilege of going out on the following weekend night.

As teens get older, reducing the number of restrictions on their activities and choices allows them to develop internal control and common sense. Adolescents do not magically become responsible and rational at age 18 or when they are handed a high school diploma; it is a process that takes time. Teenagers whose parents loosen their hold as the teen matures have the most successful adolescent-to-adult transition.

One Final Thought

Parenting is the price we pay for wanting to reproduce ourselves. There is no return policy. Often what we get depends on what we are willing to spend, cognitively, emotionally, and physically. We only truly find out the worth of our input after our teenager becomes an adult. Almost always, parents find that their efforts were well rewarded.

Sample Family Contracts

Change these contracts as needed to reflect your family's issues and needs.

Family Contract

Date: _____ Family members: _____

The family policies for mornings are: _____

_____

_____

Consequences for not following these policies are

(*use codes listed at end of contract*):_____

Expectations for school attendance are: _____

_____

_____

Consequences for not meeting these expectations are:_____

After-school policies are: _____

_____

_____

Consequences for not following these policies are:_____

Household responsibilities are: _____

_____

_____

Consequences for not completing these tasks are: _____

Weekend policies are: _____

_____

_____

Consequences for not following these policies are:_____

General behavioral expectations are:_____

_____

_____

Consequences for not meeting these expectations are:_____

Nonnegotiable expectations are: _____

_____

_____

Consequences for not meeting these expectations are:_____

Privileges and Consequences

PRIVILEGES

_____

_____

Allowance:_____

Special requests: _____

_____

_____

CONSEQUENCES

Fill in the blanks, then code each section above with agreed-upon consequences.

A: Loss of allowance, amount:_____

B: Extra chore: _____

C: Loss of _____ privilege for _____ days

D: Loss of _____ privilege for _____ days

E: Loss of _____ privilege for _____ days

F: Added activity: _____

G: Grounded for _____ days. Grounding includes _____ .

H: Total shutdown (includes the following restrictions): _____

_____ Days: _____

I. Other:_____

Parent responsibilities:

_____

_____

We, _____, as members of

the _____ family, agree to the terms of this family contract. We also agree to follow all policies without unnecessary conflict. Any changes to this contract will be made during a family meeting.

We, the children of this family, acknowledge the responsibility of our parents to enforce this contract and agree to comply with all rules and accept all consequences for failure to follow stated rules and policies.

Signed: _____ Date: _____

Signed: _____ Date: _____

Signed: _____ Date: _____

Signed: _____ Date: _____

Request for Special Privilege

I, _____ as a member of the _____

family, request the following item or special privilege: _____

_____

I am willing to _____ in order to receive this.

Signed: _____ Date: _____

Agreed: _____ Date: _____

Parent Contract

A parent contract can be helpful in making changes to specific parental behaviors and may be useful in increasing cooperation with teens.

I, _____, parent of _____ ,

agree to _____

as requested. In exchange (*optional*) _____

will do the following: _____ .

Signed: _____ Date: _____

Signed: _____ Date: _____

Teen Contract

I, _____, agree to the following change in my behavior:

_____

This purpose of this change is: _____

_____

I also agree to discuss any difficulties I may have in carrying out this change with my parents, who agree to support my efforts and honesty.

Signed: _____ Date: _____

Signed: _____ Date: _____

References

Afifi, T. D., & McManus, T. (2010). Divorce disclosures and adolescents' physical and mental health and parental relationship quality. *Journal of Divorce and Remarriage, 51,* 83–107.

Ahrons, C. (2004). *We're still family: What grown children have to say about their parents' divorce.* New York: HarperCollins.

Amato, P. R. (2001). Children of divorce in the 1990s: An update of the Amato and Keith (1991) meta-analysis. *Journal of Family Psychology, 15,* 355–370.

Amato, P. R., & Keith, B. (1991). Parental divorce and the well-being of children: A meta-analysis. *Psychological Bulletin, 110,* 26–46.

Aquilino, W. S., & Supple, A. J. (2001). Long-term effects of parenting practices during adolescence on well-being outcomes in young adulthood. *Journal of Family Issues, 22,* 289–308.

Ashner, L., & Meyerson, M. (1990). *When parents love too much: What happens when your parents won't let go.* New York: Wm. Morrow.

Associated Press. (2007, October 12). *Police: Mother bought guns for Pennsylvania boy charged with school plot.* Retrieved from http://www.foxnews.com/story/0,2933,301379,00.html

Aunola, K., Nurmi, J.-E., Onatsu-Arvilommi, T., & Pulkkinen, L. (1999). The role of parents' self-esteem, mastery orientation and social background in their parenting styles. *Scandinavian Journal of Psychology, 40,* 307–317.

Azizi, A. (2009). When a mother has cancer: Myriad issues for children and adolescents. *Clinical Journal of Oncology Nursing, 13,* 238–239.

Baldwin, D. R., McIntyre, A., & Hardaway, E. (2007). Perceived parenting styles on college students' optimism. *College Student Journal, 41,* 550–557.

Baumrind, D. (1971). Current patterns of parental authority. *Developmental Psychology Monographs, 4,* 1–103.

Baumrind, D. (1991). Parenting styles and adolescent development. In J. Brooks-Gunn, R. Lerner, & A. Peterson (Eds.), *The encyclopedia of adolescence* (pp. 746–758). New York: Garland.

Beardslee, W. R. (2002). *When a parent is depressed: How to protect your children from the effects of depression in the family.* Boston: Little, Brown.

Bowen, M. (1978). *Family therapy in clinical practice.* New York: Jason Aronson.

Bradley, M. J. (2002). *Yes, your teen is crazy!* Gig Harbor, WA: Harbor Press.

Buchanan, C., Maccoby, E., & Dornbusch, S. (1996). *Adolescents after divorce.* Cambridge, MA: Harvard University Press.

Buehler, C., Benson, M. J., & Gerard, J. M. (2006). Interparental hostility and early adolescent problem behavior: The mediating role of specific aspects of parenting. *Journal of Research on Adolescence, 16,* 265–292.

Chase-Lansdale, P. L., Cherlin, A. J., & Kiernan, K. E. (1995). The long-term effects of parental divorce on the mental health of young adults: A developmental perspective. *Child Development, 66,* 1614–1634.

Crespi, T. D., & Sabatelli, R. M. (1997). Children of alcoholics and adolescence: Individuation, development, and family systems. *Adolescence, 32,* 407–417.

Crosbie-Burnett, M. (1991). Impact of joint versus sole custody and quality of co-parental relationship on adjustment of adolescents in remarried families. *Behavioral Sciences and the Law, 9,* 439–449.

Crosbie-Burnett, M., & Giles-Sims, J. (1994). Adolescent adjustment and stepparenting styles. *Family Relations, 43,* 394–399.

Csikszentmihalyi, M., & Schneider, B. (2000). *Becoming adult: How teenagers prepare for the world of work.* New York: Basic Books.

Daniels, L. (Producer & Director). (2009). *Precious* [Motion picture]. United States: Lionsgate.

Darling, N. (1999). *Parenting style and its correlates.* Retrieved from http://www.athealth. com/Practitioner/ceduc/parentingstyles.html#Baumrind91

Darnall, D. (1998). *Divorce casualties: Protecting your children from parental alienation.* Lanham, MD: Taylor.

Demo, D. H., & Acock, A. C. (1996). Family structure, family process, and adolescent well-being. *Journal of Research on Adolescence, 6,* 457–488.

Dogan, S. J., Conger, R. D., Kim, K. J., & Masyn, K. E. (2007). Cognitive and parenting pathways in the transmission of antisocial behavior from parents to adolescents. *Child Development, 78,* 335–349.

Donenberg, G. B., Wilson, H. W., Emerson, E., & Bryant, F. B. (2002). Holding the line with a watchful eye: The impact of perceived parental permissiveness and parental monitoring on risky sexual behavior among adolescents in psychiatric care. *AIDS Education and Prevention, 14,* 138–157.

Erikson, E. (1993). *Childhood and society.* New York: W. W. Norton. (Original work published 1950)

Fagan, M. A. (2003). Research submissions exploring the relationship between maternal migraine and child functioning. *Headache, 43,* 1042–1048.

Fauber, R., Forehand, R., Thomas, A. M., & Wierson, M. (1990). A meditational model of the impact of marital conflict on adolescent adjustment in intact and divorced families: The role of disrupted parenting. *Child Development, 61,* 1112–1123.

Fisher, M. (2006, July 31). Are you a toxic parent? *Washington Post Magazine.* Retrieved from http://www.washingtonpost.com/wp-dyn/content/discussion/2006/07/17/DI2006 071700858.html?nav=topnav

Forehand, R., Neighbors, B., Devine, D., & Armistead, L. (1994). Interparental conflict and parental divorce: The individual, relative, and interactive effects on adolescents across four years. *Family Relations, 43,* 387–393.

Forward, S., & Buck, C. (1989). *Toxic parents: Overcoming their hurtful legacy and reclaiming your life.* New York: Bantam Books.

Furedi, F. (2002). *Paranoid parenting: Why ignoring the experts may be best for your child.* Chicago: Chicago Review Press.

Gonzalez, A., Greenwood, G., & Wen Hsu, J. (2001). Undergraduate students' goal orientations and their relationship to perceived parenting styles. *College Student Journal, 35,* 182–192.

Goodman, S. H., & Gotlib, I. H. (1999). Risk for psychopathology in the children of depressed parents: A developmental approach to the understanding of mechanisms. *Psychological Review, 106,* 458–490.

Grazer, B. (Producer), & Berg, P. (Director). (2004). *Friday night lights* [Motion picture]. United States: Universal Pictures.

Grolnick, W. S. (2003). *The psychology of parental control: How well-meant parenting backfires.* Mahwah, NJ: Lawrence Erlbaum.

Guo, J., Hawkins, D., Hill, K. G., & Abbott, R. D. (2001). Childhood and adolescent predictors of alcohol abuse and dependence in young adults. *Journal of Studies on Alcohol, 62,* 754–762.

Guthrie, E. (2002). *The trouble with perfect.* New York: Random House.

Hall, C. W., & Webster, R. E. (2007). Multiple stressors and adjustments among adult children of alcoholics. *Addiction Research and Theory, 15,* 425–434.

Helseth, S., & Ulfsæt, N. (2005). Parenting experiences during cancer. *Journal of Advanced Nursing, 52,* 38–46.

Henderson, S. H., & Taylor, L. C. (1999). Parent–adolescent relationships in nonstep-, simple step-, and complex stepfamilies. In E. M. Hetherington, S. H. Henderson, & D. Reiss (Eds.), *Adolescent siblings in stepfamilies: Family functioning and adolescent adjustment* (pp. 79–100). Malden, MA: Blackwell.

Hendrix, H., & Hunt, H. (1997). *Giving the love that heals: A guide for parents.* New York: Pocket Books.

Henry, C., Robinson, L., Neal, R., & Huey, E. (2006). Adolescent perceptions of overall family system functioning and parental behaviors. *Journal of Child and Family Studies, 15,* 319–329.

Hetherington, E. M. (1999). Family functioning in nonstepfamilies and different kinds of families: An integration. In E. M. Hetherington, S. H. Henderson, & D. Reiss (Eds.), *Adolescent siblings in stepfamilies: Family functioning and adolescent adjustment* (pp. 184–191). Malden, MA: Blackwell.

Hetherington, E. M., & Kelly, J. (2002). *For better or for worse: Divorce reconsidered.* New York: W.W. Norton.

Holmes, T. H., & Rahe, R. H. (1967). The Social Readjustment Rating Scale. *Journal of Psychosomatic Research, 11,* 213–218.

Inhelder, B., & Plaget, J. (1958). *The growth of logical thinking from childhood to adolescence.* New York: Basic Books.

Jacob, T., & Johnson, S. (1997). Parenting influences on the development of alcohol abuse and dependence. *Alcohol Health and Research World, 21,* 204–209.

Jacobson, K. C., & Crockett, L. J. (2000). Parental monitoring and adolescent adjustment: An ecological perspective. *Journal for Research on Adolescence, 10,* 65–97.

Jaser, S. S., Langrock, A. M., Keller, G., Merchant, M. J., Benson, M.A., Reeslund, K., et al. (2005). Coping with the stress of parental depression II: Adolescent and parent reports of coping and adjustment. *Journal of Clinical Child and Adolescent Psychology, 34,* 193–205.

Johnson, J. G., Cohen, P., Kasen, S., & Brook, J. S. (2006). Maternal psychiatric disorders, parenting, and maternal behavior in the home during the child rearing years. *Journal of Child and Family Studies, 15,* 97–114.

Juskalian, R. (2010, December 16). The kids can't help it. *Newsweek.* Retrieved from http://www.newsweek.com/2010/12/16/the-kids-can-t-help-it.html

Kenyon, D. B., & Koerner, S. S. (2008). Post-divorce maternal disclosure and the father–adolescent relationship: Adolescent emotional autonomy and inter-reactivity as moderators. *Journal of Child and Family Studies, 17,* 791–808.

Kever, J. (2006, October 15). New research indicates the brain keeps developing well into teen years, maybe even into mid-20s. *Houston Chronicle.* Retrieved from http://www.chron.com/disp/story.mpl/life/4257373.html

Klimes-Dougan, B., Lee, C. S., Ronsaville, D., & Martinez, P. (2008). Suicidal risk in young adult offspring of mothers with bipolar or major depressive disorder: A longitudinal family risk study. *Journal of Clinical Psychology, 64,* 531–540.

Koop, C. E. (n.d.). *Life affords no greater responsibility.* Retrieved from http://iwise.com/11v3J

Lamborn, S. D., Mounts, N. S., Steinberg, L., & Dornbusch, S. M. (1991). Patterns of competence and adjustment among adolescents from authoritative, authoritarian, indulgent, and neglectful families. *Child Development, 62,* 1049–1065.

Lee, S. M., Daniels, H., & Kissinger, D. B. (2006). Parental influence on adolescent adjustment: Parenting styles versus parenting practices. *Family Journal, 14,* 253–259.

Leman, K. (2002). *Adolescence isn't terminal (it just feels like it!).* Carol Stream, IL: Tyndale House.

Leonard, N. R., Gwadz, M. V., Arredondo, G. N., Riedel, M., Rotko, L., Hardcastle, E. J., & Potere, J. C. (2007). Description of a behavioral intervention to reduce substance use and related risk and increase positive parenting among urban mothers with alcohol and other drug problems. *Journal of Child and Family Studies, 16,* 531–544.

Lerner, R. M. (2007). *The good teen: Rescuing adolescence from the myths of the storm and stress years.* New York: Stonesong Press.

Littwin, S. (1986). *The postponed generation: Why American youth are growing up later.* New York: Wm. Morrow.

Maccoby, E. E., & Martin, J. A. (1983). Socialization in the context of the family: Parent–child interaction. In P. H. Mussen (Ed.), *Handbook of child psychology* (pp. 1–101). New York: John Wiley & Sons.

Maier, A. M. (1992). *Mother love, deadly love: The Texas cheerleader murder plot.* New York: Carol.

Marmorstein, N. R., & Iacono, W. G. (2004). Major depression and conduct disorder in youth: Associations with parental psychopathology and parent–child conflict. *Journal of Child Psychology and Psychiatry, 45,* 377–386.

Marquardt, E. (2005). *Between two worlds: The inner lives of children of divorce.* New York: Three Rivers Press.

Mason, P. T., & Kreger, R. (1998). *Stop walking on eggshells: Taking your life back when someone you care about has borderline personality disorder.* Oakland, CA: New Harbinger.

Maxym, C., & York, L. B. (2000). *Teens in turmoil: A path to change for parents, adolescents, and their families.* New York: Penguin Books.

Mayberry, D., & Reupert, A. (2009). Parental mental illness: A review of barriers and issues for working with families and children. *Journal of Psychiatric and Mental Health Nursing, 16,* 784–791.

McArdle, S. (2009). Exploring the development of perfectionistic cognitions and self-beliefs. *Cognitive Therapy and Research, 33,* 597–614.

McKinney, C., Donnelly, R., & Renk, K. (2008.) Perceived parenting, positive and negative perceptions of parents, and late adolescent emotional adjustment. *Child and Adolescent Mental Health, 13,* 66–73.

Merrill, A. R., & Merrill, R. R. (2003). *Life matters: Creating a dynamic balance of work, family, time, and money.* New York: McGraw-Hill.

Montgomery, C., Fisk, J. E., & Craig, L. (2008). The effects of perceived parenting style on the propensity for illicit drug use: The importance of parental warmth and control. *Drug and Alcohol Review, 27,* 640–649.

Mordoch, E., & Hall, W. A. (2008). Children's perceptions of living with a parent with a mental illness: Finding the rhythm and maintaining the frame. *Qualitative Health Research, 18,* 1127–1144.

Morris, A. S., Silk, J. S., Steinberg, L., Myers, S., & Robinson, L. R. (2007). The role of the family context in the development of emotion regulation. *Social Development, 16,* 361–388.

Mowbray, C. T., & Mowbray, O. P. (2006). Psychosocial outcomes of adult children of mothers with depression and bipolar disorder. *Journal of Emotional and Behavioral Disorders, 14,* 130–142.

National Association for Children of Alcoholics. (1998). *Children of alcoholics: Important facts.* Retrieved from http://www.nacoa.net/impfacts.htm

National Institute on Alcohol Abuse and Alcoholism. (n.d.). *Children of alcoholics—Are they different?* Retrieved from http://alcoholism.about.com/cs/alerts/l/blnaa09.htm

National Survey on Drug Use and Health. (2009). *Children living with substance-dependent or substance-abusing parents: 2002 to 2007.* Retrieved from http://www.oas.samhsa.gov/2k9/SAparents/SAparents.htm

Neal, J., & Frick-Horbury, D. (2001). The effects of parenting styles and childhood attachment patterns on intimate relationships. *Journal of Instructional Psychology, 28,* 178–184.

Netter, G. (Producer), & Hancock J. L. (Director). (2009, November 20). *The blind side* [Motion picture]. United States: Warner Brothers.

Neuharth, D. (1998). *If you had controlling parents: How to make peace with your past and take your place in the world.* New York: HarperCollins.

Nicholson, J. M., Fergusson, D. M., & Horwood, L. J. (1999). Effects on later adjustment of living in a stepfamily during childhood and adolescence. *Journal of Child Psychology and Psychiatry, 40,* 405–416.

Nielsen, L. (1999). College aged students with divorced parents: Facts and fiction. *College Student Journal, 33,* 543–572.

Nurco, D. N., Blatchley, R. J., Hanlon, T. E., O'Grady, K. E., & McCarren, M. (1998). The family experiences of narcotic addicts and their subsequent parenting practices. *American Journal of Drug and Alcohol Abuse, 24,* 37–59.

Osborn, T. (2007). The psychological impact of parental cancer on children and adolescents: A systematic review. *Psycho-Oncology, 16,* 101–126.

Pa. mom charged with changing daughter's grades. (2009, June 27). Retrieved from http://cbs11tv.com/watercooler/mom.changes.grades.2.1062776.html

Park, R. J., Senior, R., & Stein, A. (2003). The offspring of mothers with eating disorders. *European Child and Adolescent Psychiatry, 12,* 110–116.

Parker-Pope, T. (2010, June). Science of a happy marriage. *Ladies' Home Journal,* 62–66.

Parsons, T. (2003, December 14). Alcoholism and its effect on the family. *AllPsych Journal.* Retrieved from http://allpsych.com/journal/alcoholism.html

Peris, T. S., & Emery, R. E. (2004). A prospective study of the consequences of marital disruption for adolescents: Predisruption family dynamics and postdisruption adolescent adjustment. *Journal of Clinical Child and Adolescent Psychology, 33,* 694–704.

Pfeffer, C. R., Karus, D., Siegal, K., & Jiang, H. (2000). Child survivors of parental death from cancer or suicide: Depressive and behavioral outcomes. *Psycho-Oncology, 9,* 1–10.

Pickhardt, C. (2006). *The everything parent's guide to children and divorce: Reassuring advice to help your family adjust.* Avon, MA: Adams Media.

Robinson, B. E., & Kelley, L. (1998). Adult children of workaholics: Self-concept, anxiety, depression, and locus of control. *American Journal of Family Therapy, 26,* 223–238.

Rosenfeld. A., & Wise, N. (2000). *The over-scheduled child: Avoiding the hyper-parenting trap.* New York: St. Martin's Press.

Rothrauff, T. C., Cooney, T. M., & An, J. S. (2009). Remembered parenting styles and adjustment in middle and late adulthood. *Journal of Gerontology: Social Sciences, 64B,* 137–146.

Ruschena, E., Prior, M., Sanson, A., & Smart, D. (2005). A longitudinal study of adolescent adjustment following family transitions. *Journal of Child Psychology and Psychiatry, 46,* 353–363.

Rutter, M. (1990). Commentary: Some focus and process considerations regarding effects of parental depression on children. *Developmental Psychology, 26,* 60–67.

Sachs, B. E. (2005). *The good enough teen: Raising adolescents with love and acceptance (despite how impossible they can be).* New York: HarperCollins.

Sher, K. J. (1997). Psychological characteristics of children of alcoholics. *Alcohol Health and Research World, 21,* 247–253.

Sherman, M. D. (2007). Reaching out to children of parents with mental illness. *Social Work Today, 7*(5), 26–30.

Skaggs, M., & Jodl, K. (1999). Adolescent adjustment in nonstepfamilies and stepfamilies. In E. M. Hetherington, S. H. Henderson, & D. Reiss (Eds.), *Adolescent siblings in stepfamilies: Family functioning and adolescent adjustment* (pp. 127–148). Malden, MA: Blackwell.

Skorupa, J., & Agresti, A. A. (1998). Career indecision in adult education of alcoholics. *Journal of College Counseling, 1,* 54–66.

Slicker, E. K. (1998). Relationship of parenting style to behavioral adjustment in graduating high school seniors. *Journal of Youth and Adolescence, 27,* 345–372.

Spera, C. (2005). A review of the relationship among parenting practices, parenting styles, and adolescent school achievement. *Educational Psychology Review, 17,* 125–146.

Staal, S. (2001). *The love they lost: Living with the legacy of our parents' divorce.* New York: Dell.

Stein, J., Riedel, M., & Rotheram-Borus, M. J. (1999). Parentification and its impact on adolescent children of parents with AIDS. *Journal of Family Processes, 38,* 193–208.

Stein, J., Rotheram-Borus, M. J., & Lester, P. (2007). Impact of parentification on long-term outcomes among children of parents with HIV/AIDS. *Family Process, 46,* 317–333.

Steinberg, L. (2001). We know some things: Parent–adolescent relationships in retrospect and prospect. *Journal of Research on Adolescence, 11,* 1–19.

Steinberg, L. (2002). *Adolescence* (6th ed.). New York: McGraw-Hill.

Steinberg, L., Lamborn, S. D., Darling, N., Mounts, N., & Dornbusch, M. (1994). Over-time changes in adjustment and competence among adolescents from authoritative, authoritarian, indulgent, and neglectful families. *Child Development, 65,* 754–770.

Steinberg, S. J., & Davila, J. (2008). Romantic functioning and depressive symptoms among early adolescent girls: The moderating role of parental emotional availability. *Journal of Clinical Child and Adolescent Psychology, 37,* 350–362.

Strage, A., & Brandt, T. S. (1999). Authoritative parenting and college students' academic adjustment and success. *Journal of Educational Psychology, 91,* 146–156.

Strauch, B. (2003). *The primal teen: What new discoveries about the teenage brain tell us about our kids.* New York, NY: Doubleday.

Strauss, V. (2006, March 21). Putting parents in their place: Outside class. *Washington Post,* p. A8.

Timko, C., Cronkite, R. C., Swindle, R., Robinson, R. L., Turrubiartes, P., & Moos, R. H. (2008). Functioning status of adult children of depressed parents: A 23-year follow-up. *Psychological Medicine, 38,* 343–352.

Tomori, M. (1994). Personality characteristics of adolescents with alcoholic parents. *Adolescence, 29,* 949–959.

Turner, E. A., Chandler, M., & Heffer, R. W. (2009). The influence of parenting styles, achievement motivation, and self-efficacy on academic performance in college students. *Journal of College Student Development, 50,* 337–346.

Turner, R. A., Irwin, C. E., & Millstein, S. G. (1991). Family structure, family processes, and experimenting with substances during adolescence. *Journal of Research on Adolescence, 1,* 93–106.

Turney, D., & Tanner, K. (2001). Working with neglected children and their families. *Journal of Social Work Practice, 15,* 194–204.

Visser, A., Huizinga, G. A., Hoekstra, H. J., Van Der Graaf, W. T., Gazendam-Donofrio, S. M., & Hoekstra-Weebers, J. E. (2007). Emotional and behavioral problems in children of parents recently diagnosed with cancer: A longitudinal study. *Acta Oncologica, 46,* 67–76.

Wallerstein, J. S., & Blakeslee, S. (2003). *What about the kids? Raising your children before, during, and after divorce.* New York: Hyperion.

Wallerstein, J. S., Lewis, J. M., & Blakeslee, S. (2000). *The unexpected legacy of divorce: The 25 year landmark study.* New York: Hyperion.

Wegscheider, S. (1981). *Another chance: Hope and health for the alcoholic family.* Palo Alto, CA: Science and Behavior Books.

Weiss, L. H., & Schwarz, J. C. (1996). The relationship between parenting types and older adolescents' personality, academic achievement, adjustment, and substance use. *Child Development, 67,* 2101–2114.

Weissman, M. M., Warner, V., Wickramaratne, P., Moreau, D., & Olfson, M. (1997). Offspring of depressed parents: 10 years later. *Archives of General Psychiatry, 54,* 932–940.

Woititz, J. G. (1990). *Adult children of alcoholics* (Expanded ed.). Deerfield Beach, FL: Health Communications.

Wolf, A. E. (1991). *Get out of my life, but first could you drive me and Cheryl to the mall? A parent's guide to the new teenager.* New York: Noonday Press.

Woodcock, J., & Sheppard, M. (2002). Double trouble: Maternal depression and alcohol dependence as combined factors in child and family social work. *Children & Society, 16,* 232–245.

Wrigley, D. (2007). *Four killed when SUV crashes into train near Baytown.* Retrieved from abclocal.go.com/ktrk/story?section=news/local&id

Yahoo! Answers. (n.d.). *Is it ok to let teens drink alcohol?* Retrieved from http://answers.yahoo.com/question/index?qid=20081209040641AAt3VAd

Young-Eisendrath, P. (2008). *The self-esteem trap: Raising confident and compassionate kids in an age of self-importance.* New York: Little, Brown.

Zill, N., Morrison, D. R., & Coiro, M. J. (1993). Long-term effects of parental divorce on parent–child relationships, adjustment, and achievement in young adulthood. *Journal of Family Psychology, 7,* 91–103.

Index